MARCION
THE GOSPEL OF THE ALIEN GOD

MARCION

THE GOSPEL OF THE ALIEN GOD

Adolf von Harnack

Translated by John E. Steely and Lyle D. Bierma

THE LABYRINTH PRESS
Durham, North Carolina

Harnack, Adolf von, 1851–1930.
    [Marcion. English]
    Marcion : the gospel of the alien God / Adolf von Harnack : translated by John E. Steely and Lyle D. Bierma.
        p.   cm.
    Translation of: Marcion. 2nd ed.
    Includes bibliographical references.
    ISBN 0-939464-16-0 :
    1. Marcion, of Sinope, 2nd cent.   I. Title.
BT1415.H313   1990
273'.1'092 – dc20   89-49024
                                                    CIP

Printed in the United States of America

CONTENTS

FOREWORD TO THE SECOND EDITION

In 1923 I followed the first edition of this work with the *Neue Studien zu Marcion* (Texte und Untersuchungen, Band 44, Heft 4). There I took note of the numerous critiques of this work and at the same time more precisely grounded my position with reference to the views of W. Bauer and H. Freiherr von Soden. In the present new edition I have not returned to this task, but instead have formed some of my statements more exactly and have sought to guard against misunderstandings.

The new edition is enhanced by several fragments, the most important of which is the Laodicean epistle of the Vulgate, which I have unmasked as a Marcionite corruption (see the *Sitzungsberichte der Preussischen Akademie der Wissenschaften*, 1 November 1923).

The problem which Marcion's biblical text presents cannot move closer to a solution until the so-called W text and the text of Tatian are more definitely known and more exhaustively studied. I have learned this anew from the excellent study by Pott, though I am unable to agree with him on some important conclusions. My chief aim here has been to reconstruct Marcion's biblical text as fully and as reliably as the tradition will allow; I ask therefore that everything else in the book concerning the overall history of the biblical text be regarded as provisional.

My study of Marcion is a monograph. In the generation just past, patristic texts have been published in great abundance, and there is no lack of religio-historical studies of concepts and forms; but where are the monographs? They are lacking for almost all the important fathers and heretics. The old monographs, so far as such are even available at all, have for a long time been inadequate, and therefore they are no longer being read. But an understanding of earliest church history and an interest in it cannot be awakened and maintained without competently written monographs. Today the living work of the teacher must do it all, for texts and compendia alone cannot create understanding and interest. *Videant consules!* It is an obligation of honor for the younger and the coming generation to express, by writing monographs, their gratitude for the texts and preliminary labors that have been placed at their disposal. If these monographs are not written, the writing of the history of the early church will be stunted in the next generation.

Adolf von Harnack
Berlin, September 1924

FOREWORD TO THE FIRST EDITION

Fifty years ago the theological faculty of the University of Dorpat offered a prize for an essay on "Marcionis doctrina e Tertulliani adversus Marcionem libris eruatur et explicetur." I undertook the task and on the University's Founders' Day, 12 December 1870, received the prize. At that time the faculty requested me to revise and publish the work. This was not done at that time, but I have constantly kept the theme in view and have enlarged upon it. Now I present this monograph; of course, not a single sentence of the youthful work has remained exactly as it was in the original essay.

Through Marcion I was introduced to textual criticism of the New Testament, to the history of the early church, to the historical interpretation of Baur's school, and to the problems of systematic theology; there could be no better introduction! He is therefore my first love in church history, and this inclination and veneration have not been weakened in the half-century that I have lived through with him, not even by Augustine.

Marcion as textual critic is not neglected by present-day scholarship, and in the history of dogma also he is repeatedly given careful attention — in my textbook in this discipline more in detail than in others — but not one of the problems that are present here has yet been exhaustively treated. Important elements have remained unnoticed, and a monograph such as Marcion deserves is still lacking, for the task has not been fulfilled by Meyboom's work (*Marcion en de Marcioniten*, 1888).

Marcion affords us the key for unlocking a number of the difficult problems that are presented by the transition of the church from the postapostolic to the old catholic period. Here one can dismiss every individual Gnostic without loss, but we cannot omit Marcion if we wish to understand the dynamic development, indeed the metamorphosis, that occurs in the time of that transition — not only because catholicism is constructed as a defense against Marcion but, in a still higher degree, because it appropriated from this heretic something fundamental.

Still greater is Marcion's hitherto sadly neglected significance in the general history of religion, for he is the only thinker in Christianity who took fully seriously the conviction that the Deity who redeems one from the world has absolutely nothing to do with cosmology and cosmic teleology. The new life of faith and freedom was for him something so "alien" as over against the world that he based its emergence upon the same doubtful/daring hypothesis by which Helmholtz proposed to explain the emergence of organisms on the earth.

Thereby Christ acquired such an exalted and isolated position as founder of the true religion as is found in no other religious system, and the Pauline/Johannine dialectic with reference to the world and God, law and grace, moralism and religion, was heightened, but at the same time "cancelled," so that a *new religious foundation* on the basis of the Pauline gospel came into view. Paul himself was no religious founder; but that element in his religious conceptions that could be understood as a new religious creation and was understood thus also by his Judaistic opponents,—that Marcion seized upon and molded.

This significance of Marcion would have been recognized long ago had people not erroneously identified the "alien" God whom he introduced with the "unknown" God who in Marcion's time in fact had already long been the "known" God, and had people not left a part of the sources almost wholly unnoticed. Some have adduced Marcion's emendations of the gospel and Paul's letters and the reports of the church fathers about his teaching; but his great work *Antitheses* with its numerous exegetical comments, as well as *the biblical text that he allowed to stand*, have been little noted up till now.

I have assembled the material year after year and have striven for completeness, but on specific points there are still many problems here on which still more work must be done. Here beckon tasks that have a rightful claim upon the energies not being devoted to the almost exhausted problems offered by the Apostolic Fathers, for it is fitting and proper to make as clear as possible the most significant phenomena in church history between Paul and Augustine.

Having three chief vocations, I have had to write this work in stolen hours, indeed in half-hours, and I often have doubted that it would ever be completed. Yet the completion of the work has been granted to me, and I can only hope that the traces of its painful emergence are not too evident. . . .

I take this occasion also to express my hearty thanks to my honored colleague, Prof. Carl Schmidt, for his friendly support in the publication of this work.

Adolf von Harnack
Berlin, 27 June 1920

EDITOR'S NOTE

Because of the length and complexity of the appendices to Harnack's *Marcion* and because scholars will need to consult those appendices in the original form in which Harnack presents them, the editor and translators have decided not to include the appendices in the present edition. References to them, however, have been retained as an aid to further study.

I

INTRODUCTION

*The Religio-Historical Presuppositions of the Christian
Proclamation of Marcion and the Internal Situation in Christianity
at the Time of His Appearance on the Scene*

The man to whom the following pages are devoted was the founder of a *cf. Foreword, on Paul.* religion; his own contemporary and first literary opponent, Justin the Apologist, recognized him as such. Marcion, however, was one of those founders of religions who do not know themselves to be such. This self-deception was more excusable in him than in any other, for the apostle Paul had no more devoted pupil than Marcion, and it was Marcion's intention to know no other God than the one who had appeared in the Crucified One.

1.

In the first century of our era, one could read in Athens and in Rome, and presumably in some other cities as well, altar inscriptions that ran "To the unknown gods," or "To the gods of Asia, Europe, and Africa, to the unknown and alien gods," and perhaps also "To the unknown god."[1]

These inscriptions, prompted by fear, were intended to forestall unwelcome attacks by overlooked or foreign deities; the attribute "unknown" did not conceal any theological mystery.

Since the time of Socrates, however, there had been in the philosophy of religion, even though not under this name, an "unknown and alien God." He was unknown because he had no name; he was alien because he did not belong to the gods of the fathers. But the most important thing was that he had to be thought of in the *singular* and as the *true one*, and that he therefore devalued and dissolved all other gods.

Precisely thereby the unknown God became a notably great mystery and became the well-known God. Of course in name he was still the unknown one; in fact, he now acquired this name or a similar one—for the patriotic tradition and the people were not acquainted with him—but with reference to him the religious consciousness became more and more eloquent, and with reference to the other gods ever more silent and disparaging. Out of the negative attribute "unknown" it developed an abundance of positive attributes, and it no longer knew what to do with the gods that were known. This "unknown God" has nothing to do with the "unknown gods of Asia, Europe, and Africa." He is separated from them by the breadth of a world and he lives in a sphere entirely different from theirs. He is much more remote and much closer at hand!

Nevertheless, they and he are brought together, so the book of Acts tells us, and by no less a person than the apostle Paul in Athens. The fact that this was possible for him or, as some think, for his narrator—it makes no essential difference—is also a sign of the times, i.e., of syncretism. At that time people were reinterpreting numerous prophecies of a very earthly kind into supraterrestrial ones. So also Paul reinterpreted the phantasmal or only "possible" gods into *the* unknown God. However, he at once represented this unknown God as only *unrecognized* and then preached about him as the Creator and Guide of the world.

The great church followed him in this. It continued to speak of the unknown god then only when it had in mind the blindness of paganism toward him or when it had reason to emphasize the exaltation of this God above human reason and knowledge. Otherwise it knew him through his revelation in the world, in history, and in Jesus Christ; it knew him and called him by name.

But the Christian Gnostics, following Hellenic mystics and philosophers, took the concept "unknown" seriously; their God, although the Father of Jesus Christ, was actually the unknown one, for over the long course of speculation about him from Plato onward, the connection of this God with the world had by degrees been not only loosened but completely dissolved. On the basis of inner experiences and observations which became ever more persuasive, they were increasingly unable to relate the pure, good, and exalted God whom they found within their bosoms to the external world which is so bad. Finally the link is completely broken: *the unknown God is not the creator of the world.* Precisely for this reason he is the Unknown One. The attributes of God, stemming from this inwardness, as spiritual, holy, and good, exalted him so high above the world that he could no longer be thought of as its creator and governor. In the same process, however, the world came to be utterly devoid of value, since not only all value but all true being also is to be sought in the Unknown One. The world became a prison, a hell, something without meaning, an idle fantasy, indeed a Nothing. All these judgments are basically identical: the world had lost its right to be, so that the palpable fact of its existence evoked every conceivable form of hostile judgment and condemnation.

The Gnostics, however, still maintained an important reservation in this connection. Man, standing in the midst of the world and belonging to it in body and soul, possesses in his spirit a spark of the very being and life of the Unknown God. This property connects him so closely with God that this God is after all not an alien to the spirit and is unknown only in a relative sense. The Unknown One needs only to appear to the darkened and weakened spirit and the spirit immediately recognizes and apprehends him. Thus there is something divine that is present in this world of time and space and senses, and this awareness could not fail to affect one's view of the world; something supraterrestrial and worthwhile is somehow concealed in this cosmos.

All the prominent Gnostics thought along these lines. They were able to employ these ideas to heighten their self-esteem to an immeasurable degree. Correspondingly, the saving act of the Unknown God who had become manifest could only appear as the fulfillment of a binding obligation, an act that only gives assistance to what is really the self-redemption of the spirit that is after all divine.

Then there appeared on the scene a religious thinker who was utterly serious about the main principle of this entire religious perspective. *He did not stand within its line of development*, and he was not entangled in its halfway measures; for just this reason he was able to be completely serious about the matter. He proceeded from different presuppositions, from the Old Testament, from biblical Christianity, from Paul. He had come to know God in the manifestation of Jesus Christ, completely and exclusively as the Father of mercy and the God of all comfort. Therefore he was sure that no other expression about God is valid, and indeed that any other is only error of the most grave and grievous sort. Hence he proclaimed this God consistently and exclusively as the *good Redeemer*, but at the same time as the Unknown God and the *Alien*. He is *unknown* because in no sense can he be recognized in the world and in man; he is *alien* because there are simply no bond and no obligation that connect him with the world and with man, *not even with man's spirit*. This God enters into the world as an *outsider* and an *alien Lord*. He is a *tremendous paradox*, and religion itself too can only be experienced as such if it is to be the true religion and not a false one. Now, actually and for the first time in the history of religions, "the unknown and alien God" had appeared, prompted by merciful love alone, on a redemptive mission in a world that did not at all concern him, because he had made nothing in it. Those who in their subaltern and fearful piety had erected altars to "the unknown and alien gods" were far from thinking of such a God as this.

The man who proclaimed this God was the Christian Marcion from Sinope. All Christians at that time believed that they were aliens on earth. Marcion corrected this belief: it is *God* who is the *alien,* who is leading them out of their homeland of oppression and misery into a completely new paternal house, one that had not even been imagined previously. This identifies *one line* to which Marcion belongs: *he developed with utmost consistency the religion of inwardness.* He culminates a five-hundred-year development in the internalizing of religion. But Hellenism rejected this conclusion; for Gnostics and Neo-Platonists, otherwise so different from each other, were in agreement in the conviction that God is indeed the "unknown" but not the "alien."[2] But Marcion also belongs to a second and a third line, and they are his true connections. In order to assign to him his proper place in these three lines, one must be more explicit.

2.

Beginning in the days of the emperor Claudius, this new religion moved out of Palestine into the rest of the empire. Its strength and appeal lay not only in the proclamation of Jesus Christ the crucified and resurrected one, but also in the abundance of polar religious elements that it had embraced from the very first. As the loftiest manifestation of late Judaism, it adopted all these traditions and perceptions, with a Christian label, into its new concept of life, namely faith (including the ideas that were determinative for the formation of the community and cultus). By virtue of this action, *it was from the very outset an eminently syncretistic and, for precisely this reason, from the very outset also the catholic religion.* As the definitive outcome of the religious history of an eminently religious people it was not tailored to the pious demands of one particular circle but was adapted to the numerous and manifold demands of the widest circles, diverse because of their different situations and varied education. In the course of its development it could become more complicated but not more multifaceted than it already was upon its entrance into the Roman empire.

Because of this burden, the Christian religion never had a youthful existence, and indeed not even a natural development. From the very first it was burdened with a maximum of polar religious ideas.

This religion preached a previously unknown God, and at the same time it preached the Lord of heaven and earth whose existence was suspected by all and who was already known to many.

It sought disciples for a new Lord and Savior who quite recently had been crucified under Tiberius, but at the same time it asserted that he had already participated in the creation and had been revealed since the time of the patriarchs, in the human breast and through the prophets.

It proclaimed that all that its savior brings and does is new, and at the same time it handed down an ancient sacred book which it had seized from the Jews in which everything that is required for knowledge and life had been prophesied since time immemorial.

It provided an inexhaustible abundance of lofty myths, and at the same time it preached the all-embracing Logos whose being and works those myths represent.

It proclaimed the sole efficacy of God and at the same time the self-governance of the free will.

It placed great emphasis upon pure spirit and truth, and yet it produced a harsh and obscure literalism as well as sacraments that addressed religious sensuousness and mysticism.

It interpreted the cosmos as the good creation of the good God and at the same time as the evil dominion of the wicked demons.

It proclaimed the resurrection of the flesh, and at the same time it regarded and treated this flesh as the worst of enemies.

In a previously unheard-of fashion it sensitized the conscience by means of the announcement of the imminent judgment day of the wrathful God, and at the same time it proclaimed this God, for whom it maintained the continuing validity of all the utterances of the Old Testament, as the God of all mercy and love.

It demanded, under threat of condemnation, the strictest conduct of life in restraint and renunciation, and it promised a perfect forgiveness for all sins.

It encountered the individual soul as if the latter stood alone in the world, and it called all men into a unified fraternal society as comprehensive as human life and as deep as human need.

It erected a religious democracy and from the very outset was concerned with subjecting it to strong authorities.

Even in its further development no other religion was ever more multifaceted, more complicated, and more "catholic" than this religion was— openly and, even more, latently—already in its very beginnings, and this in spite of its concise confession, "Christ is Lord."

What is the source of this complexity, this *complexio oppositorum*, which is not perceived by the superficial glance and which is ascribed only to the later development of this religion? The answer is simple enough: the religion that Jesus Christ proclaimed also transmitted, along with the Old Testament, the complicated religious material of late Judaism, flowing out of numerous sources, with all its various levels, as the new religion's "faith."

This "catholicism" was not in the spirit of the founder; we know that to him all traditions, doctrines, and forms were essentially the same, if only God was acknowledged, his will followed, and his kingdom given room. It was quite far from Jesus Christ's intention to set up a broad band of "doctrine," since he, bringing forth the old and proclaiming the new, always had in view only practical religion itself at its decisive main points. And besides this, he was and remained a Jew in the sense of the prophets, in the fact that for him what mattered exclusively was the kingdom of God and "righteousness" before God, only that he measured it by a different yardstick from that used by the scribes and the Pharisees.

Apparently the Palestinian Jewish-Christian communities also felt as he did. They too had no God-world dogmatics. The tremendously complicated and disparate material that had been brought together in late Judaism still remained for them without structure; it was not doctrine but only "material" with un-defined validity, out of which one could create, according to one's preference, suggestions, admonitions, and speculations. On Jewish soil the proclamation of Jesus Christ was only the fulfillment of the ancient messianic promises. A centuries-old tradition and practice had put Judaism in the position of keeping itself immune to the new material that was received, as far as dogmatics was concerned; that is, it could indeed use the riches of this material but ultimately still not burden the simplicity of the ancient *belief*. This attitude and this skill automatically passed over also to Jewish Christianity.

But this changed—at a single stroke, one can say—when the Christian preaching passed over onto Greek soil. Judaism itself had already experienced this alteration when it came into contact with Hellenism; but since Judaism still formed a strict unity both nationally and cultically, the "Alexandrian" alteration remained hidden, suspect, and ineffective, just as historically it represented but an episode in Judaism.

Wherein did the alteration consist? A religion became a philosophy of religion—for only as such did the loftier Greek spirit understand it. It was subordinated to the Logos. At the same time, however, came the requirement to elaborate "logically" by assigning priorities within a unified whole everything that had been handed down simply as divine revelation.

But this "revealed" material was a body of material of unmanageable abundance. Unmanageable above all was the main part, the Old Testament. Who could comprehend this wealth, if it should be considered *sub specie* under the form of word, this profusion of utterances about God and about his external and internal working, this multiplicity of stories and teachings, of instructions and expressions of consolation? Who could harmonize the various stages and levels that the sacred documents encompassed, which nevertheless had to be harmonized if all was inspired by one and the same spirit? Along with the Old Testament there flooded into Christianity a stream of apocalypses, teachings about wisdom, and speculations, every wave bearing on its crest an ancient name which seemed to be sanctified by the instrument of revelation.

One is amazed that the Greeks submitted to all this as holy revelation. Only here one thing was connected with another and all ultimately depended on the six-day creation, the Psalms, and some prophetic pieces. As numerous witnesses show, these and only these made a deep impression on the souls and the spirit of the Greeks, one which caused them to acknowledge as God's word all the rest that was joined indissolubly with these revelations. In this regard some of them freely confessed that it was not the preaching of Jesus Christ that first convinced them, but the Old Testament, or its kernel, had been for them the bridge that had led them to Christianity and continued to keep them there. "I would not believe the gospel if I had not been moved by the authority of the Old Testament" was undoubtedly the confession of numerous Greek Christians of the earliest period. Of course these were not the loftier spirits; the Old Testament and the Christian proclamation succeeded in penetrating the upper level of the Greek spirit only when this upper level was already in the process of disintegration.

What had been messianism and eschatology in Palestine was revealed on Greek soil to be a religion whose content—as a result of the saturation of late Judaism with religious material—was maximal.

Down to the present day the most important task of the catholic churches was and is to maintain for the Christian religion the entire abundance of religious capital, especially the *complexio oppositorum* as it has been briefly sketched above, and along with it also its unprecedented religious universality. The entire history of dogma has developed out of this task. The ordering of the cultus and of the system of absolution is arranged in terms of the task, and indeed even the complicated constitution it has constructed is to be understood in its entirety only from this perspective. However, it was not the early church but only the Aristotelian dialectic of medieval scholasticism that was able after many centuries to gain intellectual mastery in a unitary way over the whole body of disparate and conflicting materials.

It is obvious that at no stage of its development could this *entire* body of material be or become a "private religion." However high might be the standing of the individual, however profound and capable of development might be his spirit, his life of impressions, and his religious experience, and however many unreasonable demands his loose thinking might tolerate, still for his inner life he could always choose only parts from this antithetical complex. To the *whole* he was able to offer only reverence and obedience, and so it is still today. This fact necessarily produced an intermediate entity as the bearer of the whole. Every higher religion demands a hypostatized fellowship; but here it was doubly demanded, because only such a fellowship was strong enough here to understand and to represent the whole and because the ancient *national* community of Israel rejected the new development—and *the church* was such a fellowship. The church, at one time the specific congregation of Jerusalem, appeared already in the apostolic age alongside Christ and over the other local congregations and the individual; this is an evidence of its intrinsic indispensability. The individuals live on its wealth, are nourished in various ways from that wealth, and obediently leave the understanding of the whole and the responsibility for the whole to the church, that is, to the newly emerging class of professional theologians.

But the insight that a *real* manifestation on earth must correspond to this "ideal" church was first developed in the course of two centuries out of the necessity *to maintain in force* the *entire* antithetical complex of the Christian message and to *defend* it against abridgments and expansions. The visible catholic church is therefore no "accidental phenomenon" in the development of the Christian enterprise, and it is not merely the product of that development in collaboration with the surrounding world and its pervasive forces. Instead, it was required from the very beginning onward, if all the polar elements were to be maintained in force beside and with one another, elements which were already contained in the earliest proclamation of this religion. *The church provides a basis for the immense expansion of Christian syncretistic theology.*

But at no time did the drive within the thoughtful religious man to adapt himself *inwardly* to what was presented to him as religion as a totality accept suppression, or, if that adaptation was not possible, to excise what was self-contradictory, incomprehensible, or offensive. Thus one must expect that from the beginning of church history onward, and continually, there were those who sought to make themselves at home in the religion by means of *excision, accen-*

tuation, and coherent organization of the material. It was their intention to teach a *clear* Christianity and to summarize this in a "faith" that required no self-contradictory or offensive ideas. This could indeed be achieved by means of the allegorical method, and with its help one could hold together much that was disparate; but still this method was not everywhere and always applicable, and besides, it was not to everyone's taste.

The incipient catholic church gave to such men, who developed their own religion out of the total tradition and then set it in opposition to the church, the name of "heretics," i.e., those who followed what they themselves "chose."

Here already we must think of the most prominent Christian missionary of the earliest period, the apostle Paul. His position is such a unique one because he was the father not only of the catholic church but of "heresy" as well.

Paul constantly placed the highest value upon keeping his preaching in harmony with that of the "original apostles," i.e., with the great aggregate of the Christian proclamation. However much he might emphasize his apostolic independence, full agreement with the ancient proclamation in its entire breadth and many-sidedness was not to be jeopardized thereby. He built the great church upon the foundation of the prophets and apostles with the cornerstone Christ, i.e., the church of the total tradition. However, on the other hand, he not only threatened it by the decided emphasis upon "his gospel," but he silently or explicitly excised from the complex tradition a significant part and he so accentuated other elements that their polar opposites were in danger of being lost. *He blazed the trail to a clear understanding of the Christian message*; but this is precisely what that message as universal and as *complexio oppositorum* will not tolerate. He gave to the concept of the law a new content and destroyed the old one; he ruled out the religious significance of "works"; he accentuated the "new" in such a way that the Old Testament threatened to lose its present significance; he had the "spirit" so to triumph over the "letter" that the latter appeared transitory and of no value; he interpreted both "sin" and "redemption" from one single point of view and therewith denied to all other perspectives any validity.

In sum: he was not satisfied with the juxtaposition of the religious and the moral, the theocentric and the anthropocentric, the predestinationist and the ergistic, the dramatic and the quiet elements, as this juxtaposition was taken over from late Judaism by the Christian proclamation. Starting from the belief in the crucified Son of God, he strove after a doctrine of faith which from the perspective of redemption would illumine and clearly explain the conflicts of the inner life and the course of history. Whether he himself was influenced in this by Greek Gnosticism is a controversial point which need not be discussed here. Even if one affirms this in a certain sense, Paul's religious independence still remains great enough.

But curiously, at first he had no noteworthy success with the reductions and the vigorous simplifications that he offered; we sense their presence within the development of postapostolic Christianity only as a *ferment*. His great success

was essentially limited to the establishing of the right of the Gentiles to become Christians; for the rest, his preaching had its effect along with that of the many nameless ones who, more or less uncritically, caused the broad stream of polar religious elements to pour over the world as the Christian proclamation. What is called Paulinism was more prophecy of the future than a decisive impetus in the church which was being developed into catholicism. Most of the postapostolic Christian authors down to Irenaeus show only slight Pauline influences. In a certain sense each of them still goes his own way; but on the other hand they all are in harmony, because the proclamation of none of them consciously excludes that of the other. They all draw it from the immense reservoir of late Judaism into which the Christian spring also had emptied. None of them except "John" crystallized what he expresses; one gets the impression that each one of them could have brought forth something else. No one is a "heretic," and no one makes the others into "heretics." There was as yet no clear theology that worked with special emphasis and exclusive elements.

¹One gains this impression from reading the writings of Luke, Peter, James, and the so-called Apostolic Fathers: Clement, Ignatius, Barnabas, and Hermas. Off to the side, however, there are already, alongside and after Paul, Christian "heretics," and from the time of Hadrian onward they are a significant force.

For all of them it is characteristic that they did not wish to allow the *syncretism of religious motifs*—for the *complexio oppositorum et variorum* [collection of opposites and various elements] is nothing but the syncretism of religious motifs—to exist, but set in opposition to this syncretism a more or less unequivocal and clear religious experience and teaching. In doing this they rightly recognized that the source of this impure syncretism lay above all in the Old Testament, in its frequently inferior "letter" and in the instances of arbitrary interpretation to which it gave occasion. They all therefore rejected the Old Testament, sometimes totally, sometimes in some of its major parts.

But here one notes the paradoxical fact that these "heretics," while they sought to be freed from the Old Testament, from late Judaism, and thus from the syncretism of religious motifs, and to give to Christianity a clear expression, once again introduced a syncretism from another side. They all borrowed, though in different ways, from the myth and mystery complexes of thought. Orthodox Judaism, though appearing itself already to many outsiders as liberal, regarded these complexes as pagan and demonic. To the representatives of the entire Christian tradition, too, they were alien and unacceptable. In the "Gnostics" we encounter a remarkable phenomenon in that, starting out from the saving significance of the person of Christ and therefore as a rule following Paul, they gave to Christianity a coherent structure by eliminating numerous religious and ethical motifs, but therein they accomplished the *most significant borrowing from alien mystery-speculations*.

Up to the present time this fact has not been clearly understood³ in its historical and religio-philosophical context, and therefore it has not been given adequate explanation. How does it happen that the first unambiguous Christian theologians were *Gnostics*, that is, that they introduced into the Christianity that stemmed from Judaism those alien myths and the speculations associated with them?

In my opinion, the reason for this lies in the fact that Judaism had not developed a *normative theology* with and alongside its sacred documents, i.e., with and alongside its "law." It did indeed express and append to the letter of the Old Testament an abundance of religious motifs and theological speculations in its apocalypses and books of wisdom, and particularly in its Greek literature—all this passed over into the Christian proclamation as a formless mass—but the systematic necessity was, so to speak, already exhausted by the "law." Consequently, in the realm of systematic theology Judaism did not basically go beyond the *one* principle: "Hear, O Israel, the Lord thy God is one God." And even this principle was threatened by the introduction of a new religious motif, without its being rightly recognized, because there was not any *theological* ecclesiastical bookkeeping in Judaism at all.

Since now the "law," and with it the sense of nationality, had lost its validity in the new Christian communities—what a difference from the Jewish communities!—a new binding force had to enter in, in order to counter this process of dissolution: in the course of the second century the catholic church found it in the combined ideas of *"the faith" and "the apostolic tradition,"* and out of these ideas, after the creation of the collection of apostolic writings and of the apostolic office of the bishops, carefully and gradually distilled the comprehensive catholic doctrine. Nevertheless, the first effort at a conclusion, as Origen proposed it, was a failure, ecclesiastically considered, and it had to be subjected to a thorough revision in the period that followed. The failure, however, was not catastrophic, because the formal authorities of the sacred writings and of the apostolic authority of the church in association with the quite brief apostolic confession of faith were strong enough to overcome shocks and to maintain the consciousness of an unlimited and still assured and dependable religious possession.

But the "heretics," in this respect akin to the apostle Paul, did not wish to delay establishing their doctrine, that is, their religion's success in the intellectual arena and the centralizing of its organization.[4] Already this demand shows that they were Greeks—as a teacher of the faith Paul grew beyond his people. However, not only were they Greeks, but the leaders among them must already have been Greek Gnostics before they became Christians, that is, they must have stemmed from that new intellectual and religious atmosphere that had developed out of the combination of oriental and Hellenic mystery-wisdom, not without some influence from the late Pythagorean, late Platonist, and late Stoic philosophy, some generations earlier.

This "Gnosticism" is manifested in the great diversity of its material, its cultic practices, and its sociological patterns. However, in its Christian form it is a unified entity, and in this form it anticipates the stage into which the non-

Christian Greek religious philosophy first moved with Jamblichus. The Christian Gnostics of the second century anticipate this stage in that they are *philosophers of revelation* and connect the dramatic and vertical post-Platonic God-world system, as well as the lofty hymn of the spirit, its descent, and its ascent, to the Christian proclamation. Therewith the supremacy of this proclamation is conceded; for Jesus Christ is the redeemer of the spirits, that is, he is the divine power who ends the unnatural connection between spirit and matter that has taken place through the great fall and in which the spirit lies bound in chains, and he makes possible the spirit's return to its native country.

The Christian proclamation was seized by the Gnostics—here we speak only of the major ones—with the lofty seriousness and the holy enthusiasm of Paul, whom they honored as their leader. But it became completely embedded in the dualistic system, which originally and again at the end of the drama is thought of in pantheistic terms, because the Kenoma which is thrown back again upon itself is nothing. The correctness of this combination appeared to be guaranteed by Paul himself, for there were enough passages found in his epistles about God, soul, spirit and flesh, the god of this world, mysteries of the world and of history, and so on, that could hardly be interpreted by a Greek in any sense other than the sense of that system. Moreover, there appeared in those epistles some speculations that were hardly different from the aeon-speculations. But these Gnostics could not dispense with the aeon-speculations, since only the proof of a pleroma of spirits with successively lower levels of divinity could explain the actual condition of the world as an unnnatural and baleful mixing of good and evil. These Gnostics had to confront with sharp criticism the Old Testament at every point; for its fundamental beginning point—the creation story—was wholly unacceptable to them because this story regarded as good what they condemned as evil: the world in its present condition and indeed in its very being. But for the Old Testament they substituted the lofty drama of a primordial pretemporal event and the exalted hymn of the spirit. Why should these be incompatible with the Christian proclamation, which in its sublimity and in its moving and joyous drama shows itself to be akin to them? And does not the confession "Christ is Lord" demand precisely that this Lordship of his over the universe and over history be interpreted in just such a way as this speculation does here?

The situation in which the Christian religion, politically detached from Judaism, found itself in the time of Hadrian was the most critical in all its history. On one side stood the formless, uncrystallized Christian proclamation, bound to the Old Testament but in fact dependent upon late Judaism with the abundance of its materials and of contradictory motifs, determined to draw everything into the "apostolic" sphere and to preserve it in spirit and in letter. On the other side stood important teachers who offered a clear and firm Christian knowledge of God and the world, in which the redemption wrought through Jesus Christ held the highest position and which developed the loftiest of the

Greeks' speculations about the ultimate polar opposites that are the moving
forces in the world. The former strictly maintained the authority of the Old
Testament, and the latter rejected it; but the situation was made still more difficult for the former by the fact that they themselves sensed, with an ever-
increasing keenness, the difficulties that this book contained. Does it belong to
the Christians alone, or to the Christians and the Jews? Which of its parts must
be taken literally today? None (thus the Epistle of Barnabas, which treats the
literal interpretation of the Old Testament as a work of the devil), or all, or
some? May one assume something of a temporary divinely willed validity of
certain parts? Was the law given in order to increase sin? Must one allegorize
everything? How should allegorizing be done? Is the significance of the book
exhausted in what is typological or prophetic? Is not much of it set forth in order
to characterize and to punish the Jews? and so on. Of course within the catholic
tradition there was general agreement that the ceremonial law did not apply to
Christians, but the validation of this principle was itself dubious, and beyond the
principle itself there were the most painful divergences, even to the point of contradiction. Thus the "apostolic" people entered into the great crisis with some
grave uncertainties besetting them.

Marcion saw himself as called to liberate Christianity from this crisis.
*No syncretism, but simplification, unification, and clarity of what bore the
Christian label*—this is the second line in which he appears with his preaching
of the alien God and his founding of a church. A plain religious message
was to be set in opposition to the immense and ambiguous complex of what
was handed down in tradition. Here, however, Marcion not only stands with
Paul, but also together with the Gnostics and over against the church; and
just so he most sharply rejects, in opposition to these Gnostics, the new
syncretism which they introduced in the mistaken opinion that the material
brought in from the mystery-speculations was adequate to the true Christian
idea and hence worthy of admiration. Thus here also, as is true in his ruthless carrying through of the *paradoxical* character of religion, Marcion is the
consistent one; *true religion must be plain and transparent, just as it must
also be alien and absolute-paradoxical.*

3.

Religion is redemption—the indicator of the history of religion in the first
and second centuries points to this position; no longer can any be a god who
is not also a savior. The new Christian religion splendidly addressed this
awareness, and the apostle Paul had already so shaped it that he made Christ
as *redeemer* the central point of his entire Christian proclamation. But his concept of God, nourished on the Old Testament, shows, in comparison with his
concept of Christ, a tremendous overflow of additional meaning. Whether he
was right or wrong in this may be left aside here. What is beyond any contradic-

tion is that the Father of Jesus Christ for Paul is by no means simply coterminous with Christ the redeemer. He is not only the Father of mercy and the God of all comfort, he is also the inexhaustible, who dwells in light unapproachable, the creator of the world, the author of the Mosaic legislation, the sovereign guide of history, particularly of the Old Testament. Further, he is the wrathful and punishing one and finally the judge who stands at the door with the great day of judgment. Of course, Paul had already stricken out much of the old Jewish concept of God, partly by means of allegorical exposition, partly by means of an historical-philosophical way of looking at things which made it possible, on the basis of the idea of the education of the human race and of an accommodation that was necessary for salvific aims, to eliminate numerous offensive elements. Thus not only the ceremonial law was set aside but also a great number of intolerable Old Testament utterances. And beside Paul there stood numerous other teachers who worked at the task of interpreting and shaping the Christian concept of God in terms of the savior Christ. Marcion also stood in this line; but he advanced along it to the most extreme degree of consistency. Nothing at all could be allowed to stand alongside redemption; it is something so great, so exalted, so incomparable, that the person who has it and brings it *cannot be anything other* than the redeemer. *The Christian concept of God must therefore be stated exclusively and without remainder in terms of the redemption wrought by Christ. Thus God may not and cannot be anything other than the God in the sense of merciful and redeeming love.* All else is rigidly to be excluded; God is not the creator, not the lawgiver, not the judge; he does not become wrathful and does not punish but is exclusively love incarnate, redeeming, and blessing. Thus the yearning of the times for the God of redemption and its lofty estimate of redemption is given the sharpest conceivable expression.

Religion is the paradoxical message of *the alien God*; it is simply a *clear* and *unitary* message, and it is the *exclusive* message of the God who is the redeemer. Every one of these declarations, which fit together into a harmonious whole, responds to the powerful longing and striving of the times, expresses it in maximal fashion, and brings it to the highest fulfillment by demonstrating this fulfillment to have occurred in the coming of Christ. In the preaching of Marcion "of the *good and alien* God, the Father of Jesus Christ, who through faith redeems to eternal life mankind, wretched, utterly alien to him, out of the strongest bonds—*namely, out of the nature that was foisted upon him and out of the captivity of this nature under a condemning law*"—it found its most concise and yet all-encompassing expression. The paradox of the religion, its unmistakable power, and its exclusive character as redemption are here summarized. Men do not return to their father's house through redemption; instead, a glorious foreign land is opened up to them and becomes their homeland.

The interest that is aroused by the appearance of Marcion on the scene of the history of religion and of the church is herewith indicated. No other religious personality in antiquity after Paul and before Augustine can rival him in significance. Therefore everything that is preserved for us from him or is handed down in tradition about him is worthy of our careful attention. And this is not, after all, a small amount; we possess (1) the accounts of his alleged "system" as given by his opponents; we know (2) the scope of his Bible, and many selections from it are handed down to us verbatim; we know (3) about the principles of his biblical criticism, and numbers of his emendations are available to us; finally, (4) extensive remnants of his great work *Antitheses* have come down to us, together with numerous explanations of biblical passages.

But up until now there has been little exploitation of these sources; in particular the second and the fourth have been unduly neglected, and yet they are the most important. As a result of this neglect, Marcion's Christianity appears to be more unbiblical, more abstract, and more lifeless than it was in fact, especially since people have allowed far too much weight to be placed upon his adversaries' accounts as over against Marcion's own statements. Who, for example, has paid any attention to the fact that Marcion left standing a number of utterances in which the concepts "just," "righteousness," "justify," and "judgment" are employed with reference to the good God? Who up to the present time has discovered the great difference which even according to him existed between the original apostles and the Judaistic pseudoapostles? Who traces out his attitude toward the law and the Old Testament beyond the bare acknowledgment that he rejected them? In all these and many other problems, historical writing has long been essentially satisfied with repeating the brief and emphatic items of information given by his opponents. People still today operate within the context provided by these opponents; they intend to show that he was a dualist, but this can be refuted from what he allowed to stand in the New Testament. The task, however, is posed for an authentic writing of history to show from this same material what he then really intended. This is more, deeper, and richer than what has been indicated up to the present time. And it is a joy to occupy oneself with a deeply religious man of intellectual purity, one who rejects all syncretism, allegory, and sophistry.

II

MARCION'S LIFE AND CAREER[1]

According to a reliable tradition, Marcion was a native of Sinope, the most important Greek commercial city on the south shore of the Black Sea, and thus a fellow countryman of the Cynic Diogenes, a point upon which Tertullian plays (*adv. Marc.* I 1).[2] The date of his birth may have been about the year 85 or somewhat later.

There were Jewish communities in Pontus in the early days of the empire. Paul's fellow-worker, Aquila, came from there (Acts 18:2), and so did the Bible translator of the same name, a Jewish proselyte. The latter was an exact contemporary of Marcion; indeed, if one may trust Epiphanius, this Aquila too was born in Sinope (Iren. in Eus. HE V 8.10; Epiph., *de mens. et pond.* 14f.).[3]

It is remarkable that from this city there emerged simultaneously the sharpest adversary of Judaism and the most scrupulous translator of the Jewish sacred scriptures.[4] Here one would like to learn something more in detail about the propaganda of Judaism and its antithetical effects, but the tradition is silent on this point.

Marcion and Bible translator Aquila are not after all antithetical in every respect; there rather exists a certain affinity between them. Marcion too proposes to take nothing away from the letter of the Old Testament, and in his way he is as literal as Aquila. His ecclesiastical opponents indeed noted this about him and held it against him. The question suggests itself as to whether Marcion had not at some time been closely related to Judaism. One detects nothing of the Hellenistic spirit in him, *the Jewish expositions of the Old Testament are well known to him*, and his entire attitude toward the Old Testament and Judaism can best be understood as one of resentment. In the *Neue Studien zu Marcion* (p. 15) I have already proposed the hypothesis that Marcion or his family came out of Judaism; Jewish proselyte status preceded the conversion to Christianity, a step which is not indeed surprising but was rather the rule in the conversions of the earliest period. A further argument for this view is the fact that he explains the messianic prophecies in the same way as do the Jews.[5] Thus his Christianity is built upon a resentment towards Judaism and its religion. For this reason it was possible for him to have an experience very similar to that of Paul, only that it went much further than did the apostle's; the latter only broke with the law and not with the lawgiver and the Old Testament.

The first epistle of Peter presupposes Christians in Pontus, and the famous letter of Pliny to Trajan tells us how numerous and strong the Christian com-

munities there were already in the time of Trajan. According to recent studies
this letter was written in or near Amisus.[6] The "deaconesses" whom Pliny mentions allow us to conclude that there was an established organization of the communities there at the beginning of the second century.

Hence the otherwise unsuspicious account of Hippolytus that Marcion was
the son of the bishop (or a bishop) of Sinope has nothing against it; in fact, Marcion's development becomes more understandable to us if he was a Christian
from his early years and was a member of the great church. All his life he, as
distinguished from the Gnostics, worked for the great community, i.e., for all
of Christendom, and he never intended to be a sectarian. Further, his familiarity
with the Old Testament and his respect for the very letter of the Old Testament,
even though it turned into aversion, is more easily explained if he had grown
up with the Holy Book.

But the other report that Hippolytus also provides, that Marcion was excommunicated in Sinope by his father because he had seduced a virgin, does
not deserve any confidence. Hippolytus himself did not repeat it in his later anti-
Gnostic work, the *Refutation*; Irenaeus, Rhodon, Tertullian, the Alexandrians,
and Eusebius are silent about it. It certainly arises out of the polemical theme;
Hippolytus says quite generally that the heretics had seduced the church, the
pure virgin.[7]

On the other hand, one need not doubt that Marcion was excommunicated
by his own father. The report is so singular in the history of the heretics that
for this reason alone it deserves to be believed. But if Marcion was excommunicated in Sinope, the reason would have been his false teaching, and this
is in fact also the meaning of the legend that he had seduced a virgin.

There cannot have been excommunications, in the sense of the later
church's practice, as early as Hadrian's time; they implied more then in some
respects and less in others. More, because they could be so severe that the person expelled was handed over to Satan; less, because the judgment of the ex-
communicating congregation was not automatically effective in other congregations as well. But we certainly may assume that only a grave instance of false
teaching occasioned the excommunication; for only in the most extreme case
would it be decided in those times to expel a brother if he still acknowledged
Christ as his Lord. Thus Marcion must already at that time have held the basic
features of his teaching which was so intolerable to the great church.[8]

He betook himself to Asia Minor; this was itself a journey for purposes
of propaganda. An indisputable source tells us that he took along with him
some letters from some brothers in Pontus. These could only have been
letters of recommendation, from which fact it is clear that he had followers
in his home country and thus that his exclusion there had not taken place
without some conflict. But in Asia Minor too (Ephesus, says the source;
probably Smyrna also, and perhaps Hierapolis), where he sought recognition
from the leaders of the churches and laid before them his interpretation of

the gospel, he was rejected and repelled. It is probably at that time that his encounter with Polycarp took place—or was it only later in Rome?—an encounter related by Irenaeus (following Papias?). Polycarp sharply rebuffed the man yearning for recognition: "I recognize you as the first-born of Satan." Marcion must already have proposed his "two gods" doctrine and the rejection of the Old Testament and tried to insinuate them into the community when Polycarp countered him in this cruel fashion.

Now Marcion betook himself to Rome. Pontus, Asia Minor, Rome: already at this time this signified in ecclesiastical matters an ascending sequence. Anyone who wished to gain influence upon the whole of Christendom had to go to the world capital.[9] He travelled thence in his own ship; for we hear from the best sources (Rhodon in Rome, Tertullian) that he was a well-to-do shipmaster and was known in Rome as such.[10] This journey probably took place in the first year of Antoninus Pius, and it certainly was about this time. A report from Hippolytus tells that Marcion had already sent a woman disciple thence in advance to prepare for his arrival. This is obscure.

In spite of the rebuffs in Pontus and in Asia, Marcion felt and knew himself still to be a member of the Christian community and therefore a "brother." According to his conviction he represented the gospel as it was given to Christendom and as Christendom ought to represent it. Therefore he joined the Christian group in Rome and upon his entrance into their company gave to the community 200,000 sesterces. In Rome people must have known nothing at first about his earlier history and his doctrine, but even if they soon became acquainted with it, there was no necessity immediately to exclude him. They could wait. The gift of money may also have contributed to the delay in criticizing the new member of the community, and Marcion himself may have begun cautiously in propagandizing for his doctrine. Even for the period after his break with the great church it is characteristic that not a single abusive or angry word about the church and its members is handed down to us.[11]

But it is also possible, and indeed rather probable, that Marcion first conducted himself circumspectly in Rome in order to lay the foundations for his teaching most securely in serious labor. The production of the *authentic* text of the gospel and of Paul's epistles, i.e., their purging of the Judaistic interpolations, and then the composition of the great critical work *Antitheses*, which was to demonstrate the irreconcilability of the Old Testament with the gospel and its origin from a different God, were tasks of such scope and difficulty that they could be achieved only in quiet, persistent labor. Since they are based upon the text that is more strongly attested for us in Rome and the West than in the East, it is probable, if not certain, that Marcion first composed his fundamental works in Rome. Since the break with the Roman church and the great propaganda effort that followed the break both presuppose these works, Marcion must have completed them in the year 144, for the break comes in this year (at the end of July). Thus probably as a mature man, during the approximately five years between 139 and 144, Marcion created his New Testament and his *Antitheses* in Rome; still the possibility must be left open that this had already been done during his stay in Asia Minor.

As soon as he had finished them, he appeared before the Roman community and demanded that their presbyters (it is significant that the source, Hippolytus, does not mention a bishop) take a stand with reference to these works of his and thus to his teaching. A formal hearing was held—the first of this kind that we know of in early church history, but on the other hand a parallel to the so-called apostolic council. In the hearing Marcion took as his point of departure Luke 6:43 ("the good and the corrupt tree"). The saying in Luke 5:36f. ("new wine, old wineskins"), which in his mind was even clearer, appears also to have played a part already at that time; at any rate, it too provided a foundation for Marcion's statements. In fact both statements are, in their sharply antithetical nature, especially suited to serve as beginning points for the Marcionite teaching.

The hearings ended with a sharp rejection of the unprecedented teaching and with the expulsion of Marcion; the presbyters also gave the 200,000 sesterces back to him. Two generations later not only Hippolytus in Rome but also Tertullian in Carthage knew about this impressive action. It will always remain memorable that at the first Roman synod of which we know, there stood before the presbyters a man who expounded to them the difference between law and gospel and interpreted their Christianity as a Jewish kind. Who does not think here of Luther?![12]

Perhaps at that time, or perhaps only later, a letter (supposedly from the archives of the Roman church) was attributed to Marcion—Tertullian reports this—in which he himself had confessed that he earlier had shared the faith of the great church. The authenticity of the letter need not be doubted. Even if it shows that when he came to Rome Marcion knew himself still to be in unity of faith with the Roman Christians (which, in fact, his joining the community and his gift of money proved), still this should not occasion any surprise;[13] for Marcion indeed assumed that his doctrine was the genuine Christian doctrine and that therefore—up until the contrary was proved—it surely would find acceptance with the Christian communities. Therefore Tertullian's effort to fashion the letter into a snare for Marcion is fruitless. Further, it can be justified on moral grounds that after he had been rebuffed in Pontus and in Asia, Marcion did not come to Rome at first as a reformer; instead, he intended first to investigate and to provide for his teaching a sure basis and foundation in the hope that in this form it would be recognized by the community of the world capital and then by all of Christendom.

It was certainly with a heavy heart that Marcion received the judgment that excluded him and rejected his teaching as the worst kind of heresy, but he now drew the implications from that action and began his reformatory work of propaganda on the broadest scale. Only a few years later, around the year 150,

Justin wrote in his *Apology* that this propaganda had spread to the whole human race, and he placed Marcion alongside the arch-heretic Simon Magus, after he had already begun his literary battle against this "apostle of the demons" in his now-lost *Syntagma Against All Heresies*. Tertullian also writes (*adv. Marc.* V 19): "Marcion's heretical teaching has filled the whole world."

Marcion's career hardly lasted longer than some fifteen years after the year 144; no source reports that he was still living in the time of Marcus Aurelius. We do not know when and where he died. The legend given by Tertullian to the effect that on his deathbed he repented and asked to be readmitted to the church does not deserve to be believed.[14]

Unfortunately we know nothing at all of the years of Marcion's greatest activity. We see only the fruits, the extraordinary spread of the Marcionite church in all the provinces of the empire already in the age of the Antonines, for in opposition to the great church Marcion, conscious of being the called successor of Paul, established, not unstable sects, but *one* great *church*, consisting of ordered and well-established congregations, *the* church of Jesus Christ. It was for just this reason that Justin placed him alongside Simon Magus. Only the *one* significant report has come down to us that Marcion joined forces in Rome with the Syrian Gnostic Cerdo and that the latter gained an influence over him. Some church fathers, following Irenaeus, have greatly exaggerated this influence in order to minimize Marcion's originality and to surbordinate him to ordinary Gnosticism;[15] but the main part of Marcion's doctrine, the contrast of the good, alien God and the just God, does not come from Cerdo. Instead, the latter proclaimed the opposition of the good and the evil Gods, as did other Gnostics, and he was a Syrian representative of common Gnosticism. So far as we know, the Marcionite church never claimed Cerdo as its founder; on the contrary, it revered Marcion as exclusively holding that honor. Hence the relationship of dependence in which Irenaeus and Hippolytus have placed Marcion is based upon an error or a falsification. But on the other hand it is possible that certain features of Marcion's teaching, which are most loosely connected with the chief doctrine and which are on the other hand most closely related to Syrian Gnostic doctrines (the interpretation of the relationship of flesh and spirit; the strict Docetism), go back to the influence of Cerdo. If this must be admitted, still it is improbable that, as Epiphanius asserts, Marcion was first influenced by Cerdo after his break with the Roman community or even "took refuge in the heresy of Cerdo." Those features of kinship show up clearly in the criticism of the text of the gospel and of Paul's epistles as well as in Marcion's *Antitheses*, but these works (see above) hardly were only composed after the break with the church.[16]

The date of this break, immediately after the hearings with the presbyters of the Roman church—that is, the founding of their reformation church—remained in the memory of the Marcionite church. It occurred in July in the year 144, for counting from it the Marcionites reckoned the span of time between Christ and Marcion at 115 years and six and one-half months.

It cannot be concluded, at least not with any degree of probability, from a passage in Clement (*Strom.* VII 18.107) that Marcion had personal contact with Valentinus and Basilides. Moreover, the disconnected account in the Muratorian Fragment to the effect that Valentinus and some other person had written a new psalmbook for Marcion remains utterly obscure. If the Christian teacher Ptolemaeus, whom Justin mentions in the so-called *Second Apology*, is identical with the Roman Valentinian of the same name (which is not unlikely), then Marcion could have had contact in Rome with this man.

III

MARCION'S POINT OF DEPARTURE

The point of departure for Marcion's criticism of the tradition cannot be mistaken. It was provided *in the Pauline contrast of law and gospel, on the one side malicious, petty, and cruel punitive correctness, and on the other side merciful love*. Marcion had immersed himself in the basic ideas of Galatians and Romans and found in them the perfect illumination of the nature of the Christian religion, the Old Testament, and the world. It must have been a bright day for him, but also one full of horror at the darkness that had again darkened this light in Christendom, when he came to see that Christ represented and proclaimed an entirely new God; further, that religion is simply nothing other than devout belief in this redeemer-God who transforms man; and finally, that the totality of world events down to the present time is the evil and contradictory drama of a deity who possesses no higher value than does the obtuse and loathesome world itself, whose creator and ruler this deity is.

In this recognition all of Paul's religious antitheses were given the sharpest expression, which however by this intensification was far removed from the apostle's own intentions. Marcion remained faithful to these intentions only in the blissful certainty of the *gratia gratis data* with its contrast with the *justitia ex operibus*, and in the awareness of a liberation that transcends all reason in contrast to a dreadful lost condition. In this conviction the universality of redemption, as over against its limitation to one people, was necessarily included as well. *The religious principle that embraces all higher truth in the contrast of law and gospel is also the principle of explanation of the totality of being and becoming*.

This knowledge, in which the religion of redemption and inwardness was elevated in an incomparable fashion to the ethical metaphysics that governs everything, had as its inevitable result the abandonment of the Old Testament. But it is hardly possible for us any longer to sense what this must have meant for a devout person who, like Marcion, had grown up with the general Christian tradition (and indeed, perhaps earlier with the Jewish tradition). The reassessment of the Old Testament that resulted in its rejection could have been achieved only with the most profound disturbance and the keenest pain on his part; for he found it necessary to consign to the flames what he formerly had revered, and along with the law he had to condemn also the prophets and the psalms which still contained so much that seemed to agree with the gospel or to prepare the way for it. Error! Error! Even their most elevating and comforting words are only pretense and delusion! Even from them there peers forth, now unmasked, the frightful countenance of the cruel God of the Jews, the creator of the world; for when Paul preached that Christ is the end of the law and that it had been given in order that sin might abound, he meant not only the law in its narrower sense, but the entire old order of salvation with all its representatives, and even Christ says that not only the law but the prophets as well preached only as far as John, and thus that they no longer possess any validity.[1] And nothing that loses its validity can be divine.

Christ himself proclaims this in his gospel, but he confirms the Pauline gospel in general and in detail. Did he not break the law again and again in his life and through his teachings? Did he not declare war against the teachers of the law? Did he not call the sinners, while those teachers desired only righteous men as their pupils? Did he not declare the greatest prophet of the Old Testament God, John the Baptist, to be an uninformed man, one who had taken offense at him? And most of all, did he not bluntly and curtly declare that only the Son knows and reveals the Father and thus that all who had come before him had proclaimed a false God?

These assertions are marked by an inexorable certainty and clarity; thus also the explanation of two programmatic utterances of Jesus is clear and admits of no doubt. When he spoke of the two trees, the corrupt and the good, which are able to produce only such fruits as are given by their very nature, he can mean thereby only the two great divine authors, the Old Testament God, who creates nothing but bad and worthless things, and the Father of Jesus Christ, who produces exclusively what is good. When he forbids the placing of a new patch on an old garment and the pouring of new wine into old wineskins, he thereby strictly forbids his people in any way to connect his preaching with that of the Old Testament; the latter rather must always be kept at a distance, since it is alien and antagonistic to him from the very beginning.

The Old Testament is abandoned—for the moment the new religion stood naked and bare, uprooted and defenseless. It must renounce all proof in terms of age, all historical and literary proofs in general! But a deeper reflection taught him that precisely this defenselessness and lack of proof are demanded by the very nature of the case and therefore provide support for its true nature. Grace is "freely given," so Christ and Paul teach, and this is the entire content of religion. But how could grace be freely given if the one who bestows it had even the slightest obligation to provide it? But if he were the creator of men and if from the beginning he were their educator and lawgiver, he would have *had* to take an interest in them. Only a wretched sophistry, conducted disgracefully in relation to God, could relieve the deity of this obligation! Thus he cannot have any natural or historical connection with men to whom he shows mercy and whom he redeems; thus he cannot be the world-creator and lawgiver; thus also neither the Old Testament nor any other dreamt-up prehistory can have any claim to validity. *Therefore it is demanded by the nature of his redemption that the redeemer-God, who is God in truth, had not appeared to men in any revelation of any kind before his appearance in Christ*; he may be understood only as absolutely *Alien*. But it also follows therefrom *that the inimical realm from which the redemption through Christ frees men can be nothing less than the world itself, together with its creator*. Now since Marcion remained true to the Jewish-Christian tradition in identifying the creator of the world and the God of the Jews and saw in the Old Testament not a book of lies but the truthful account of actual history—a remarkable limitation of his religious anti-Judaism—*for him the God of the Jews, together with all his book, the Old Testament, had to become the actual enemy.*

Once again, one should observe here how completely everything in this perspective is determined by the Christian religious principle, which to be sure is not able fully to establish its sway over the times because it cannot cast off the chains of the Old Testament, even though those chains are broken. Here the principle of the good, as the redeeming power and exclusively as such, is elevated to the highest principle. The remarkable thoroughness with which this is done, *and with which this principle is opposed not so much by "matter" as by fundamentally the multiform evil ethos of the "world,"*[2] forms an unappealing contrast with the hesitancy which, in spite of the negative judgments expressed, still is not able to break away from the Old Testament. In that time Greeks like Celsus most especially were able to sense this contrast; for the Christians of every variety, all of whom lay in the shackles of the Old Testament, he simply could not feel any sympathy. They saw only that Marcion scorned the Old Testament, but did not see that he was thinking within its framework.

But after Marcion had found the basic principle and the basic opposing principle, new tasks began for him. He now had to expound the true and so badly misunderstood content of the preaching of Jesus and Paul for knowledge and for life. In view of the disparate and varying ideas of faith of most Christians, which followed the tradition of late Judaism, and in view of the varied philosophical ideas and false dualisms of the Christian Gnostics, this was an immense task. It would have been immense even if the material from which the content was to be drawn, clearly delineated and transmitted without any doubt as to its authenticity, had lain ready before him. But here in fact he encountered a state of affairs that could induce doubt even in the most courageous and vigorous investigator. He found no Christian writings that possessed absolute authority to place alongside the Old Testament, which he could not use in the exposition of the Christian message. No: he had at his disposal four Gospels which, when he had reflected and labored in Asia Minor and Rome, already possessed an authority in the churches in those places, an authority that approached the absolute level. Then there were those Pauline epistles from which he had learned all of his Christianity; in the Roman community they enjoyed an apostolic reputation. Finally, there was still a larger number of Christian writings: the Acts of the Apostles, the Revelation

of John, other Christian prophetic writings and letters of various authors
under the names of apostles and pupils of apostles, which enjoyed a validity
not exactly defined but nevertheless important. But how much there was in
these writings that was divergent, varied, contradictory, and how uncertainly
did they testify to the pure gospel that Christ had come as the Son of an
alien God as *spiritus salutaris* in order to free sinners from the captivity to
their father and lord, the creator of the world, and to bless them! Marcion
had to begin his great undertaking on behalf of Christianity as a critic and
restorer, for the matter and the witnesses lay concealed in deep obscurity. In
fact, no Christian critic has ever been confronted with a more difficult task:
to show from New Testament writings that humanity must be redeemed and
has been redeemed from its God and Father! Marcion did not allow himself
to be frightened off; over against the old books, the law and the prophets,
he placed the new books, the book of the gospel,[3] and the letters of Paul.

IV

THE CRITIC AND RESTORER: MARCION'S BIBLE

Marcion, confident of his own faith as genuinely Pauline, saw the main body of Christendom around him in an internal struggle in which all seemed to be lost. While he was convinced that Christ had abolished the Old Testament and its God and had proclaimed an alien God, Christianity continued to equate the two Gods and to construe them out of the Old Testament, and thus it was "Judaistic" through and through. Further, books under the celebrated names of the original apostles supported, by their accounts, this error and apparently demanded its acceptance. Finally, — worst of all — even in the letters of Paul it is inescapably clear that there is much that unequivocally confirms the false belief that Christ is the Son of the creator of the world and that he promoted the will of this his Father in his own work.

How did this happen, and how could it happen, when in some chief passages in the Pauline letters the truth was so unequivocal and clear? *A great conspiracy against the truth must have begun immediately after Christ left the world and must have carried through its intentions with striking success.* No other explanation can suffice here. Marcion seized upon this explanation. In order to prove it, there was simply nothing at his command, as his statements show, but the recollection of the battle that Paul had waged against his Judaistic opponents, and even of this battle he, Marcion, knew nothing but what could be read in the apostle's letters.

It is important not to overlook this fact. Marcion was never able to appeal to other witnesses. There was no longer any living echo of these struggles; he knew of no continued action in the battle beyond what was known from the epistles, and no new documents were at his command that could give him information about the intentions either of Paul or of his adversaries.[1]

But in Paul himself, particularly in his epistle to the Galatians, so it seemed to Marcion, there were two guiding stars which one needed only to follow in order to find the sure way out of the labyrinth of the poor traditions: (1) Paul explains that there is only *one* gospel and that he represents it *alone, as he had also received it in particular*; and (2) he further says that all the others are proclaiming a *Judaistic* gospel and that therefore he simply must oppose them all as those who are held captive by the false belief that the Father of Jesus Christ is identical with the creator of the world and the God of the Old Testament.

For Marcion the following insights emerged from these explanations:

(1) The gospel that Paul means must, according to his own words, be free

from all Judaism; that is, not only must it have no connection with the Old Testament, but it must take an antagonistic stance with respect to it. Thus anything that purports to be Christian and yet exhibits a connection with the Old Testament is false and forged.

(2) From this he concludes at once that even the letters of Paul must have been corrupted, since in their present condition they exhibit much that is Judaistic.

(3) But further, he concludes from the Pauline epistles that the entire apostolic age had been moved exclusively by *one* major topic, that of the struggle of the Judaistic Christians against the true (i.e., the Pauline) gospel. The prologues to the epistles of Paul are the clearest evidence of this historical perspective of his, whether they stem from Marcion himself or from one of his pupils; for in them these epistles are considered exclusively from the perspective of how the communities to which they are addressed stand on the Pauline-Judaistic struggle. The author actually succeeds in forcing upon all of them this theme; the "falsi apostoli" either precede Paul in the mission or invade his mission; the communities either allow themselves to be captivated by them or else remain true to Paul's gospel.

(4) Marcion identified the "falsi apostoli" following Galatians 1:6–9, 2:4, and II Corinthians 11:13,14. From these passages, which he combined into one, he concluded that a large number of unauthorized and unnamed Judaizers had appropriated unto themselves the office of apostle in the church and had staged a propaganda campaign which had met with the greatest success in the entire empire, and in fact must have begun its unwholesome activity immediately after the resurrection. They are indeed definitely distinguished from the original apostles (Marcion follows Galatians here); but he is convinced that the latter played a deplorable role in the matter. He formed the following conception of them: Jesus had chosen them (the Twelve; Luke 6:13ff; Tert. IV 13) and had devoted the greatest care to them; but even during his lifetime he had not been able to bring them to the abiding belief that he was the Son of an alien God and not of the Old Testament God. When Peter at Caesarea gave his great confession to the Sonship of his Master, the latter had to enjoin him to silence because Peter held him to be the Son of the creator of the world (Tert. IV 21). Although the heavenly voice at the transfiguration clearly exhorted them to listen not to Moses and Elijah but to Christ, Peter did not understand this, as his foolish suggestion to build *three* tabernacles shows (IV 22). Of course the disciples had a slight glimmer of knowledge of "the truth of the gospel" and proper conduct when one of them asked Jesus to teach them to pray; he would not have made this request if he had still believed in the God of the Old Testament (IV 26). Again, this is demonstrated when Jesus defended their practice in contrast to that of John's fasting disciples (IV 11: "Christ defended his disciples, because they rightly conducted themselves differently, being consecrated to another and a different deity"). But they fell back again immediately, and it is they whom Jesus means when he speaks in words of lamentation about the "unbelieving generation"

(Tert. IV 22). The resurrection of Christ appears to have led them for a short time along the right road, and they were even persecuted by the Jews as "heralds of a different God" (IV 39); but everything very quickly became dim and obscure for them again, especially since they never even overcame their fear of men. Therefore when Paul began his battle against the false apostles, they did not make common cause with these latter, to be sure, but they did not support the witnesses of the truth. Instead, they revealed themselves to be half-Judaists (Peter and the other apostles supported by those understood to be "in alliance with Judaism," Tert. V 3), as men of the law ("Peter is a man of the law," Tert. IV 11), as timorous patrons of the pseudoapostolic mission (Tert. V 3), indeed, as those who through intrigue and deception are scarcely able to escape the suspicion that they are guilty of the depravation of the gospel ("Marcion complains that apostles are suspected [for their prevarication and dissimulation] of having even depraved the gospel," Tert. IV 3; ANF III, 348). In their lack of understanding they themselves have mixed "legalisms" with the tradition of the words of Jesus (Iren. III 2.2: "For [they maintain] that the apostles intermingled the things of the law with the words of the Savior," ANF I, 415), and nothing beneficial could come from their missionary activity since they did not know the full truth and, still influenced by the Jewish mind, have proclaimed the gospel only in fragmentary form (Iren. III 13.2: "They did not know the truth"; III 12.12: " . . . that the apostles preached the Gospel still somewhat under the influence of Jewish opinions. . . ," ANF I, 434).[2] Therefore, not only through the choice of Judas but also, though in a different way, through the choice of the twelve, Christ experienced a grievous disappointment. Consequently, if "the truth of the gospel" were not to go down to defeat, a new witness and missionary had to be raised up. The original apostles were not confirmed false teachers, but they had been mired in grave confusion; indeed, they had slipped ever further into it, so that they were not even frightened by the "peddlers" of the gospel (II Cor. 2:17).

(5) Paul says unequivocally that he is an apostle who has been called directly by Christ himself, that his gospel has not come to him through human mediation, that he rather has received it through revelation and in fact through an experience of being caught up into the third heaven, i.e., into a heaven which lies far above the terrestrial heavens. From this Marcion concludes that Paul had been called as *the* apostle of Christ, in order to counteract the false preaching, and further, that there must be in existence *one* gospel which is written by no man but is given directly from Christ—Marcion appears to have formed no clear conception of how this was done. The followers of Marcion sometimes thought of Christ himself as the author and sometimes Paul (Adamant., *Dial.* I 8; II 13f.; *Carmen adv. Marc.* II 29); but Tertullian reports (IV 2) only that "Marcion ascribes no author to his gospel." Especially worthy of note is the fact that Marcion must have regarded it as self-evident (since he thus interpreted certain of Paul's expressions) that Christ had provided for an authentic *written* gospel—so

destitute was he of all historical skill and so forcefully did he himself create history. The abandonment of the Old Testament certainly (along with the general conceptions of the time with reference to what a trustworthy religion finds essential) led him to this fixed idea; for a *littera scriptura* must be available, and if the creator of the world had provided such, then the alien God must all the more do so. How inadequate the oral tradition is was indeed most clearly exhibited by the unreliable missionary preaching of the twelve apostles.

There must be an authentic written gospel—at the moment in which Marcion was convinced of this, a grave temptation confronted him in view of the state of the gospel literature which he found at hand, namely, the temptation to write such a gospel himself! Here in particular there is shown with special clarity the remarkable interweaving of criticism and fidelity to history that characterized this unusual spirit and in addition the interweaving of an energy such as only the founder of a religion has, with the modesty of a pupil. As certain as it is that his church very soon highly honored him, the founder, (it saw him sitting at the left hand of the enthroned Christ—Paul was on the right hand; it counted time from the day when in Rome he finally had broken with the Judaistic church; it called him "*the* bishop" [Adamant., *Dial.* I 8]), it is just as certain that Marcion himself never laid claim to the vocation and rank of a prophet or an apostle, and he never made anything of his own authority or even of revelations that he had had. He knew himself simply as a pupil of Paul; he intended only to walk in Paul's tracks, and as he believed himself to be far from teaching a piety and mysticism of his own (see below), so also he certainly would have regarded it as the gravest sacrilege to author the true tradition of the gospel.

There had to be an authentic written gospel, for Paul says so. But where is it? It must be found among the four Gospels that are handed down, for Christ cannot have allowed it completely to disappear. It was no idiosyncrasy of Marcion to insist upon only *one*; instead, the situation that he found existing was an intolerable calamity and dilemma, which had only recently made its incursion into some of the chief churches and in which certainly the least of the churches could not have been comfortable—that situation wherein Christianity was expected to develop the authentic tradition of Christ out of four Gospel-books. What a contradiction within itself this is! At best the placing of these four books alongside each other was something temporary; the next requirement is that they be brought into a unity through a process of editing. But to do such editing surely was as far from Marcion's mind as was the creation of the authentic gospel. His task was only to reproduce the pure tradition; a "re-editing" would be an attack upon that tradition.

Which of the four Gospels is the authentic one? Tertullian tells us that Marcion, in his *Antitheses*, examined each of them, and this may also be inferred from the information given by Irenaeus and Origen. First of all, Marcion reached the conclusion that the original apostles themselves had written nothing at all (Adamant., *Dial.* II 12: "they did not proclaim in writing")—we do not know the source for this conclusion. It immediately follows from this that the names of "Matthew" and "John" for two of the Gospels are clearly forgeries.

However, it is not merely the names that are falsified.[3] All four Gospels, as they now exist, are, in their superscriptions[4] and their contents, forgeries of the Judaists (Tert. IV 3: "Marcion . . . tries [scil., in the *Antitheses*] to destroy the standing of those Gospels that have been published as genuine and under apostolic names, in order to gain for his own gospel the credit that he takes away from them").[5] However, one of them must not be forged but, like the epistles of Paul, only adulterated, for otherwise the gospel of truth would indeed have perished. Marcion decided for the Gospel that "the Judaistic tradition" falsely identified as that of *Luke*.[6]

The choice must not have been easy for Marcion; he set forth in his *Antitheses* the reasons for it and for the rejection of the other Gospels, together with the interpolations in the "genuine" Gospel. Unfortunately, we do not possess this statement of his reasons. It is, of course, beyond question that he had to reject the Gospel of Matthew at once, and in the Fourth Gospel the Prologue ("he came unto his own"), the high estimate of John the Forerunner, the wedding at Cana, and so on. The whole of the mysticism that is native to late Judaism also must have been extremely distasteful to him from the very outset, even though he must have been attracted by such a saying as "All who came before me are thieves and murderers," and a good bit besides. The choice therefore had to fall on either Luke or Mark. For the latter, there was the fact that he did not offer any prehistory, but against him was the scantiness of the words of Jesus, to which Marcion must have been especially sensitive. In Luke's favor, the "Gentile-Christian" and the ascetic character, and also, in spite of the surrender of the name, the traditional and historical connection with Paul weighed heavily; but on the other side the prehistory was, in Marcion's eyes, an immense *skandalon* of adulteration. When he nevertheless decided on this Gospel and not on Mark, the reason perhaps lay only in external circumstances. The first Gospel to reach Pontus probably was the Gospel of Luke; Marcion would have been familiar with it before any others, if indeed it was not for some years his only gospel in his Pontic homeland. So he may have clung to the gospel book which he had first come to know.

The survey yields the following results: after the twelve apostles had already mixed Judaistic materials into the oral tradition of the gospel, the "protectores Iudaismi" had put forth into the world three false gospels (and under false names at that) and had adulterated the true gospel which Paul had used as the foundation of his missionary preaching, as well as the letters of the apostle. They placed the name of Luke at the head of the adulterated authentic gospel book, for this name must be false; Paul, according to his own statements, had received his gospel from Christ himself.

Now if the true gospel and the letters of Paul have been adulterated, then, however difficult the task may be, it is the highest obligation to free them from this falsification. To be entrusted with this obligation—not with an "innovation" but with the "restoration of the previously adulterated rule [of faith]" (Tert. I 20)—therein consisted the reformatory consciousness of Marcion, and it was as "restorer" that his church celebrated him. But for this task he did not appeal to a divine revelation, any special instruction, nor to a pneumatic assistance; he did not undertake it as an enthusiast but, being supported by internal reasons, only with the means of philology.

From this it immediately follows that for his purifications of the text—and this is usually overlooked—he neither could claim nor did claim absolute certainty. But this is evident also from the history of his text; his pupils constantly made alterations in the texts—sometimes more radical than his own, sometimes more conservative—perhaps under his very eyes, but certainly after his death. We are told this most definitely by Celsus, Tertullian, and Origen, and also by Ephraem, and we possess examples of it. Thus the Marcionite church did *not* receive from its master the gospel and the ten letters of Paul with the instruction to revere the re-established text as a *noli me tangere* [do not touch], but the master gave to them the liberty, indeed perhaps left behind him the obligation, to continue the work of establishing the correct text. This freedom went so far that later Marcionites without embarrassment included the (purified) Pastoral Epistles in the collection of Paul's letters—thus Marcion must not have rejected them but only remained silent about them—and that they did not hesitate even to accept some individual fragments from other Gospels.[7] This latter step cannot be very surprising; for even though Marcion rejected these Gospels as forgeries, their affinity with the Gospel of Luke, even in the latter's "genuine" sections, cannot have escaped him. Thus if they contained some undoubtedly reliable material alongside the many forgeries, then Marcion could hardly raise any objection against one's subsequently employing them with caution in his church. In fact, it is not wholly ruled out that he himself had noted the interpretations of sayings of the Lord which Matthew presented, even if (see below) almost all agreements of his Lukan text with the Matthaean text (against the original text of Luke) are to be traced back to conformations which the copy of the Gospel of Luke that he had corrected in Rome already exhibited.

Probably in Rome, but perhaps already earlier, Marcion undertook the great task of the restoration of the texts. In Appendices III and IV I have investigated the tradition of the texts, restored the texts themselves so far as possible, and shown that the so-called W-text underlies Marcion's efforts and that the abundance of readings that earlier were regarded as Mariconite are simply Western readings—in a word: almost all those that are dogmatically neutral (even if they otherwise lack the attestation)—for it cannot be proved that Marcion intended also to provide a critical correction of the text of a purely stylistic kind, even though some passages could be interpreted thus. Now and then (though this is not certain) he has yielded to the inclination to underscore and to clarify; in some passages in which his emendations are not clear to us, a tendentious intention that we are no longer able to identify may have prevailed. However, Marcion most probably began his work with the "purging" of the letters of Paul, for only from this starting point could he find the norm for the criticism of the variegated tradition as it lay before him in the "adulterated" third Gospel. For the following I ask that the reader constantly consult the texts cited in the Appendices.

What principles, now, did Marcion follow in his work on the texts? We are still in a position to answer this question satisfactorily on the main point, in spite of the fact that the Marcionite canon of the Bible has been handed down to us in such fragmentary form and in spite of our necessary uncertainty as to whether numerous specific sections were omitted from Marcion's collection or have simply been passed over by Tertullian (or other witnesses).[8] In making a judgment one must always keep in view the fact that in Marcion's mind, what he omits are additions from the hand of the Judaistic pseudoapostles and what he inserts had been dropped out by them.[9] In the apostle's part of his canon Marcion demonstrably employed the following tendentious emendations:

Galatians. In 1:1, following "through Jesus Christ", Marcion strikes out the words "and (through) God the Father" and thus derives from the resultant text the indication that Jesus had awakened himself from the dead. In his interpretation of the relationship of the Father and the Son, which was close to Modalism, this very thing must have been welcome to him. The emendation is interesting in that it took as its point of departure a difficulty in the existing text.

In 1:7 Marcion adds to the expression that the gospel has no other alongside it the words "according to my gospel" (cf. Rom. 2:16). He was interested in noting, at the beginning of the epistle, the identity of his gospel with Paul's own gospel and thereby excluding the "Judaistic" gospel as well as a number of evangelical writings. The further change in the same verse, "(some) want (you) to change the gospel of Christ into a different gospel" (for "(some) want to change the gospel of Christ"), lies on the borderline between a tendentious emendation and a variant reading.

Chapter 1:18–24 probably were omitted because Marcion could not allow these connections of the apostle with Peter and the Jewish-Christian communities to stand; they must have been inserted by the "*pseudoapostoli et Iudaici evangelizatores*" (Tert. V 9). Chapter 2:1,2 were at the most only slightly altered, yet in all probability the "with Barnabas" was omitted; Marcion did not wish to see Paul's apostolic sovereignty influenced from any quarter.

The introduction to the apostolic council either was omitted or was reformed (2:6–9a). In 9b and 10, "fellowship" was left out, whereby the nature and spirit of the information became different, and the "and Barnabas" was omitted as well. By means of the latter omission and by the retention of the plural "we remember," the obligation laid upon Paul becomes an agreement which binds the two sides. Thus by means of minor excisions a considerable shift in meaning is achieved.[10]

Chapter 3:6–9,14a were stricken out, as we are explicitly told in the tradition, for only the Judaists could have introduced Abraham here. Verses 10–12 in Marcion's version, with the excision of the Old Testament quotation introduced by "it is written" and revised, read as follows: "Learn that he who is righteous through faith shall live, for whoever is under the law is under a curse, and the one who does these things lives in them," but the text here is not entirely assured. The long statement in 3:15–25 concerning the testament, Abraham, his seed, and the law was removed in its entirety; similarly, in v. 29 the words "then you are the seed of Abraham" were excised.

In Chapter 4:3 the words "still, from a human standpoint I say," which have been moved from 3:15 to this place, are unclear; in 4:4 Marcion excised the words "born from woman, born under the law." How Marcion understood 4:8,9 is not altogether clear, but it is certain that instead of "to beings not by nature gods" he wrote "to beings by nature gods." This is one of his striking emendations; for him it was important to see the heathen gods designated as gods of nature, while it was unsatisfactory for him to have them identified as "not gods" (because of the demiurge and his angels).

Chapter 4:21–26 bring the great intervention (together with a rearrangement of the text) which demands special attention; unfortunately, we know the text here only in part, but it is certain that Marcion allowed the name of Abraham to stand here. The most important alterations are the substitution of the concept representation or exhibition for covenants, elimination of Jerusalem, the insertion of Ephesians 1:21, and—if the text actually read thus or came from Marcion himself—the addition: "in which we are promised the holy church, which is our mother," together with the introduction of the synagogue of the Jews. The fact that the name of Abraham has been permitted by Marcion to stand here cannot be attributed to carelessness, since he obviously has carefully considered and worked through the section. Thus he does not shy away from using the Old Testament positively under certain circumstances. His insertion here of Ephesians 1:21 and the solemn confession of the church as mother can be understood, if at all, only to mean that he intended here to create a liturgical text of fundamental significance. It is especially important that he did not choose to speak of two Testaments, but substituted for that term the word "exhibitions" (demonstrations). In connection with allegory this word does not acknowledge any obligations with respect to the Old Testament, and it also avoids any reminiscences of "prophecies"; "If one allegorizes them, one can recognize in Abraham's sons of the slave woman and the free woman the two basically different institutions which led to the synagogue and the church."

Chapter 4:27–30 (the quotation from Isaiah about the unfruitful, Isaac and Ishmael) must have been eliminated.

If in 5:14 (see the Appendices) Marcion's reading is " 'in you,' not among the Jews," then here this reading has penetrated into the Western ecclesiastical tradition (for it is attested by numerous Western witnesses). This is certain because the removal of the immediately following ἐν τῷ is surely tendentious (the words "you shall love your neighbor as yourself" should not appear as an Old Testament quotation), but this same excision is also found in the very same Western witnesses!

The "the others" in 6:17 is probably a tendentious emendation for "the rest." "The others" are to be understood to be the Jewish-Christian enemies of the apostle.

I Corinthians. Here only a few tendentious excisions may be *proven*.[11] In 3:17 Marcion replaces "God will destroy him" with "he will be destroyed"; the good God destroys no one. In 10:11 he probably wrote "these things happened randomly" instead of "all these things happened as a type"; the "type" had to be eliminated. In 10:19 he was concerned with the proscribing of all sacrifices, while for him the nonexistence of the idols (cf. Gal. 4:8–9) was unacceptable. Thus he wrote: "any meat sacrificed to any idol or an offering to an idol is something" for "is an idol anything? No, . . ." In chapter 15 there are four tendentious emendations that can be demonstrated: (1) in the introduction to the chapter he struck out, for understandable reasons, in verses 3–4 "that which I also received" and "according to the Scriptures"; (2) in verse 20 he wrote "Christ has been raised" into "is known to have risen" because he did not like the idea of an "awakening" of Christ (see Gal. 1:1); (3) in verse 38 the later Marcionites put "spirit" in place of "body" in the sentence: "But God gives it a body as he wishes." Finally, (4) in verse 45 Marcion wrote "the last (man), the Lord, became a life-giving spirit" for "the last Adam became . . ." Jesus should not in any sense be described as "Adam." It is probable that Marcion did not leave out, at least not altogether, the appearances of the resurrected one that are cited at the beginning of the chapter.

II Corinthians. In 1:3 Marcion did not read "and Father" after "the God"; was this tendentious? Certainly the omission of "to God" in 2:15 is intentional: for the good God there is not an aroma as there is for the creator of the world. In 3:14 ("their minds or purposes are hardened"), the substitution of "(the purposes) of the world" for "their" is a very significant emendation, for since Marcion interpreted "the world" as meaning the creator of the world, he has Paul say that the purposes of this God had been hardened. Marcion must also have altered what follows to make it correspond to this. In 4:10 the emendation "death of God" for "death of Jesus" is tendentious in a modalistic direction. It is questionable whether in 4:11 "for the sake of Jesus" was intentionally omitted. In 4:13 the Old Testament saying has been removed. The later Marcionites judged the "tribunal" of Christ (5:10) to be unsuitable and excised it. Marcion wished to hear nothing of a defilement of flesh and *spirit* (7:1); he put "blood" in place of "spirit."[12]

Romans. In 1:16 Marcion did not have the "first" after "to the Jew" in his text. Since this is obviously a tendentious excision, and yet the word is missing also in G g and in fact even in B, therefore an influence of the Marcionite text upon the catholic text here is to be assumed. Further, in 1:17 Marcion cut out the words "as it is written: he who is righteous through faith shall live,"[13] and in 1:18 "of God" after "wrath," the former as a quotation of Scripture, the latter because the good God does not show wrath. Then he eliminated 1:19–2:1 completely because this bit of natural religion had to go counter to his opinions, just as did the idea that men are given up by God to the most dreadful vices as punishment. Similarly, he struck out 3:31–4:25 entirely, for the idea of "we uphold the law" was just as intolerable to him as was the Abraham-theology. In 6:9 he replaced "he is raised" with "he is risen" (see above), and in 6:19 he wrote "present (your) members to God to serve in righteousness" with "present (your) members subject to righteousness," for a person should place himself at God's service alone. The excision in 10:3 is related to this. There Marcion wrote "being ignorant of God" instead of "being ignorant of the righteousness of God." In 7:5 "in you" instead of "in your members" is probably a tendentious emendation; according to Marcion, under the creator of the world sin was active not only in the members but in the whole man. Chapter 8:19–22 ("the anxious waiting of the creation") must have been incomprehensible or offensive to Marcion. He eliminated it, as well as the entire section 9:1–33, because of its friendliness toward the Jews and its Old Testament references, and finally also the long section 10:5–11:32, which must have appeared to him as intolerable for the good God. In 11:33 he erased "knowledge" after "wisdom of God" (what his reason was is not clear), as well as the "unsearchable judgments," because the good God does not judge. For the same reason the "but give place to the wrath" in 12:19 has been eliminated, as has the "it is written." Marcion reversed the order of verses 18 and 19. The absence of chapters 15 and 16 is not to be charged to Marcion but to the copy from which he worked (see below, in Appendix III). Later Marcionites inserted 16:25–27; the wording of these verses which we read in our Bibles today is an emendation of the Marcionites (loc. cit.). Thus here again the Marcionite text has exerted an influence upon the catholic text.

I Thessalonians. There is tendentious insertion ("their own") in 2:15 with "prophets". In 4:4 "in holiness" alongside "honor" is erased; the former probably appeared to Marcion to be, in reference to one's conduct with respect to one's wife, too lofty an expression. In 4:16 "of God" is intentionally removed from the connection with "sound of a trumpet" ("last" is added) and is put with "shout of command," and "in Christ" has been intentionally excised after "the dead"; here Marcion had in mind the general resurrection. The fact that in the same verse it is said of the dead that "will be raised" (instead of "will rise") is perhaps an intentional emendation by Marcion, although some other witnesses also have it here. The elimination of "wholly" before "spirit, soul, and body" in 5:23 also can easily be explained in terms of Marcion's doctrine. In the same verse "and savior" is added to "lord"; thus Marcion placed special weight upon this designation – or was it here a part of the tradition that was handed down to him?

II Thessalonians. In 1:8 the omission of the flaming fire is tendentious, as is the replacement of the words "inflicting punishment" with "submitting to punishment." The good God himself does not pronounce judgment but is only present at the judgment. Therefore in 2:11 also Marcion does not write "God sends them a powerful delusion" but "they have a powerful delusion." Further, he was not willing for "so that they believe what is false" to stand, as he in fact has also erased from Romans 1 the abandonment of men to their sins.

The Laodicean Epistle (Ephesians). One wonders whether Marcion allowed 1:21 to stand here, since he had already inserted the verse at Galatians 4:24. In 2:2 the absence of "of the spirit" is probably to be taken as intentional; in 2:11 later Marcionites appear to have stricken out "in the flesh." In 2:14,15 the omission of "his" after "in (his) flesh" is tendentious and so is that of "in" before "dogmas, ordinances"; it was not in *his* flesh that Christ took away the emnity, and it was not that the commandments consisted in dogmas but by means of the (new) dogmas God has set aside the law of the commandments. Thus Marcion contrasted the "dogmas" with the "commandments" and saw in the former the principles of the Christian faith. In 2:20 Marcion tendentiously erased "and prophets" after "apostles" because the former could not be a part of the foundation of the new Christian edifice. Marcion's most important erasure is found in 3:9; there he omitted the "in" before "the God who created all things" and thus acquired a *locus classicus* for his doctrine that the redemptive dispensation of the good God had been concealed from the creator of the world from time immemorial. On the tendentious insertion of ἡμῖν in 4:6 see Appendix III. In 5:22ff. Marcion did some abbreviating; this section on marriage was generally unacceptable to him. In verse 22 the "your own" before "husbands" was probably omitted, as also "as to the Lord" and "(Christ is) himself the savior of the body." He worded the sentence in verse 28 thus: "He who loves his flesh loves his wife as Christ also loved the Church" (i.e., not sexually). He struck out verse 30, which appeared to him to be utterly unfitting for Christ. He wrote "for this (church)" instead of "for this reason," relating it to the church, and omitted the words "and he will be united in marriage to his wife": "For the sake of the church a man will leave father and mother, and the two (i.e., the man and the church) will become one flesh." Since catholic manuscripts also are lacking the words "and become one with his wife in wedlock," here again an influence of Marcion's text upon the catholic text is to be assumed (see Appendix III). In 6:2, in the commandment to honor one's parents, Marcion tendentiously removed the words "this is the first commandment with a promise" as well as the following verse ("that it may be well with thee," etc.). Tendentious also is the excision (verse 2) of "your" with "father" and "your" (verse 4) with "children." The Marcionites should themselves not be fathers; thus the commandment must be converted into a general one which treated the relationship of the fathers as the older generation to the children as the younger generation.

Colossians. The long saying about the preexistent Christ (1:15–17) has been summarized by Marcion in the short sentence "he who is the image of the invisible God, and he is before all things," for Christ could have no connection with the creation. In 1:19, "in himself" instead of "in him" is tendentious and is to be understood in terms of the relative Modalism of Marcion; similarly in 1:20 "himself" in place of "him." In 1:22 Marcion excised the "of the flesh" after "in (his) body" (= church); for Christ does not have flesh. An ingenious change is found in 2:8: in the phrase "through philosophy and empty deceit" Marcion changed the "and" into "which is." Here we see how disparagingly he judged all philosophy; he believed that the expression chosen by Paul had been falsified because it was too weak. In 4:14 he probably eliminated the words that stand with "Luke," "the beloved physician"; he did not want any praise to be given to Luke, from whom indeed he had wrested the gospel.

Philippians. In 1:15 Marcion altered the words "and some because of goodwill" to read "and some because of the glory of the word" (or "goodwill of the word"), intending thereby to strike at vain Christian scholastic wisdom. In 1:16 Marcion gratuitously inserted the words "and now some out of struggling"; presumably the "out of selfish ambition" was not enough, and he probably wanted expressly to see the ecclesiastical rivalries proscribed. In the famous passage 2:7 he omitted "being born" and "(being found in the form) as (a man)" and thus achieved the Christological image that he desired. In 3:9 he probably wrote "having a righteousness not of my own from the law, but that which is through him from God" (or "that which is through him, the righteousness of God"); thus he expressed even more forcefully his opposition to the law.

In the gospel Marcion undertook the following excisions and emendations:[14]

Chapters 1–4. After eliminating 1:1–4:15 Marcion – probably in order to separate Jesus from Nazareth as completely as possible – changed the position of the pericope of Jesus' appearance in Nazareth (see the critical apparatus on 4:16ff. in Appendix IV) with that of the healing of the demon-possessed in Capernaum (4:31ff.), after he had altered the former pericope and shortened it (by omission of the preaching;[15] later Marcionites inserted Bethsaida in place of Nazareth, in order to sever any connection of Jesus with this city; in 4:34 Marcion himself omit "Nazareth"). Chapter 4:27 certainly was omitted here (see on 17:17f.). Among the major omissions, to which the baptism of Jesus also had to fall victim, that of the temptation narrative is especially striking. This narrative was certainly too "human" for Marcion; his Christ was above such assaults.

In determining the tendentious excisions made by Marcion in the gospel there exists the difficulty that Tertullian almost never indicates whether he had not found the pericopes at hand or whether he had passed over them as a result of his critical labors. But if one assembles these pieces, compares them with what certainly was eliminated by Marcion, and notes precisely the transitions in Tertullian (in Epiphanius also), in many cases it appears probable that there was an excision. In some cases this is a very high probability, even if one considers the fact that Marcion did not everywhere proceed consistently. Here I assemble these pericopes, leaving aside those that are utterly unimportant:

4:36–39 (general; healing of Peter's mother-in-law): probably not excised.

4:41 fin. ("They knew that he was the Christ"): uncertain whether it was omitted.

4:44 (preaching in the synagogues): uncertain whether omitted.

5:37 The words "and the wineskins are destroyed" probably were omitted.

5:39 ("The old wine is better"): *certainly omitted.*

6:17 It is very probable that Judea and Jerusalem were excised.

6:19b ("power went out of him"): uncertain.

6:23a (rejoicing and leaping for joy on the day of judgment): *probably* omitted.

6:30b (ask nothing back from the robber): hardly omitted.

6:32,33 (no credit for doing good to those who love us): hardly omitted.

6:34b (sinners and receiving interest): hardly omitted.

6:47–49 (house with and without foundations): hardly omitted.

7:29–35 (the children playing, the relation of the people to John the Baptist and to Jesus): *probably omitted.*

8:19 (his mother and brothers come): *omitted.*

8:28 ("of the Most High" beside "God"): probably omitted.

8:32–37 (the story about the swine within the story about the demon-possessed man): uncertain.

8:40–42a, 49–56 (story of Jairus): uncertain whether omitted.

9:23 (taking the cross upon oneself): uncertain.

9:25 (injuring one's soul): uncertain.

9:26b,27 (coming of the Son of Man in glory with his train of angels. "There are some standing here" etc.): *probably omitted.*

9:31 (prediction of Moses and Elijah): *probably omitted.*

9:36 (conclusion of the transfiguration narrative): uncertain.

9:49,50 (those who drove out devils in Jesus' name): uncertain.

10:12–15: *the lamentations over the cities probably omitted.*

10:21: Marcion omitted "Father" and "and the earth" in the prayer of Jesus. The agreement of the reports given by Tertullian and Epiphanius here is especially clear and important.

10:24: "they wanted to see" (said of the prophets) certainly omitted; in its place, read "they did not see."

10:25: "eternal" after "life" certainly omitted.

10:27 ("and your neighbor as yourself"): uncertain; 26 and 29 were omitted (see below).

10:29–37 (the good Samaritan): uncertain.

10:38–42 (Mary and Martha): uncertain, but one probably may assume that Tertullian passed over this and the preceding story because he knew nothing objectionable in the Marcionite exposition.

11:4: We do not have evidence that Marcion read the second half of the fifth petition.

11:23 (He who is not with me is against me): uncertain.

11:24–26 (continuation of the Beelzebul story): uncertain.

11:29 (Jonah) and 30–32 (Jonah, the queen, and Solomon): omitted.

11:34–36 (eye and light): uncertain.

11:42 fin. (these you ought to do and not to leave the other undone): omitted.

11:44,45 (the Pharisees, "unmarked graves," and the lawyer's question): uncertain.

11:49–51 (the saying about God's wisdom, unjust bloodshed from Abel to Zechariah): certainly omitted.

11:53,54 (the Pharisees' intentions toward Jesus): uncertain.

12:4: The omission of "to you" or of "my" is intended to remove any identification of Jesus' disciples as the *friends* of Jesus.

12:6,7 (God's care for the sparrows; the higher value of persons): certainly omitted.

12:8,9: Instead of "before the angels of God" Marcion wrote "before God."

12:24: The words "and God feeds them" probably were omitted.

12:25,26 (adding a cubit to one's stature): uncertain.

12:28 (clothing the grass of the field): omitted, but "of little faith" retained.

12:32: The "your" after "Father" was omitted.

12:33,34 (disposing of possessions, almsgiving, treasure in heaven): uncertain.

12:49b,50 ("I came to cast fire on the earth," "I have a baptism," etc.): uncertain.

12:52 (five in a house): uncertain.

13:1–5 (the slain Galileans; the tower of Siloam): certainly omitted.

13:6–9 (the parable of the fig tree): certainly omitted.

13:22–24 (the narrow gate): uncertain.

13:29–35 (the meal in the heavenly kingdom; message to Herod; the saying about Jerusalem that slays the prophets): certainly omitted.

14:1–6 (healing of the man with dropsy): uncertain.

14:7–11 (reproof of the ambitious; warning not to take a high place for oneself): uncertain.

14:15 ("Blessed is he who eats bread in the kingdom of God"): uncertain.

14:25–35 (hating father and mother; bearing the cross; thoughtless undertaking of building or of war; renouncing all; salt that has lost its taste): uncertain.

15:10 ("the angels" is lacking before "of God"): certainly omitted.

15:11–32 (the lost son): certainly omitted.

16:9b (reception into the eternal habitations): uncertain.

16:10 (faithfulness in little and in much): uncertain.

16:15b (what is exalted in men's sight is an abomination before God): uncertain.

16:29,30 (Abraham omitted): intentionally eliminated. According to Marcion, in verses 27–31 God himself is the one who is addressed and the one who speaks.

17:5,6 (faith like a grain of mustard seed): uncertain.

17:7–10 (the unprofitable servant): uncertain; "worthless" certainly was omitted.

17:11–19 (the ten lepers): 4:27 was inserted into this pericope (see above; why this was done is not clear), and something was omitted; it is uncertain, however, what was omitted. In any case, the "in Israel" of 4:27 was eliminated.

17:23,24 (the manifestation of the Son of Man as the lightning): uncertain.

17:33–37 (seeking and losing one's soul; two shall be in one bed, etc.): uncertain.

18:23–30 (discourse about wealth and the promise to the disciples who have left all): uncertain, but verses 29 and 30 were certainly eliminated.

18:31–33 (announcement of the passion): certainly eliminated.

18:34 (the disciples' lack of understanding): probably excised.

18:37 ("inhabitant of Nazareth"): certainly excised.

19:9b (Zacchaeus): "son of Abraham" certainly eliminated.

19:10: Was the "to seek and" before "to save" intentionally omitted?

19:27 (slaughter of the enemies): certainly eliminated.

19:28 (journey to Jerusalem): uncertain.

19:29–46 (entrance into Jerusalem, cleansing of the temple): certainly excised.

19:47,48 (Jesus teaches in the temple; the scribes seek to kill him): uncertain.

20:9–18 (the wicked vineyard-keepers): certainly excised.

20:37,38 (Moses calls God the God of the patriarchs; God a God of the living): certainly eliminated.

20:40 ("they dared not ask him anything more"): uncertain.

20:45–47 (warning against the idle and ambitious Pharisees who devour widows' houses): uncertain.

21:1–4 (the widow's mite): uncertain.

21:18 ("not a hair of your head will be lost"): certainly excised.

21:21–24 (the command to the Jews to flee; woe to those with child; Jerusalem's destruction): certainly eliminated.

21:35b,36 (the day of judgment will come upon all; watch so that you may escape the terror): uncertain.

22:2 (the scribes seek to kill Jesus, are afraid of the people): uncertain.

22:3 (Satan enters into Judas): uncertain.

22:6,7 (Judas seeks an opportunity to betray him; the day of the Passover arrives): uncertain.

22:9–13 (description of Jesus' direction about preparing the room for the

Passover): uncertain.

22:14: The words "when the hour came" appear to have been omitted.

22:15: The "this" before the "Passover" perhaps intentionally omitted.

22:16 ("I shall eat it no more until it is fulfilled in the kingdom of God"): certainly excised.

22:17,18 (blessing and passing of the cup): certainly omitted, but it probably was already lacking in the earlier text that Marcion had before him.

22:19b ("Do this in remembrance of me"): uncertain.

22:20: "new" modifying "covenant" omitted.

22:23-30 (The question as to who is the betrayer and the dispute among the disciples over rank; Jesus' saying about true greatness; promise for the disciples as future judges): uncertain, but Marcion could not have allowed verse 30 to stand.

22:35-38 (Had the disciples ever lacked anything? the swords): certainly eliminated.

22:39,40 (journey to the Mount of Olives): unattested, but it cannot have been completely omitted.

22:42-46 (the striving in prayer in Gethsemane; the sleeping disciples): probably excised.

22:48 ("Do you betray the Son of Man with a kiss?"): uncertain.

22:49-51 (the story of the cutting off of the servant's ear): certainly omitted.

22:52-62 (saying to the guards; Peter's denial): unattested, but verses 31-34 require that Peter's denial be narrated.

22:65,68,71: unattested, probably by accident.

22:70: Marcion probably eliminated the words "that I am."

23:4,5 (Pilate finds no guilt; Jesus' adversaries describe him as an agitator): uncertain.

23:13-17 (Pilate's dealings with the high priests, etc.): uncertain.

23:26 (Simon of Cyrene): uncertain.

23:27-31 (the lamenting women of Jerusalem; the green tree): uncertain.

23:34b (dividing of Jesus' garments): eliminated, but Epiphanius found it again in his Marcionite gospel.

23:35 (reviling): uncertain.

23:36-42 (drinking the gall; "save thyself"; the inscription on the cross; the thieves): uncertain. The thieves probably were eliminated from the story.

23:43 ("Today you will be with me in Paradise"): certainly excised.

23:46: Later Marcionites perhaps erased the words "Father, into thy hands . . ."

23:47-49 (the centurion, the people, the acquaintances, and the women present at Jesus' death): uncertain.

23:54 (that the sabbath was approaching): uncertain.

24:2 (the stone rolled away): uncertain.

24:8 ("They remembered his words"): uncertain.

24:21b–24 (account of the travellers to Emmaus about what had happened on Easter morning): uncertain, but perhaps omitted.

24:27 (Jesus recapitulates the prophecies): certainly excised.

24:28,29 (They arrive at Emmaus; Jesus is invited to remain with them): unattested.

24:32–36 (conversation of the two disciples; return to Jerusalem; the report; the Lord appears to Peter; Jesus' entrance into the circle): uncertain.

24:39: "touch me and see" certainly eliminated.

24:39: "flesh and" is omitted, which is very strange.

24:40 (He shows them his hands and feet): certainly omitted.

24:44–46 (Jesus opens the Scriptures to the disciples): certainly excised.

24:47 ("beginning from Jerusalem"): probably excised.

24:48–53 (sending out of the disciples; Bethany): certainly omitted.

Besides the excisions, which constituted the greater part by far of his emendations, there are found also the following other changes in the gospel text that were made by Marcion:

5:18ff.: Here it was perhaps noted that the healing of the paralytic took place on a sabbath.

6:43: The bad tree is mentioned before the good one.

7:28: Here Marcion reinterpreted the text to fit his view by making it read "the prophet John is greater than all those born of women."

8:20–21 ("mother and brothers"): restructured into an abrupt and negative question of Jesus; in place of "the word of God" Marcion inserted "my words."

9:26a: Read "whoever is ashamed of me, I also will be ashamed of him."

9:30: "they stood with him" instead of "they talked (with him)" (Moses and Elijah should not speak with Jesus); later Marcionites again read it as "they talked (with him)."

9:41: "to them" is added in order to make the disciples appear as the "faithless generation."

9:54f.: Marcion here inserted the additions: "as Elijah also did" and "and he said: you do not know of what kind of spirit you are."

10:21: Marcion perhaps had the tendentious reading "some things that are hidden" in place of "that you have hidden these things."

10:25ff.: This story was tendentiously related in such a way that it was not the lawgiver but Jesus who uttered the saying about the love of God (which was not identified as an Old Testament saying); thereby a considerable abbreviation was necessitated (see above). The Marcionites whom Epiphanius knew again had the authentic text.

11:3: Marcion altered the fourth petition and wrote "your bread." (His reading of a petition for the Holy Spirit as the first petition is not an emendation but the original text of Luke.)

11:4: For "do not lead" Marcion wrote "do not allow us to be led into temptation."

11:42: The tendentious reading "the call" for "the justice." The agreement of the reports given by Tertullian and by Epiphanius is especially worthy of note.

12:4: Marcion wrote "do not fear those who have the power only to kill you, yet after this have no authority."

12:8,9: A stylistic alteration (in addition to the excision of the angels; see above).

12:46: Here "he will punish severely" probably was erased and "he will separate" or a similar word inserted.

12:46: Instead of "he will place" Marcion inserted "he will be placed" in order not to have God appear as a judge.

13:28: Here the patriarchs were eliminated and "the righteous" inserted in their place; further, "cast out" was replaced by "held outside" (according to both Tertullian and Epiphanius).

14:21: In place of "being angry" the tendentious reading "motus" ("being moved"?).

16:12: In place of "that which is your own" the tendentious reading "mine" (thus also some Itala-codices and minuscule 157).

16:17: In place of "of the law" the tendentious reading "of my words."

16:26: In place of "those wishing to cross over" there is the reading "to cross over here" (tendentious?).

16:28,29: "that place" added (for elucidation?).

18:19: According to Origen and Epiphanius (but not to Tertullian), "the Father" was added to "God."

18:20: Marcion probably wrote "and he said: I know the commandments" for "you know the commandments" in order not to have to hear the Old Testament commandments from the lips of Jesus.

20:35: For "those who are counted worthy" Marcion wrote "those whom God counts worthy" and referred the words "of that age" to "God" in order to secure a prooftext for the distinction between the two Gods.

21:13: To "to bear witness" Marcion added "and salvation."

21:19: "save yourselves" for "gain your lives" (patterned after Matt. 24:13?).

21:27: In place of "in a cloud" the tendentious reading "from the heavens."

21:32,33: Marcion wrote: "the heavens and the earth will not pass away except all (this happen); indeed the earth and the heavens will pass away but my word remains forever."

23:2: Added "destroying both the law and the prophets" and "misleading both the women and the children."

23:3: Marcion wrote "the Christ" in place of "the king of the Jews," since Jesus answers this question of Pilate in the affirmative.

23:56: Marcion has the tendentious reading "according to the law" for "according to the commandment."

24:25: Marcion wrote "those things that he spoke" (later Marcionites, "I spoke") "to you" for "those things that the prophets spoke."

24:37: Marcion wrote "ghost" for "spirit."

As to the *formal* procedure, first of all one must distinguish between *additions*, *excisions*, and *emendations* in the texts.

The great majority of corrections consists of *excisions*, from the excision of a single word or particle all the way[16] to that of large sections. The gospel of Luke has lost the opening chapters in their entirety down to 4:32, with the exception of 3:1; the epistle to the Romans has lost almost half of its material. How much was omitted in the other epistles and in the gospel unfortunately cannot be determined, since the sources do not permit a definite judgment on the matter. Marcion assumed that the Judaizing forgers had most gravely corrupted the texts by making additions of all sorts.

The number of *additions* made by Marcion is so very slight that one is skeptical about the few cases in which such must be assumed; yet they are well attested.[17] Thus as a rule Marcion did not assume that the Judaistic pseudoapostles had made erasures in the authentic texts, or he regarded it as impossible to remedy these excisions. This is a tribute to his critical labors, as is the observation that he did not employ any of the apocryphal material. The few additions, which are by no means certain in all the passages, are found in Galatians 1:7 ("according to my gospel"), I Corinthians 1:18 ("wisdom"), I Thessalonians 2:15 ("their own"), I Thessalonians 5:13 ("and savior"), Philippians 1:16 ("and some from struggling"), Luke 9:41 ("towards them"), Luke 9:54f. ("as Elijah also did" and "you do not know of what kind"), Luke 16:28,29 ("that place"), Luke 18:19 ("the Father," doubtful), Luke 18:20 ("and he said"), Luke 21:13 ("and salvation"), Luke 23:2 ("destroying both the law and the prophets" and "misleading the women and the children").[18]

Highly significant, on the other hand, is the number of passages in which Marcion assumed that *changes* had been made by the forgers. Here he attributed to them the most cunning methods and employed all his skill in order to get behind their alleged tricks, to expose them and to correct them.

(1) He assumed that they had exchanged certain words for others that sounded like them or were similar in spelling in order to get a different meaning; hence he made the following corrections: in Galatians 2:20, "redeeming" for "loving"; in Galatians 4:8, "to beings by nature gods" for "to beings not by nature gods"; in Galatians 5:14, "in you" for "in one (word)"; in II Corinthians

7:1, "blood" for "spirit"; in Colossians 1:19, "in himself" for "in him" (see also verse 20); in Luke 11:42, "the call" for "the justice"; in Luke 18:20, "I know" for "you know." In I Corinthians 10:11 he probably changed the "type" with the preceding "all things" into "unformed." These emendations are the conjectures of a skilled philologist.

(2) He was convinced that the forgers often had changed the active and passive voices for their own tendentious purposes; hence he wrote the following: in I Corinthians 3:17, "he will be destroyed" for "God will destroy him"; in I Corinthians 15:25, "they are placed" for "he has placed" (if indeed this is not just a reading of the later Marcionites); in Luke 10:21, "some things that are hidden" for "that you have hidden in these things"; in Luke 11:4, "do not allow us to be led into temptation" for "do not lead"; in Luke 12:46, "he will be placed" for "he will place"; in Luke 20:35, "those whom God counts worthy" for "those who are counted worthy." Included in this category also are the several passages (though he is not consistent in this; see I Corinthians 6:14) where instead of allowing the language to speak of Jesus' being raised from the dead, he has it speak of his rising or of his raising himself. Other critical substitutions are those of pronouns (e.g., in Luke 11:3 Marcion wrote "your bread" for "our"; in Luke 16:12, "mine" for "that which is your own"), of particles (the most important is in Colossians 2:8, where Marcion has "through philosophy as empty conceit" while the authentic text reads "and" and not "as"), and of persons (thus in the conversation in Luke 18:18ff., resulting in an entirely different meaning); cf. also the conversation in Luke 8:20f.

(3) According to Marcion, the forgers also made certain changes, though not a great many, in the order of sentences, clauses, or phrases. Hence in Luke 6:43 he put the bad tree before the good one, and in Romans 12, verse 19 before verse 18; see also Galatians 4:3, I Thessalonians 4:16, etc.

(4) He assumed that the forgers, without any deceptive cover, insolently and brazenly altered specific ideas and even a considerable number of sentences. Therefore he felt compelled to recognize and give utterance to the individual concepts and phrases that had been altered as well as to reshape long clauses completely. With regard to the former, see, for example, Galatians 4:24, where he could not allow the two instances of "covenants" and in their place inserted "representation" or a similar word (if this emendation is not to be credited only to his followers); Galatians 6:17, "the others" for "the rest"; I Corinthians 10:19, "an offering to an idol" for "an idol"; I Corinthians 15:20, "is known to have risen" for "has been raised" (see above); I Corinthians 15:45, "Lord" for "Adam"; II Corinthians 3:14, "of the world" for "their"; II Corinthians 4:10, "of God" for "of Jesus"; Romans 6:19, "to God to serve in righteousness" for "subject to righteousness"; Romans 7:5, "in you" for "in your members"; Romans 10:3, "being ignorant of God" for "being ignorant of the righteousness of God"; I Thessalonians 4:16, "will be raised" for "will rise"; II Thessalonians 1:8, "submitting to punishment" for "inflicting punishment"; II Thessalonians 2:11,

"they have" for "he sends"; Philippians 1:15, "because of the glory of the word" for "because of goodwill"; Luke 7:28, "all those born" for "in those born"; Luke 8:21, "my word" for "word of God"; Luke 9:30, "they stood with him" for "they talked with him"; Luke 12:46, "he will separate" or something similar for "he will punish severely"; Luke 13:28, "the righteous" for the patriarchs; Luke 14:21, "being moved" or something similar for "being angry"; Luke 16:17, "of my words" for "of the law"; Luke 21:19, "save yourselves" for "gain your lives"; Luke 21:27, "from the heavens" for "in a cloud"; Luke 21:33, "my word remains forever" for "my words will not pass away"; Luke 23:3, "the Christ" for "the king of the Jews"; Luke 23:56, "according to the law" for "according to the commandment"; Luke 24:25, "those things that he spoke to you" for "those things that the prophets spoke"; Luke 24:37, "ghost" for "spirit." The number of provable *extensive* alterations is not great. The most important is in Galatians 4:21–26; cf. Galatians 3:10–12 and Colossians 1:15–17. Luke 8:20f. and 10:25ff. can also be included here.

As to the motives that prompted the excisions and emendations, in most cases these are evident when one calls to mind Marcion's chief doctrines.[19] The most important motives were:

(1) The creator of the world and God of the Old Testament may not appear as the Father of Jesus Christ. He is "just" and malevolent; his promises apply only to the Jewish people and are earthly.

(2) The Old Testament cannot have prophesied anything that is fulfilled in Christ. It cannot have been invoked as an authority by Christ or Paul.[20] The law and the prophets are to be interpreted literally.

(3) The good God must have been hidden from the creator of the world until the former's appearing.

(4) He, the good God, must not be thought of as the director of the world or as the God of earthly providence.

(5) He may not appear as judge but exclusively as the merciful one and as redeemer.

(6) His redemption and his promises are related exclusively to eternal life.

(7) The Son of the good God, Christ, is to be understood modalistically in his relationship to the Father.

(8) He had nothing about him that was earthly and thus no flesh and no physical body; therefore he cannot have been born and cannot have had relatives.

(9) He did not fulfill the law but abolished it, exposed the radical opposition between law and gospel, and established his redemption upon faith alone.

(10) He demanded of men their total separation from the world and from the works of the creator of the world.

(11) He raised up only *one* genuine apostle after the original ones had proven themselves to be unteachable. The gospel of Paul is the gospel of Christ.

(12) He will not appear again as judge but at the end of time will announce

the great separation that has been made.

One can, without any difficulty, read these twelve self-contained motives in Marcion's excisions and emendations.[21] In addition, he allowed himself to be prompted by some other motives of a second rank, which however as a group have an inner harmony with those listed above. Only a very few excisions are obscure as to the motive prompting them, for in most cases a closer examination will reveal the motive. For example, at first glance one is puzzled by the fact that the parable of the prodigal son (Luke 15) is cut out; surely the main thrust of the parable would have appealed to Marcion, but just as surely the setting of it ("return to the Father's house!") would have been unacceptable to him. The cleansing of the temple (Luke 19) could be a welcome thought to him, but the words, "My house is a house of prayer," were unacceptable to him, as Epiphanius correctly perceived. Of course it may be objected that he would have needed only to strike out this saying, but upon closer reflection one will have to say that in fact Christ expressed, through the act of cleansing the temple itself, an evaluation of the temple which Marcion could not possibly accept. And in the final analysis, it remains altogether obscure in numerous cases why in one instance Marcion has taken radical steps and has excised entire sections and in another has effected a thoroughgoing alteration by means of slight and delicate emendations. He cannot have been guided by a tradition, for he did not possess any such but remained throughout the dogmatic critic. Hence it is a mistake to suppose that in the excision of the infancy narratives he had been influenced by the earlier tradition which had not known these narratives; he also excised the baptismal narrative, which nevertheless belongs to the earliest stratum of tradition and most probably was already present in Q.

One cannot, however, gain a clear picture of Marcion's attitude toward the text from his excisions and emendations; one must rather take into account also what he allowed to stand. Of course, a great many inconsistencies and cases of incompleteness then appear, but only on this basis—and this is a point that the critics have overlooked heretofore—is it possible to penetrate into his thoughts and to give color and life to his teachings. It will also be shown that his teachings *in their dependence upon the gospel and the apostle* are not to be grasped and exhausted with some characterizing catchwords and antitheses, but that they possess an intrinsic and conceptual depth which alone renders them valuable (cf. the chapter on doctrine).

Finally, in the definition of Marcion's critical point of view and procedure it must not be overlooked that he was a conscious and decisive opponent of allegorical interpretation. This is confirmed by numerous detailed testimonies which tell us that Marcion had given fundamental consideration to the question (see below on the *Antitheses*). He explicitly declared: "One must not allegorize the Scripture," and he interpreted this principle to mean that neither the Old Testament nor the gospel nor the apostle may be allegorized. Origen describes the Marcionites (*Comm. XV.3 in Matth.*, T. III, p. 333) as "slaves to pure history," and from another witness we learn that for him even the gospel was not intellectual but simple; hence it may be allegorized only where it obviously contains parables. Whether Marcion himself was able to maintain this position in its purity is another question,[22] but in any case there was no theologian in the early church who rejected allegorical interpretation as consistently as did he. For the Old Testament this resulted in the fact that in his explanations of the most important Old Testament passages, especially the prophetic and messianic ones, he was in agreement with the interpretations of the Jews, since he too assumed that the prophecies are in part already fulfilled (in David, Solomon, etc.), and in part they refer to an earthly kingdom and to the Messiah of the Jews who would yet come as a warrior-king. This agreement with the Jewish exegesis was for Marcion's opponents a grave *skandalon*; a Christian was already condemned if this association could be proved against him. But for us it remains a psychological riddle how a critic who on the one hand rejected the fantasies of allegorism, bore upon his shield the legend of "pura historia" and altered not a line in the Old Testament—indeed, acknowledged the entire text of the multilayered book as unadulterated history,[23]—was able on the other hand to criticize the Christian writings in such large scope as forged or corrupted and to undertake so confidently their restoration! Not only allegorism but dogmatism too can move mountains!

In this connection Zahn (*Kanonsgeschichte*, I, pp. 625f., 717) has posed the question whether and how Marcion's conduct can be justified from a moral perspective. He starts out from the admission that in general Marcion had a clear conscience, but then continues:

> It is difficult to believe, however, that this good conscience and the positive belief that by his critical operations he was helping the original Paul (and the original gospel) to come to expression again accompanied him always in his labors. When he artificially joins clauses or sentences which in the text which he possessed lay far apart, in order to bring out an entirely different idea; when he several times proposes rearrangements which if correct would presuppose an utterly pointless procedure on the part of the alleged Judaistic forgers; when he very frequently turns an idea into its exact opposite by the addition or subtraction of syllables or words, this artificial and often petty procedure cannot be reconciled either with a good conscience or with sound reason. Today it is hardly possible any longer to arrive at a sure decision in choosing between these two bases for explanation; but we should not take it amiss in those who stood nearer to Marcion when under the impact of his spiritual significance they were more doubtful of his honesty than of his rationality and therefore more often accused him of audacious forgery than of fanatical blindness.

That is a proper statement of the problem. In my opinion, the solution that would be more favorable to Marcion's character is rendered less likely, first of all, by the fact that two reasons for mitigation of the judgment which have been offered—even Zahn allowed the second of them—can hardly come into consideration. One may not appeal, on behalf of Marcion's conduct, to the development of the synoptic gospels as though that development provided a perfect analogy (thus Baur and his school, because they traced the great differences among these gospels to "Tendenz-criticism"). Neither may one appeal to the proliferation of manuscripts that already existed in Marcion's time. The divergences among the Synoptics in the main are based on oral tradition and only in a secondary measure on tendentious emendations. While these divergences are often decisively important and now and then even appear audacious and thus they do exhibit some points of kinship with Marcion's procedure, yet there is still a great difference between what he did and the variations that exist among the Synoptics. At the most one may say that what Luke and Matthew permitted with respect to Q and Mark in individual passages has been elevated by Marcion to the level of a principle of his critical method. The other suggestion, however, that the proliferation of manuscripts could excuse Marcion's conduct, does not apply at all; for we know nothing about whether this state of affairs made any impression upon him at all. Rather, so far as we are able to judge, it is probable that he held essentially to *one* given text, for it is nowhere clearly attested that he undertook the comparison of variant texts, even if it may be suspected in some passages.

Consequently, while his critical procedures remain unique in their tendentious arbitrariness, still it may be possible to excuse him to a certain degree because he wrote in an age in which authoritative texts had to suffer a great deal not only through proliferation but above all through falsifications. Only a few years later Dionysius of Corinth complained that his letters had been falsified behind his back by the heretics, and Irenaeus, invoking the name of the Christ who will return, adjured his copyists to leave his books intact. Hence we may concede to Marcion that he could believe the gospel and the epistles of Paul to have been adulterated through and through. But in my judgment, and in opposition to Zahn, there still is no reason for doubting Marcion's subjective honesty, that is, his conviction that what he had done was right and proper. If he had been a swindler, more than one way would have been open to him to give his falsifications a high or even an absolute authority. He could have appealed to the "Spirit" and claimed that the Spirit had given the books to him, or he could have concocted a secret tradition from which he had received the original gospel and the original epistles, or he could have asserted that he had found a manuscript that contained these writings. In those times every one of these ways could easily be taken and would have been successful—examples of such are not lacking. But he took none of them, and thereby he showed that he was not a charlatan.

But how then is the riddle of this "critical" literary work to be solved? That is, how could Marcion believe in his own undertaking? Zahn explains it by saying that if Marcion was an honest man, he must have been smitten with a fanatical blindness and must have been lacking in sound judgment. Undoubtedly there is here a defect in sound reason, but everything depends on to what extent or in what degree this was lacking. If it had to be established that he issued this text of his as the authentic one down to the very last letter, then under the circumstances as given there is, of course, no possibility of sympathy with such an assertion. But we have already seen that Marcion cannot have made this assertion, for his pupils zealously continued the work of improving the text. Therefore it is highly probable that Marcion did not publish the texts that he had purified and reproduced with the claim that they were absolutely dependable but with the qualification that the work was to be revised and continued. Even so, of course, with respect to many passages the undertaking remains almost inconceivably daring; only if one remembers what many classical philologists have done in recent times by way of emendations, rearrangements, and excisions in the ancient texts—and indeed with sanguine "certainty"—does one come somewhat closer to the frame of mind in which Marcion lived and worked. It must be admitted that this was somewhat more naïve than the mental outlook of many a modern man, which itself has appeared as nothing less than naïve, but with regard to critical labors the entire age, with few exceptions, was more naïve. Hence one will have to assume that Marcion, supported by his supposedly certain comprehension of the gospel and of Paul, undertook a purification of the texts with the naïve assurance that on essential matters he would hit upon the correct text, especially since the main thing was to remove what was incorrect. The excisions are indeed the main thing in his procedure; the positive expansions and rearrangements, insofar as they are his own intellectual property, could appear as corrections to which the current status of philological criticism conceded a certain right. To facilitate the understanding of this procedure, one would be glad to hear that in it Marcion also appealed to a divine support or illumination, but it is still more rewarding to establish the actual state of affairs, according to which Marcion was so honest that he made no pretense of divine assistance in his work.

Marcion's critical procedures—most daringly negative and productive dogmatic criticism in support of given texts—is unique, and yet it has a parallel which goes fairly far. How did the author of the Fourth Gospel proceed? He too stands upon a given documentary foundation, the first three Gospels, and deals with this foundation most freely. He expands, rearranges, and corrects in details just as Marcion does. He too subjects all the material to a negative and productive dogmatic criticism, but therein he proceeds far more daringly than does Marcion in that he not only sketches long discourses but probably also invents new historical situations. But above all, he goes far beyond Marcion in the fact that he does not deduce or infer the authority for his work from the sources but in a mysterious manner gives to it an independent authority. Marcion's undertaking is intended to be a *restoration*, and as little as it is that, still it certainly is that in the judgment of its author; the Fourth Gospel, on the contrary, is set forth as *vision and tradition*. But if one asks in which of the two critics the painting-over of the historical picture is done with more thoroughness, one will

hardly be able to decide, even though John has avoided the capital error of entirely separating Christ from the Old Testament. Marcion's inner attitude
guiding his work can be understood, even if only approximately; but for that
of the author of the Fourth Gospel a certain understanding is possible for us only
if we take him as an enthusiast (a "pneumatic"), but this predication rules out,
from the outset, any full comprehension. But if one approaches the question
with the "moral" standard of measurement there can be no doubt that an
honorable moralism finds it more difficult to pronounce an acquittal in the case
of the Fourth Gospel than in that of Marcion, particularly since the latter played
with his cards on the table, and this cannot be said of the former. But in neither
case is the standard of morality appropriate, because in the one case we have
to do with an enthusiast full of the Spirit, toward whom a respectful reserve is
required, and in the other a stubborn (that is, inspired with a single thought),
sober, and energetic thinker.[24]

With an energetic and *forceful* thinker — the forcefulness of Marcion here
lies in the fact that he is not correcting some Christian texts but that he intended
to create for Christ's community a new Bible. He reworked the Gospel of Luke
and the epistles of Paul in order to combine them and to put this corpus in place
of the Old Testament. The idea of combining them in the sense of a unified
canon as well as the idea of displacing the Old Testament with a new collection
is his work,[25] and he successfully forced this work upon the great church even
though it also preserved the Old Testament and differently defined the new collection, i.e., with "original apostolic writings" and the pastoral epistles included,
and set it in the light of the book of Acts. This is to be treated in the chapter
on Marcion as organizer, but here it must be mentioned that Marcion's great
text-critical efforts are not the work of a litterateur but of a creator of a church,
who with gifted vision recognized the necessity of giving to his church, which
he had to deprive of the Old Testament, a new *littera scripta* as the basic document of its faith.

After the death of the master Marcion's pupils not only continued the work
on the text of the Bible which had been handed down to them but also sought,
first, to render the epistles of Paul comprehensible by means of prefatory
"Argumenta" and second, added a forged epistle to the Laodiceans to the Bible;
see below, Chapter VIII and Appendix III.

Perhaps only twenty years after Marcion had produced his Bible, and probably in Rome also, Tatian produced in the Greek language[26] his painstaking
work *Diatessaron* and thereby actualized the original intention which had
governed the selection and combination of the four Gospels.[27] That this work
also must have been an act of resistance to Marcion's gospel is, from the
historical situation *a priori* certain (thus apparently Tatian's Christianity touches
on Marcion's at some important points, but still it was differently grounded), but
a posteriori it cannot be proved. Points of agreement in the form of the text,
where such are to be found, are most simply explained by the assumption that

both Marcion and Tatian had the Roman text before them.

It cannot have been twenty years later when authoritative bishops in Asia Minor and Rome proceeded to set in opposition to Marcion's two-part Bible a collection that was also in two parts and to designate it as *the apostolic-catholic New Testament*. This work, created in imitation and under the impact of Marcion's creation, was hardly felt to be an odd innovation, because the four Gospels had already been in use in those churches for more than a generation. Moreover, alongside these books, Paul's letters and other ancient letters and apocalypses for a long time had been made accessible in worship and to the churches otherwise, and the book of Acts had proved itself indispensable in the struggle against Marcion.

As for the text that Marcion used for the Gospel and the letters of Paul, it may be affirmed with certainty that it was a W-text (= the I-text of von Soden). Marcion's peculiar readings that are not explained in terms of his theological views are therefore—at least for the most part—not to be regarded as readings that he has created but rather as variants of the W-text that had been handed down to him. For more on this, see Appendices III and IV.

V

MARCION'S *ANTITHESES*[1]

Although there is a great deal of material available for the reconstruction of this work,[2] up till the present time no one has succeeded in getting a certain picture, even in its basic features, of the structure of the book, and even the investigation that follows here does not lead to a fully satisfactory conclusion. It is certain that no other work of Marcion himself, other than the *Antitheses*, is known.[3] Therefore, whatever of Marcion's statements that is reliably reported in the tradition, or whatever bears the mark of his own thoughts, must stem from these *Antitheses*. Moreover, it is certain, as the title causes us to suspect and as Tertullian expressly remarks, that the contrasting of the words and deeds of the creator of the world and those of the good God (or of his Christ), and hence also the contrasting of the law (of the Old Testament) and the gospel, in the form of "singulae iniectiones" ["several devices"], formed the essential content of the work.[4] Further, Tertullian says that it was Marcion's intention for the book to be a polemical-apologetic work: it was intended that from the demonstrated contrasts and opposites, on the larger scale as well as in detail, there should emerge the necessity of distinguishing between two mutually inimical Gods and therefore of recognizing the independence of the gospel from the Old Testament and the absolute newness of the former. Finally, the work was intended to be not only a literary addition ("dos") to the gospel and a defense ("patrocinium") of the same but also an authoritative work for the community and thus its creedal book. It is true that we do not know on the basis of positive testimony that Marcion himself gave this direction, but we certainly may surmise it; for already in Tertullian's time the Marcionites had it "in the most important instrument, by which they are initiated into and hardened in this heresy." That can only mean that its authority had to be recognized by every Marcionite,[5] in fact at the time of his admission, and it was Marcion's way to place everything in his church on a clearly defined and firm foundation.[6] Marcion's gospel and apostolic corpus were only halfway understandable, even in their intentions, if they were not accompanied by the explanation that the *Antitheses* afforded; hence the former must have been accompanied by the latter from the very first.

Only Tertullian (and those who copied from him) actually *named* the work with this title.[7] Certainly a good many catholic polemicists of the later period knew it, but for us only the presbyter in Irenaeus' work, Irenaeus himself, Origen (probably also Celsus), Ephraem, and an unknown Syrian writer come into consideration. Adamantius, Jerome, Epiphanius, Maruta, Esnik,[8] and sup-

posedly the author of the pseudo-Clementine Homilies, as well as others, had
not seen it, but Adamantius has some valuable material from writings whose
authors had been acquainted with the *Antitheses*.

The work was dedicated to an unnamed comrade in the faith; at least this
is the most probable meaning of the passage in Tertullian IV 9. Here Tertullian
considers himself obliged to go into the impermissible conclusions that Marcion
has tacked on to the pericope of the healing of the leper (Luke 5:12 ff.) by way
of a detailed explanation. He comments: "Since, however, he quotes with
especial care, as a proof in his domain, a certain companion in misery and
associate in hatred himself, for the cure of leprosy, I shall not be sorry to meet
him" (ANF III, p. 355).[9] The one person was for Marcion representative, in
fact, of all his compatriots; hence, in another passage Tertullian can challenge
Marcion (IV 36): "Well, Marcion and all who are now companions in misery
and associates in hatred with that heretic, what will you dare to say?"[10] From
Tertullian IV 9 one learns two things: first, that Tertullian had before him the
Antitheses not (or at least not only) in Latin, like Marcion's Bible, but also in
Greek;[11] and second, that they contained not only antitheses in the narrowest
sense of the word but also more detailed "argumentationes" concerning the correct understanding of biblical passages.[12] Now, however, Tertullian further
remarks (IV 4; see above) that Marcion in his *Antitheses* has represented the
gospel of Luke as adulterated and that this had been done by the "protectoribus
Iudaismi" (in order to prove its harmony with the law and the prophets).
Moreover, he says explicitly (IV 3): "Marcion tries [in the *Antitheses*, of course]
to destroy the status of those gospels that have been produced specially under
the apostles' names, or even the status of the apostolic writings, in order to direct
to his own gospel [scil. the faith] that he takes away from them."[13] Thus, the
Antitheses contained also the fundamental discussions about the "Judaistic
Christians," about the "adulteration" of the gospel in the church's tradition, and
against the four gospels which therefore already in that time existed as an
authoritative collection. Thus the statements about the apostles and the apostolic
age that Marcion made on Galatians 1 and 2 must also have stood here.[14]

But once that is certain, it cannot be doubted that the *Antitheses* are the
source of much more: the great bulk of Marcionite explanations of biblical
passages which Tertullian continually sets forth in the fourth and fifth books of
his *Against Marcion* and even in the first three books[15] and which other literary
opponents of Marcion adduce; and dogmatic-critical expositions of various
kinds[16] as well as polemical, disputatious statements. Then, however, the
Antitheses were by no means only a great bundle of brief theses and counter-
theses, but the work only received its name from these; they themselves were
embedded in a work in which the gospel and the apostle, whether continuously
or—as is more probable—in numerous individual passages, were commented on
in an apologetic-polemical fashion, i.e., also *antithetically*.

However, not only passages from Luke and Paul were treated in the

Antitheses but also passages from the writings of the "Judaistic" apostles or evangelists. When one reads in Origen (*Comm. XV lff. in Matt.*, T. III, par. 333) a statement of Marcion on Matthew 19:12 (about self-mutilation), this can only have come from the *Antitheses*. The same is true with reference to Matthew 5:17; for according to Tertullian (IV 7,9,12,36; V 14) there is no doubt that Marcion expressly rejected as false the saying that Jesus had come to fulfill the law and the prophets, and he turned the saying into its very opposite. Further, from Tertullian III 12f. it clearly emerges that Marcion also set himself in opposition to Matthew 1:23 and 2:11 by disputing the fulfillment of the prophecy of Isaiah 7:14 in Jesus, on the basis of Isaiah 8:4. In view of Tertullian IV 34 it is highly probable, as Zahn (*Kanonsgeschichte*, I, p. 670) has correctly seen, that when Marcion discussed Luke 16:18, he also considered and rejected Matthew 19:3–8. In order to defend his view of the body of Christ, which he understood as the Catholic Christians understood the bodies assumed by the angels when they appeared, Marcion asked (according to Tertullian, *De carne Christi* 3) where, then, was the body of the dove in which the Holy Spirit had appeared. Since the baptismal narrative was eliminated from his gospel, he thus was here recalling the other gospels. It cannot be proved with certainty that Johannine passages were treated in the *Antitheses*. It is possible, however, that Marcion discussed the foot-washing episode (see Chrysostom, *Hom. VII in Phil.*, T.I, par. 246), and Ephraem (*47th song against the heretics*, c. 2) reports the Marcionites' ridicule of the wedding in Cana.[17] Cf. Appendix IV.

Among the sayings of Jesus that Marcion presented, there are no apocryphal ones; he kept himself strictly to the corrected third gospel. Hence it was not Marcion who, according to Clement (*Strom.* IV 6.41), offered the evangelical utterance, "Blessed are those who are persecuted on account of righteousness, because they will be perfect." It is true that Clement places the responsibility for it on perverting the good news so that one could think of Marcion, but here he probably has the Encratites in view. Indeed, the term "perfect" suggests the Encratites, not Marcion. In the case of Clement's *Stromateis* III 10.69, one can perhaps conceive of an apocryphal saying of a textual variant that we no longer possess; there it is said that according to the Marcionites' exegesis the Lord taught "by the plurality is meant the Creator, the God who is the author of existence, and by the elect one is meant the Savior, who clearly is the son of another, good God." However, this could also be an exposition, for example, of the story of the ten lepers. As to the scope of the Old Testament that Marcion used, so far as I can see he employed only those books that belong to the Hebrew canon. But I should not want to draw a certain conclusion on this point just now.

From all that has been said one cannot yet draw a clear conception of the *form* of the *Antitheses*. It still is unclear whether we may assume that the book included some continuous expositions; its relation to Marcion's Bible also presents a problem to us. That is to say, if one reads the fourth and fifth books of Tertullian's *Against Marcion*, one does not gain the impression that Tertullian had laying before him still another work besides the Marcionite Bible; he rather appears to draw the text and the expositions and excursuses of Marcion (together with the antitheses in the strict sense of the word) from a *single* work. This impression is so strong that Hahn (*Evangelium Marcions*, pp. 108ff.) and Ritschl (*Evangelium Marcions*, pp. 18, 120) have proposed the hypothesis that Marcion's *Antitheses* consisted of two parts: a predominantly dogmatic-historical part that stood before the Gospel and the apostle as a kind of introduction and a second part that had accompanied the entire text of the biblical books as scholia of an exegetical and critical sort. However, the other witnesses for Marcion's Bible had nothing else before them but the bare text, and Tertullian himself, when he speaks explicitly of the *Antitheses*, unquestionably treats them as a wholly independent work. This is clearest in IV 1, where we read: "In order to build up faith, he devised a kind of dowry for the gospel . . ., by which he might protect . . . the gospel . . . by dividing God into two. But I would have destroyed such things in special combat, hand to hand, i.e., regarding the individual insertions of the Pontic, if it had not been much more convenient to drive them back in and with that very gospel to which they attend." Thus it is Tertullian who, in undertaking in the fourth and fifth books to refute Marcion from Marcion's own Bible, has combined it and the *Antitheses*. His success in doing this is so striking that one must think that he had before him only a single document. This can hardly be explained except by assuming that the *Antitheses* in one major section or in its main part followed the important passages in the gospel and the epistles of Paul chapter by chapter. Thus Tertullian could easily find and reproduce the Marcionite exposition or comment on any given passage. This means that the biblical texts were, to a considerable extent, repeated in the *Antitheses*; this can be demonstrated particularly from the individual antitheses as they are reproduced in Adamantius. This also provides the simplest explanation of some of the uncertainties in the tradition about the specific form of Marcion's text; for it is not surprising that the texts brought over into the *Antitheses* do not always agree in details with the texts in the codex. We may assume that particularly the texts afforded by Adamantius in part do not come directly from Marcion's Bible but from the *Antitheses* in which they were cited.

As to the form of the work, at least this much now is determined: we may distinguish two parts: (1) historical and dogmatic statements which began with the exposition of the relation of Paul to the original apostles,[18] the justification for the new Bible, and the refutation of the false gospels and the book of Acts, and (2) a running commentary, though an eclectic one, of scholia[19] with "iniectiones." But since this part also was marked throughout by *one* emphasis and proclaimed, in tiresome repetition, the opposition of law and gospel and therefore of the two Gods, not only could the whole work be labeled "Antitheses" but it actually was a work of antitheses.

In the reconstruction of this work still another difficulty is caused by the fact that in his polemic, in all five books, Tertullian addresses himself not only to Marcion but in bewildering alternation also to the Marcionites, and in his discourse he introduces not only the former but also, and just as often, the latter. Indeed, often the most profound and most illuminating material that he presents from the teaching of Marcion is given in the form, "the Marcionites say" or "You say." Here it is evident that Tertullian actually confronted Marcionites; in fact, in some passages one has the strong impression that his statements and the comments of his opponents are the echo of disputations that Tertullian conducted with them in Carthage. Nevertheless, these parts cannot be separated from the quotations that are adduced from the *Antitheses*. The uncertainty that remains here, however, does not create any inconvenience in dealing with the question of Marcion's spiritual and intellectual legacy. In these cases we are not concerned with the problem of the fundamental principles in Marcion and their mutual relations — here the pupils very soon diverged from each other and complemented their master in different ways — but with the basic questions of Marcionite belief and Marcionite attitude. In these respects, however, even Apelles, who in theological matters is farthest removed from his master, remained a genuine Marcionite. What the pupils asserted about the two spheres, that of justice and that of love, and moreover about sin, law, and gospel and redemption, is so unanimous that it may be claimed with certainty as the intellectual property of Marcion himself.

A reconstruction of the *Antitheses* is impossible because in fact not even the arrangement of the work is clear. Little is accomplished by means of mere compilations of the antitheses in the narrowest sense of the word, especially since the tradition contains numerous half-antitheses which require completion, either from the Old Testament or from the gospel. But it is highly significant that in the *Antitheses* Marcion apparently never assails his opponents for having *two* written Testaments. It is always *only* the Old Testament that he attacks as the revealed *littera scripta* of false Christianity; he knows nothing at all of *two* revelational documents, one old and one new, belonging to the great church. From this it evidently follows that the church of his time still did not possess a New Testament, as in fact also clearly emerges from Justin's *Dialogue with Trypho*.[20] Over against the *littera scripta* of his opponents, the Old Testament, he places his new *littera scripta*, the Gospel and the apostle. Certainly he saw already the four Gospels as most highly treasured works in their hands, but for them these writings still did not possess the dignity of being *scriptural* documents of the *new* covenant and thus the second Testament.

The introduction to the *Antitheses* rejected the four Gospels of the great church as false, traced the apostles and their pupils to Judaism, acknowledged as valid only the apostle Paul, who had been called by a special revelation, and identified his gospel with the third gospel which had been given directly by Christ, adulterated by Luke, and now purged of its Judaistic interpolations. Apart from the force of this introduction, the strength of the *Antitheses*, so far as they did not contain exegetical interpretations of the new Bible, lay in the criticism of the Old Testament.

This criticism pursued a twofold aim: first, it was intended to bring to light the unmerciful "righteousness," harassing strictness and cruelties, passions, zeal, and wrath of the creator of the world; further, his evil partialities, pettinesses, and limitations; and finally his weakness and self-contradictions, his unprincipled whims, and his precepts and commandments which were so often ethically doubtful. This criticism reached its climax in the proof that he was even the "conditor malorum," the author of evil, the one who incites wars, is deceitful in his promises, and is wicked in his deeds.[21] Second, this criticism was intended to show that all the promises of the creator of the world are earthly and temporal and, insofar as they were not altogether insupportable, had already been fulfilled in the history of the Jewish people or would yet be fulfilled there. For this reason also the promised Messiah is an earthly warrior-king who would actually yet come; but the prophecies that pointed toward him are not numerous, since most of them have already been fulfilled in David, Solomon, and others, and are falsely assigned to the future Messiah.[22] With this criticism, in the controversy between the people of the great church and the Jews with reference to the interpretation of the Old Testament, Marcion placed himself on the side of the Jews. He readily accepted the unfavorable position into which he thus came and which was so abundantly exploited[23] by his ecclesiastical adversaries. He undoubtedly used arguments that the Jewish polemics directed against the church's exposition of the messianic passages of the Old Testament. We can assert with great probability, though not with certainty, that he drew them from that polemic; see above.

But Marcion himself was utterly lacking any deeper penetration into the spirit of the Old Testament or even a truly historical consideration of it. Meanwhile, even the moralistic-religious criticism, based simply upon the wording, has its rightful place in the face of a document that purports to be holy and normative. But it is highly remarkable that Marcion acknowledged the Old Testament as a self-contained whole, assumed that it had no adulterations, interpolations, or such, and did not even regard the book as false; instead, he believed it to be trustworthy throughout. While he condemned many primitive Christian books as Judaistic forgeries and declared the third gospel as well as the letters of Paul, in the form in which the church read them, to have suffered heavily from interpolations, he did not extend this kind of criticism to the Old Testament (see above).[24] This is all the more striking since at his time in some circles of late Judaism, but especially among the Gnostics, there were attempts at a differentiating assessment of the Old Testament, which advanced even to the point of excising individual parts and admitting larger or smaller interpolations. Here again the reserved attitude of Marcion[25] put him on the side of orthodox Judaism, whose anti-Christian contemporary historical exposition of the Old Testament he also indeed approved and apparently adopted. In this respect, particularly the rejection of any allegorical and typological explanation, which, as was shown above, is especially typical of Marcion, comes into consideration. Explicit denunciations of this dubious art, by means of which the church fathers gave expression to their whole view of history, were not lacking in the *Antitheses*.[26] Since Marcion rejected it, from the very outset he was not in a position to recognize the Old Testament and to maintain its harmony with the Christian revelation. But naturally the rejection of this harmony is with him the primary element, and the rejection of the allegorical method is the consequence.

The gripping cry of jubilation with which the *Antitheses* most probably began ("O wonder beyond wonders, rapture, power, and amazement is it, that one can say nothing at all about the gospel, nor even conceive of it, nor compare it with anything") – the only longer sentence that we possess word for word from Marcion's pen – is certainly not decisive for determining the style in which the work was composed. The other extensive fragments rather exhibit a quite sober and matter-of-fact style.

In Appendix V the remains of the *Antitheses* are brought together in full – indeed, more than in full, since much here may belong to the pupils, although it cannot be separated from the words of the master. The arrangement of the material must be arbitrary. I have excluded the detailed account of Marcion's teaching in Esnik, since it probably did not come exclusively from the master himself.

Some important items for the characterizing of the *Antitheses*, however, should be reported at this point by way of conclusion:

(1) It appears that no key word was used more frequently in the *Antitheses* than "new." It explains the cry of jubilation with which the *Antitheses* begins. One may note "new God" (Tertullian I 9; IV 20; and elsewhere); "new deity" (Origen, *Comm. in Joh.* II, 82); "the new kingdom," "new and unheard-of kingdom" (Tertullian III 24; IV 24); Christ brings the New because he has brought himself (Irenaeus IV 33.14f.); "new master and proprietor of the elements" (Tertullian IV 20); "novel doctrines of the new Christ" (IV 28); "new works of Christ" (III.3f.); "new miracle" of the power and goodness of Christ by the raising of the youth of Nain (IV 18); "a new precept" to forgive sins again and again (IV 35); "it is a new thing" to forgive all brothers (IV 16); "a novel institution of Christ" of cancelling the Sabbath commandment (IV 12); "new benevolence of Christ" (IV 10); "a new kind of patience," which is revealed in the new commandments of Christ (IV 16); "in Christ . . . any novel form of discourse, whether he proposes similitudes or refutes questions" (IV 11); "Paul a new author and advocate" (V 10); "the Spirit, the newness of the Testament" (V 11); and "new creature" (following II Cor. 5:17; Adamantius II 16f.).

(2) In the *Antitheses* Marcion referred with special emphasis and probably repeatedly to certain passages in the Old Testament and in his New Testament. Those in the Old Testament include: the account of the fall (Tertullian I 2: "morbidly brooding over the question of evil"; Tertullian II 5: "These are the

bones of contention, which you are perpetually gnawing"; Origen, *De princ.*
I 8.2; II 5.4: "the most talked-about question of the Marcionites"); the theft
of the Egyptians' silver and golden vessels (the presbyter in Irenaeus IV 30,31;
Tertullian II 20; IV 24); and Isaiah 7:14 and 8:4 (Tertullian III 12: "challenge
us, as is your custom"). His references to the New Testament point to the
passages about the good and evil trees and about the new patch and the old garment; to Luke 10:22 ("Only the Son knows the Father"; Tertullian IV 25: "In
this passage other heretics also find support"); to Galatians 2 (Tertullian V 2:
"the foremost epistle against the Jews"); to the Beatitudes (Tertullian IV 14: "I
now come to those ordinary precepts of His, by means of which He adapts the
peculiarity of His doctrine to what I may call His official proclamation as the
Christ" [ANF III, p. 365]); to Luke 18:19 ("No one is good save God alone";
Origen, *De princ.* II 5.4: "The Marcionites see in this saying as it were a shield
given especially to them"[27]); to Luke 16:16 ("The law and the prophets were until John" [Tertullian IV 33]); and to II Corinthians 3:3-13 (Tertullian V 11: "The
New Testament, which is permanent in its glory, the Old Testament, 'which was
to be done away' ").

(3) Marcion could not give expression to the most profound things that he
had to say in the briefly formulated *Antitheses*, even though there were dozens
of them, but the *Antitheses* still are especially characteristic of his strong intention to think in Christian terms. Hence, most of them may be given here without
any particular sequence assigned to them.[28] Jesus' pithy parables (of the good
and evil trees and of the new garment and the old patch, which Marcion related
to the two Gods and their divine economy and placed at the head of his expositions),[29] as well as the Pauline antitheses in Galatians and Romans, prompted
him to use this literary form.

(i) The demiurge was known to Adam and the following generations, but
the Father of Christ is unknown, as Christ himself said of him, "No man has
known the Father but the Son."

(ii) The demiurge did not even know where Adam was, and therefore
he called, "Where are thou?" Christ, on the other hand, knew even the
thoughts of men.

(iii) Joshua conquered the land with violence and cruelty, but Christ forbade all violence and preached mercy and peace.

(iv) The Creator-God did not cause blind Isaac to see again, but our Lord,
because he is good, opened the eyes of many blind persons.

(v) Moses intervened in the dispute of the brothers without being invited
and rebuked the offender: "Why are you smiting your neighbor?" He, in turn,
rebuked Moses: "Who made you a teacher or judge over us?" Christ, however,
when a man demanded of him that he arbitrate the dispute with his brother over
their inheritance, refused to take part in even so fair a cause—because he was
the Christ of the good God and not of the God who is a judge—and said, "Who
made me a judge over you?"

(vi) Upon the exodus from Egypt the Creator-God gave Moses the charge, "Be ready, girded, shod, staff in hand, sacks on shoulders, and carry away with you gold and silver and all that belongs to the Egyptians." But our Lord, the Good One, upon sending the disciples out into the world, said to them, "Have no shoes on your feet, no sack, no change of garments, no money in your purses!"

(vii) The prophet of the Creator-God, when the people were locked in battle, climbed to the top of the mountain and stretched forth his hands to God, that he might kill as many as possible in the battle; our Lord, the Good, stretched forth his hands (scil., on the cross) not to kill men but to save them.

(viii) In the law it is said, "An eye for an eye, a tooth for a tooth," but the Lord, the Good, says in the gospel, "If anyone strikes you on one cheek, turn to him the other also."

(ix) In the law it is said, "Clothing for clothing," but the good Lord says, "If anyone takes from you your coat, let him have your cloak also."

(x) The prophet of the Creator-God, in order to kill as many as possible in battle, had the sun to stand still that it might not go down until the adversaries of the people were utterly annihilated; but the Lord, the Good, says, "Let not the sun go down upon your wrath."

(xi) At the reconquest of Zion the blind opposed David, and he had them killed; but Christ of his own accord came to help the blind.

(xii) At the request of Elijah the creator of the world sent down fire; but Christ forbade his disciples to call down fire from heaven.

(xiii) The prophet of the Creator-God commanded the bears to come out of the thicket and to eat the children; but the good Lord says, "Let the children come to me, and do not forbid them, for of such is the kingdom of heaven."

(xiv) Out of all the many lepers in Israel, Elisha, the prophet of the creator of the world, cleansed only one, Naaman the Syrian; Christ, though he was "the alien," healed an Israelite whom his Lord (the creator of the world) had not been willing to heal. Elisha needed to use a material, water, for healing, and it had to be applied seven times; Christ, however, healed by means of one single, simple word, and it was done at once. Elisha healed only one leper, but Christ healed ten, and these in disregard of the legal requirements; he simply told them to go their way, to show themselves to the priests, and on the way he cleansed them—without contact and without a word, by means of silent power, by his will alone.

(xv) The prophet of the world's creator says, "My bows are drawn and my arrows are sharpened against them," but the apostle says, "Put on the armor of God, that you may be able to quench the fiery darts of the wicked one."

(xvi) The world-creator says, "You are not (any longer) to hear me with your ears," but Christ on the contrary says, "He who has ears to hear, let him hear."

(xvii) The world-creator says, "Cursed is everyone who hangs upon the tree," but Christ suffered death on the cross.

(xviii) The Christ of the Jews was destined by the creator of the world exclusively to lead the Jewish people back from the Dispersion; our Christ, however, has been entrusted by the good God with the liberation of the whole human race.

(xix) The good God is good toward all, but the creator of the world promises salvation only to those who are obedient to him. . . . The good God redeems those who believe on him but does not judge those who are disobedient toward him; the creator of the world, however, redeems those who believe in him and judges and punishes the sinners.

(xx) *Maledictio* characterizes the law, and *benedictio* characterizes faith (the gospel).

(xxi) The creator of the world commands us to give to our brothers, but Christ simply says to give to all who ask.

(xxii) In the law the creator of the world said, "I make the rich and the poor." Christ, however, blesses (only) the poor.

(xxiii) In the law of the righteous God, good fortune is given to the rich and misfortune to the poor; in the gospel this is reversed.

(xxiv) In the law God (the creator of the world) says, "You shall love the one who loves you and hate your enemy." But our Lord, the Good One, says, "Love your enemies and pray for those who persecute you."

(xxv) The creator of the world ordained the Sabbath, but Christ takes it away.

(xxvi) The world-creator rejects the publicans as non-Jewish and profane men; Christ accepts the publicans.

(xxvii) The law forbids the touching of a woman who has an issue of blood; Christ not only touches them but heals them as well.

(xxviii) Moses permitted divorce, Christ forbade it.

(xxix) The Christ of the Old Testament promised the Jews the restoration of the earlier state of things by the return of their land to them, and after death, in the underworld, a refuge in Abraham's bosom. Our Christ will establish the kingdom of God, an eternal and heavenly possession.

(xxx) With the creator of the world, the place of punishment and the place of refuge both are situated in the underworld for those who are in the bondage of the law and the prophets; but Christ and the God to whom he belongs have a heavenly resting place and haven which the creator of the world never proclaimed.

Anyone who compares the *Antitheses* with the biblical text provided by Marcion (but also with the contents of the forged Laodicean epistle and of the "Argumenta") must be amazed at the massive unity and uniformity of the few chief ideas to which everything is reduced here. According to Marcion, one should read the gospel, epistles, and Old Testament *only* in the perspective of how new is the message of the redeeming God of love, and how frightful and deplorable at the same time is the evil-righteous God of the world and of law. Never again in the history of Christianity are the gospel and the inherited capital of the Old Testament and of late Judaism so sharply reduced, so plainly interpreted and summarized in such a simple formulation as is given here. Only Luther with his justification-faith manages to rival Marcion here; but since he holds fast to the identity of the Creator-God and the Redeemer-God, he is able to combine with this faith the whole wealth of salvation history and of the "traces of God" that Marcion was compelled to abandon.

VI

MARCION'S CHRISTIANITY AND HIS PREACHING

Anyone who can read will be able to read off from the remains of the *Antitheses* and of the canon what Marcion intended and proclaimed; still it is incumbent upon us to arrange in some order what has been handed down to us and cast some light upon it.[1] For the presentation of Marcion's preaching the following provisional observations are important: (1) that nothing is known of a doctrinal system or anything of the sort that he expounded and published, that his pupils never appealed to doctrinal principles in conceptual form which he was supposed to have declared, and that everything that he left behind in written form was set forth in the *Antitheses* or in the exegeses of biblical passages given here; (2) that he never appealed to "the Spirit" or to a special revelation that had been granted to him; (3) that with regard to the sources of his teaching he rejected everything "apocryphal" and held with strict exclusiveness to the Gospel and the Apostle and to the Old Testament;[2] (4) that he abstained from adducing any sort of mystery-wisdom and any "philosophy," since he condemned these as "vain deceit"; (5) that he rejected, as a matter of principle, the allegorical and typological explanation of the texts;[3] (6) that in his church diverse doctrinal principles developed right away without leading to divisions in the church, except for that of Apelles.

Thus Marcion's proclamation of Christianity is intended to be nothing but *biblical theology*, that is, religious teaching which on the positive side is exclusively based upon the *book* that consists of the Gospel and the letters of Paul and on the negative side on that other book, which also is actually truthful, the Old Testament. Both books intend to be understood as mere writings, that is, their contents are fully contained in the letter of what is written. Marcion's Christianity — the "strange, foreign gnosi," as Clement calls it — is presented as an exclusive religion of the book. He is the first one in Christianity to find his support in two major collections of books; it is his contention, however, that they do not belong together but that the second refutes the first.

1. The Foundation

The presentation of Marcion's Christian proclamation has to be related to what was stated above in Chapter III. There is no doubt that the doctrine of the two Gods, i.e., the distinction between the law and the gospel, related to "the good tree and the evil tree." "*Famosissima quaestio Marcionitarum*" ["the most notorious question of the Marcionites"] formed the basic schema of his preaching; but what his religious feelings were, and how he determined what was essential, is not clear at first, yet this is the most basic question. Here, however, we are fortunate in having four testimonies which splendidly serve to enlighten us as to his basic Christian feelings: (1) The *Antitheses* began with the words: "O wonder beyond wonders, rapture, power, and amazement is it, that one can say nothing at all about the gospel, nor even conceive of it, nor compare it with anything." In harmony with this is the fact that repeatedly and universally the gospel is characterized as something entirely new in its contents (from the sudden and new appearance of Christ, the "new and strange disposition" (Tertullian I 2), down to the "new kind of patience" (IV 16)), as well as in its form (IV 11: "novel form of discourse"). (2) Tertullian transmits to us (I 17) the Marcionite saying: "One work is sufficient for our god; he has delivered man by his supreme and most excellent goodness, which is preferable to (the creation of) all the locusts" (ANF III, 283). (3) Tertullian and other witnesses report that the basic thought of Galatians and Romans was normative for Marcion, namely, the idea that the righteous person experiences through faith in the crucified one a "re-formation" and in this faith "out of the love of God" receives redemption and eternal life; Marcion's pupil Apelles clearly and precisely confirms this. (4) Tertullian (IV 14) tells us that Marcion characterized the Beatitudes as the "ordinary (the essential) precepts of Christ," "by means of which He adapts the peculiarity of this doctrine" (ANF III, 365); he therefore calls them in Marcion's sense the "edict of Christ" and reports further (IV 9.36) that Marcion described and addressed his comrades in the faith as "companions in misery and companions in hatred."

The nature of Marcion's Christian experience and piety breaks forth from these testimonies with luminous clarity. The first is perhaps the most important, for it teaches us that Marcion had felt in the gospel the whole force and power of the "Numinous," to use Otto's expression. But to know this is of the highest significance; for at first there is a very strong suspicion that a religious thinker who not only excluded from the deity wrath and punitive righteousness but also detached from the deity the creation of the world and even the world itself is cherishing a weak and sickly religion. If there simply can be no fear and trembling in the presence of God and if all exalted feelings that the vision of the world and of the grand march of world history beget are held to be apocryphal, indeed even irreligious, the conjecture arises that here a curiously limited and half-hearted piety has been put in the place of power. Only the mighty peal of the words, "O wonder beyond wonders, rapture, power, and amazement," and so on here can dispel every suspicion: Marcion sensed the *gospel* – but only the gospel exclusively – as a confessedly great *mysterium tremendum et fascinosum*. To him it is simultaneously light and darkness, and he stands before it, the new – indeed the only thing that is really new in all the world or in history—, in trembling and silent worship.[4] Thus "religion" here has not lost anything of its essential nature.

The second testimony establishes the exclusiveness of the gospel as the object of religion: the gospel brings redemption, and no other work can approach this redemption which is provided by an immeasurable and incomparable goodness; no other may even be joined to it.[5] The God who has performed this work cannot have created any other, and thus not even this world, whose nature and worth are characterized by the loathsome vermin that fill it and by repulsive sexuality and procreation. The world cannot be repudiated with greater scorn than with the words "and being preferred by all locusts." Redemption redeems so completely that simply *nothing* remains of the old; it makes everything new, to the very ultimate basis of things. Thus, everything that existed previously is corruptible and vain, for redemption is redemption not only from the world but also from its creator and lord.

The third testimony defines the historical actuality and the appropriation of the redemption that is given in the gospel: in faith, which signifies an inward re-formation, to lay hold upon Jesus Christ, his death and his resurrection. Within redemption and in the new life, which is also the eternal life, Christ is all in all and hence also the founder and the perfecter of faith. Before him were only false prophets, and after him there is no need of any further revelation but only of a restorative reformation.

Finally, the fourth testimony says, in connection with the foregoing, that the redemption is indeed already accomplished, that the believers, however, first possess it as an assured hope with the pledge of the Holy Spirit. They ought therefore to know that as long as they live in this wretched world under the harsh and contemptible world-creator they must be poor, suffering, mourning, and persecuted. They simply must not have dealings with the world. It is self-evident from this that they are the hated ones and that they can possess the rapturous bliss of the redemption here upon earth only in faith, but this faith is already bliss.

A greater contrast than the one in which the Marcionite believer lived is inconceivable. On the one hand, he knew himself to be redeemed not only from sin and guilt, not only from death and the devil, not only from the entire nature of the world, but also from the God and Father whom he earlier either had served in fear and trembling or, with a bad conscience, had fled in culpable thoughtlessness. On the other hand, he still lived on the earth as one hated and persecuted by this God! Who is this God?

2. The World-Creator, the World, and Man

Many uncertainties with respect to Marcion's major teachings could have been avoided by remembering that Marcion, as an exclusively biblical theologian, saw the God from whom Christ redeems the believers in those attributes that the Old Testament assigns to deity and that are found in the gospel and the epistles in connection with the God of the Old Testament. The God whom according to Marcion Christ has put in the wrong thus is not the Persian Ahriman, not merely the evil principle (Marcion sees the devil, as the Testaments teach, existing along with this deity, and he thinks of the devil as does the mass of Christendom), not the creator of darkness in opposition to the light (he created both; see Appendix V). Even less is he to be identified as Matter; he is simply the Jewish Creator-God, as the law and the prophets have proclaimed him.

Nevertheless, this recognition is subject to a limitation or modification. To be sure, it does not automatically follow that according to Marcion God created the world out of material that is primordial as he is; in that time both Hellenistic Jews and Christians generally taught that idea without embarrassment, but they thought of a matter that is devoid of qualities. Marcion, however, according to definite testimonies (see Appendix V; Tertullian, Clement, Ephraem, Theodoret, Esnik, the testimonies of the last two alone would not suffice), held matter[6] to be *evil* and formed the precise principle that the world's nature is evil because it stems from the collaboration of evil matter and the just Demiurge (thus Clement).[7] But the striking thing here is that neither in his exegeses nor in his other statements did Marcion make any use of this assumption, which he did not expand.[8] Indeed, so far as we know, outside the statements about the creation[9] he nowhere else even mentioned matter. In addition, there is the fact that apart from the evil designs of the Creator, he regarded the devil as the originator of evil. *Always, however, he has to do with only the two Gods.* If, therefore, "evil matter" appears to have to be regarded as an alien element within his perspective of belief, it is suggested that we can recognize there an influence which, according to the tradition of Syrian Gnosticism, came to him through the mediation of Cerdo. Further, in what follows we shall note the presence of another alien element, namely, the specific condemnation of the flesh and the restriction of redemption to soul and spirit (though these are actually as alien to the "alien God" as is the flesh). The suspicion is strengthened that these two closely related doctrines (that of evil matter and that of the irredeemability of the flesh) are not a part of Marcion's original conception. Nevertheless, this may not be regarded as certain, at least as far as the first point is concerned. That is to say, since in his view the creator of the world was not "evil," Marcion required in any case an evil principle alongside this creator and *for his exoneration.* This was required at the very beginning of things, at which point the devil—according to biblical tradition himself a creature of God—could not yet appear. From this perspective, matter was essential to Marcion's view, though as soon as the devil is present in the picture he can leave matter out of consideration and, in fact, he now let it drop. The lack of clarity here (matter and devil) is typical of Marcion's "stopping in the middle of a thought," indeed, of his tendency to avoid philosophical thought. [10]

But let us turn back to the creator of the world. Marcion's way of conceiving him emerges clearly from the remnants of the *Antitheses*. The particulars are given in Appendix V and need not be repeated here. From the clear summary provided by the pseudo-Clementine Homilies cited in the Appendix one can most quickly gain an overview of the limited and contradictory qualities and the offensive actions and fancies of the petty and fickle, impatient and jealous, warlike and wild Creator-God. One must not be led astray by the inferiorities and the varied detail of those Homilies; it is appropriate still to recognize that according to Marcion *iustitia*, in the sense of formal justice ("an eye for an eye, a tooth for a tooth") and in judicial practice, and miserable pettiness are the basic characteristics of the Creator-God, but wickedness is not.

This of course appears to be refuted by numerous passages in which an undisguised badness appears and by that chief passage in which Marcion simply calls the Creator-God "the corrupt tree." Only if one examines the testimonies that are compiled in Appendix V does one come to a different conclusion. Incidentally, that different conclusion is already demanded because there can be no doubt that Marcion identified *righteousness* as the *essential* characteristic of the Creator-God. Besides, he would not have found it necessary to point his finger triumphantly at passages such as "I am the one who created evil" and the like if he had held evil to be the very *essence* of the Creator.

Wherein is his malice shown?

(1) In the creation of men, in that he formed man weak, helpless, and mortal and allowed him to be tempted; and it is also shown in the fact that he even tolerates sin, death, and the devil (who is indeed his creature), as well as every kind of evil;

(2) In the numerous punitive ills that he inflicts, in the disproportion of punishment to guilt, and in the sending of ills in general;

(3) In numerous examples of harshness, cruelty, warlike rage, bloodthirstiness, and so on;

(4) In his practice of punishing the children for the sins of the fathers and allowing the innocent to suffer for the guilty;

(5) In the hardening of heart that he inflicts upon the obstinate;

(6) In the jealousy with which he kept the first men from the tree of life;

(7) In the partiality with which he favors those who worship him, even if they are wicked, allowing or even encouraging them in injustice, deception, plunder, and acts of violence of all kinds against his adversaries.

Almost all these traits are compatible with "justice" if one sees the Creator-God as a *despot* in the ancient sense and in the sense of numerous Old Testament passages, a despot who proceeds on the principle that "the will of the king is the supreme law," who seeks above all his own honor, who treasures as the highest virtues in his subjects their submissiveness and obedience, and who declares his adversaries, as impious folk, to be without rights and destroys them. Under the presupposition of these superior principles the despot can be a highly just man. Of course, in this connection there is also a negative presupposition to be added with reference to the Creator-God of Marcion's thought which, however, is also customarily applied to despots: he is supposed to be all-knowing, wholly superior, possessed of a sure fore-knowledge, beyond contradiction, complete in himself, dependable and almighty, in order in his fullness of power not to fall into follies, mistakes, and contradictions; but he is not all of this. Thus also the righteousness of the Marcionite creator of the world is disfigured with evil by these deficiencies that beset him—for example, he is simply too weak to create better men and wholly to annihilate evil. Nevertheless, this God purports to be righteous and even is so, so long as his honor is not at stake and his limitations are not crucial. Thus, wickedness is not his essence, but his *iustitia* has not grown to fit its task and, because of jealousy and weakness, under certain conditions it becomes unfairness, pettinesses, and malice.[11]

Moreover, one must not overlook the fact that Marcion also had to allow all the splendid and elevated expressions about the Creator-God that the prophets and especially the psalms contain concerning him. It is this God who said, "Fear not, for I have redeemed thee, I have called thee by name, thou are mine." Again, it is the believer in this God who says to him, "If I only have thee, I do not ask for heaven and earth." It is quite understandable that in the fragments of the *Antitheses* that are preserved, this side of the Creator-God does not emerge, since these fragments have come to us from the hands of Marcion's opponents; but even Marcion himself would hardly have dwelt long upon them, since they would necessarily have caused him some embarrassment. We know how he mastered this embarrassment where it was possible: he interpreted everything that the Old Testament contained by way of comfort, promise, and redemption to refer to an earthly redemption which has its content in a long and satisfied life and in the prospect of a temporal and earthly kingdom of pleasure and splendor. With the World-Creator there is no "eternity" in the intensive sense of the word—Marcion excised the word from the New Testament where it must be related to the life that the World-Creator guarantees, and he emptied it of force where it appears in the Old Testament. Everything is oriented to this world and to a future splendid intensification of the life of the world, in which the meaning of redemption is exhausted. It does not need to be said that with such an interpretation Marcion mishandled the most profound passages of the Old Testament and eviscerated them, and he fell far behind the understanding that was found at that time among devout and spiritually advanced Jews; but since in the canonical book, which was recognized as inspired, everything stood on *one* plane, it is understandable that there once appeared a man who read the book not from the right to left but from left to right and explained the highly developed and splendid in terms of the primitive.

In order to grasp rightly the character of the Creator-God according to

Marcion, however, the following features of the character must also be brought out: *his ignorance of the existence of the other God; his profane revealedness; the identity of his nature with the nature of the world* (even though it is the higher), *and the base and contemptible method of procreation which he has arranged or which he at least tolerates.*

The utter ignorance of the World-Creator about the other God is the worse aspect of all his ignorance; it shows him to be inferior in the most extreme degree. But since, because he does not know the other God even the sphere and the nature of that God are incomprehensible to him, true goodness is also completely closed to him. It is true that he too has "goodness," indeed is himself "good" (see below concerning the "Law"); but this is a kind of goodness that, when measured by genuine goodness, actually does not even deserve this name.

The creator of the world is "known" absolutely and therefore also can be given a name; his nature can be read off fully and without remainder from his creation and revelation. This profane revealedness which leaves no mystery shows him to be an inferior God. The shocking incompleteness, vacillation, contradictions, and unreliability exhibited by this God, however, are according to Marcion nothing less than a mystery, but precisely as in the case of men, indicative of an unprincipled weakness, a lack of character, and susceptibility to passion.[12]

This world, a product of the just World-Creator and evil matter, is an evil nature. "The Marcionites," Tertullian says (I 13), "turn up their noses and scornfully say, 'Is it not true that the world is a great creation, one worthy of a God?' " "These poverty-stricken elements," "this sorry apartment of the Creator" (I 14, ANF III, 281)—thus they labeled the world, for which they have nothing but scorn. That must have filled every Hellene, but also the Jews and the Christians, with indignation. But if for Marcion this stupid and wretched world, teeming with vermin, this miserable hole, was only an object of contempt,[13] it is Marcion's most derogatory criticism of the creator of the world when he repeatedly identified him with the world or in his exegeses substituted him for the world, equating the two. When Paul says that through Christ the world is crucified to him and he to the world, according to Marcion we are here to understand the creator of the world to be intended. The same holds true of the saying that God has made the wisdom of this world to be foolishness, as well as of the saying that the apostles have become a spectacle for the world. Marcion read II Corinthians 3:14, "the minds of the world were hardened" for "their minds" and then interpreted the world as meaning the World-Creator; and in Ephesians 2:2 he understood the αἰὼν τοῦ κόσμου τούτου to mean the aeon of the creator of the world (see Appendix V). These identifications are of great importance for our full understanding of the Marcionites' World-Creator, for they teach us that Marcion had darkened the picture of the World-Creator afforded by the Old Testament by defining, according to his own whim, in various passages the character of the creator of the world in terms of the character of the world. The wisdom of the creator of the world coincides with the wisdom of the world! Thus how contemptible is the wisdom of the creator of the world! God is the world, and the world is God—not in the pantheistic sense but in the ethical; each is the mirror of the other.

Finally, the creator of the world is responsible for the abhorrent system of procreation and for all the loathsomeness that the flesh exhibits, from its origin to its uncleanness. If one surveys all that is preserved for us from Marcion, one learns that the man who was marked by calm reflection and quiet could also become profoundly moved; but in only two places is this handed down to us by the tradition. One of these occurs when he has in view the newness and the rapturous and ineffable splendor of the gospel (in his introductory words to the *Antitheses*). The other, in contrast to that, is here, where he pronounces his judgment about the flesh and above all about its begetting and birth. In the former passage he breaks out in rejoicing that cannot find adequate words; here, he has indulged in the bitterest "perorationes" (see the testimonies of Tertullian, Appendix V), in abusive language about the flesh, its origin, its components, its experiences, "its entire outcome, that from the very beginning onward it is unclean as the faeces of the earth, that it has become progressively more unclean through the filth of its own seed, that it is unworthy, weak, criminal, burdened, miserable; and finally, as a conclusion to the whole litany of its base profaneness, that it sinks as a corpse into the earth from which it came, but even loses this name and disappears into nothingness—no longer even a name, but a nothingness which dispenses with any and every designation." This "flesh stuffed with dung," which develops out of the marital "lewd transaction," flows together in the womb from the loathsome materials of procreation, is nourished by the same refuse for nine months, comes to light through the shameful parts, and is nursed amid simpers! The "most hallowed and awe-inspiring works of nature" (thus Tertullian!) are to him a factory of filth and a seething mass of the common and loathsome! The "blasphemy of the Creator" which the church fathers charge against Marcion comes to its climax here; but it was pointed out above that through this condemnation of the flesh an element has entered into Marcion's thought which is not contained in the leading contrast of "good" and "righteous" but points to another source. [14]

In agreement with the account in Genesis, Marcion also recognized man as the goal of creation, but in the criticism of this "crown of creation" he comes to a conclusion that is altogether different from that of the Jews and of the Christians in the great church. For him, the creation of man is a grievous tragedy for which the creator alone is responsible, for:

(1) God indeed imparted to man, by the in-breathing of the soul, *his own substance* and therewith gave to him even more than his likeness and image. [15] However, not only is this divine substance itself imperfect and unstable, but evil matter is mingled with it, by God's action, through the addition of the flesh. Thus there developed, whether from a lack of goodness, foresight, or power on

the part of the creator — Marcion apparently left this question open, but probably assumed all of these deficiencies (see Appendix V) — a helpless, weak creature who was not even immortal but was exposed to death.

(2) It had hardly been created when, as always happens with despots, there arose in the creator a jealous concern lest his honor might be impaired. He showed himself therefore to be jealous of man and barred him from the tree of knowledge and the tree of life. Moreover, in his weakness he was unable to prevent one of his own angels from falling away from him, becoming evil, and striving to estrange man also from his creator.

(3) Thus the catastrophe began: man allowed himself to be led astray by the devil and became disobedient to his creator. This catastrophe utterly surprised the creator of the world, and he regretted having created man; he expelled him from Paradise in order to win him back again outside Paradise with every kind of means. Even in the mind of his originator man is a spoiled creation, a monster.

From this interpretation of the creation story it follows that the good God has no part at all in man, not even in his spirit or his soul, and that humanity on the basis of its constitution and because of being led astray by the devil[16] has fallen into a miserable, indeed an unutterably sad and hopeless state. From the very first loathsomely constituted, weak, and helpless; through the fall further weakened and in his defective knowledge still more sorely benighted, he is expelled from Paradise, thrust out into the frightful and sorrowful world, and here stands in the presence of his righteous, zealous, and wrathful "Father" who severely punishes every inclination of man toward the material, issues strict laws, and makes his rights of retribution cruelly effective.

3. The Creator of the World as the God of the Jews; Righteousness as Morality; Law, Prophets, Messiah, and Holy Scripture of the God of the Jews

Only after moving from Marcion's ideas about God as creator of the world to his ideas about God as the lawgiver does one arrive at the interest that was primary and crucial for him. For Marcion, as for Paul, the most important thing is that those whom Christ has not redeemed are under the law, and the importance of the law is so great that he substituted the creator of the world (in Romans 7:7) for the law, just as he also substituted the World-Creator for the world itself (see above).

But the lawgiver is the God of the Jews.[17] Here again Marcion follows the Old Testament without any objection. After the fall men forgot God completely, but God chose Abraham and his tribe in order to call men back. After he had given the law through Moses to Abraham's descendants, he used this same law to keep the Jewish people to himself and to win to himself those among the other

nations who, following after the devil, were wandering in the night of godless-
ness and of polytheism. Thus the heathen—although following Romans 2
a natural knowledge of the law is conceded—can return to the Creator-God in
no other way than by becoming Jews, i.e., proselytes; for all the promises of
earthly blessedness and of a future kingdom of glory on earth apply to the
chosen people. The Creator-God has a fatherly concern only for his people, the
Jews, and for others only through the mediation of this people.

The law (apart from its minutiae, the whole system of sacrificial worship
and the ceremonial aspects, which of course are inseparably connected with it)
is what is righteous and therefore what is *moral*. Marcion, like Paul, is far
removed from all antinomianism that would favor a libertine manner of life. To
be sure, he underscores what Paul has said about the law as leading to sin and
so forth, but with Paul he holds the conviction that the righteous, that is the
ethical, demands of the law are to be observed under all circumstances: no one
should kill, commit adultery, steal, or lie.[18] If, however, as we shall see, it is
not the ones faithful to the law who are saved by the good God but the gross
sinners who allow themselves to be saved and are saved, this does not imply
any reversal of values in the sense that the moral is to be held as immoral. Instead, here two basically different viewpoints, the moral and the religious, cross
in Marcion. According to the former, what is moral is just—indeed, one may
even call it good—and what is immoral is bad. According to the latter, which
is superior in Marcion's view, only that which comes from faith in Christ the
redeemer is good; the morally good, i.e., that which is just, as a matter of
course becomes the most serious hindrance to redemption, when one contents
oneself with it. For this reason the redeemer had to appear as "the rival of the
law" (Tertullian IV 9), although he, like the creator of the world, denounces as
evil that which the law forbids as evil.

Marcion's attitude toward the law therefore is not sharply distinguished
from that of Paul, if one leaves aside the ultimate presupposition of the two
Gods. He allowed to stand undisturbed the following passages from Romans
with reference to the law (not only 5:20; 7:4,5,8,23):[19]

Romans 2:12: "As many as have sinned without the law will also perish
without the law, and as many have sinned under the law will be judged by the
law"—we shall have something more to say about this passage in connection
with what he said about Christ.

Romans 2:13: "For it is not the hearers of the law who are righteous before
God but it is the doers of the law who will be made righteous."

Romans 2:14: "those who do not have the law do by nature what the law
requires."

Romans 2:20: "having the embodiment of knowledge and of truth in the
law"—thus even this is conceded by Marcion.

Romans 2:25: "For circumcision indeed is of value if you keep the law, but
if you break the law your circumcision becomes uncircumcision."

Romans 7:7: "What then shall we say? That the law is sin? By no means; but I would not know sin if not for the law."

Romans 7:12: "the law is holy and the commandment is holy and righteous and good"—with Tertullian, we are amazed that Marcion allowed this to stand; see also 7:13: "sin, order that it might be revealed as sin brought about death in me through what is good."

Romans 7:14: "the law is spiritualized"—this is the most startling concession of all.

Romans 7:25: "so I myself then serve the law of God with my mind."

In light of these passages one will not be able to cling to the superficial opinion that Marcion simply rejected the law as a manifestation of the just god and is therefore an antinomian in the full sense of the word, since the matter is more complicated than that. Marcion explained the law, that is, certain parts of it (the moral law) as *holy*, *good*, and even *spiritual*, and therefore as an inviolable norm; but he nevertheless did not derive it from the good God, because it belongs to the sinful situation and serves to increase sin. Then, however, the assumption is unavoidable that he made a distinction between "good" and good, "holy" and holy, "spiritual" and spiritual. The "goodness," "holiness," and "spirituality" of the law follows only from its contrast with evil and sin; in comparison with the goodness expressed in mercy and redemption, however, it is neither good nor holy nor spiritual. Marcion's dialectic thus is of a different kind here from that of the apostle whom he follows, for the apostle knows no goodness and holiness of a first and a second order. For Marcion, however, only the concept "wicked" is unequivocal; on the other hand, he distinguishes between a moral goodness, which has only an earthly character, and a religious goodness.[20] Paul places the tension of the unequivocally interpreted concepts "righteous" and "good" in the Deity himself; Marcion frees the Deity of this tension, knows, however, a twofold righteousness and a twofold goodness, and divides them between the two Gods. As a rule he does not describe the inferior righteousness (and thus also the creator of the world) as "good" but only as "just," and he does not call the higher goodness "just" but only "good." But seen as over against evil (sin), even the creator and his law, by contrast with sensuality and sin, can be called "spiritual" and "good."[21]

This is confirmed when one investigates the concept of law in Marcion's gospel and further compares the passages in which are found "righteousness" and "righteous." Naturally Marcion allowed the "law" to stand in the saying of Luke 16:16 "the law and the prophets until John" [See ET of Luke 16:16], and it is equally understandable that he erased it from the saying in Luke 16:17 and inserted in its place "my words"; for it is not the law but the words of the redeemer that are more enduring than heaven and earth. On the other hand, it is very strange that he not only did not erase the pericope 10:25ff. but preserved it and emended it in such a way[22] that it is Jesus who there says that it stands written in the law that one should love the Lord God with all one's heart, and so forth. Thus, here Jesus himself quotes the law and indeed with approval; hence, Marcion must have been of the opinion that the "sum total" of the law is correct. Of course, here Jesus has tacitly made the important reservation that it is the *Redeemer-God* who is the object of our love; he has, however, followed the wording of the law.[23] Still more important is Luke 16:29f. Here Jesus says to the rich man with regard to his brothers who are still living and carousing that they should hear Moses and the prophets; for even someone risen from the dead would not be able to do anything with them if they disregarded the preaching of Moses and the prophets with regard to mercy towards one's neighbors. But this constitutes an apparent recognition of the worth of the law against evil and sin that goes far beyond a patient accommodation to the law which, according to Marcion, Jesus practiced when he commanded the leper (Luke 5:14) to show himself to the priest. It must therefore be affirmed that according to Marcion the two Gods agree in that they both regard evil to be evil and the love of god and neighbor to be good.[24]

The case with "righteousness," "righteous," and "justify" and so on is the same as it is with "law". Righteousness is reprehensible only in the form in which it is practiced by the creator of the world; it is not bad in and of itself. Hence with Marcion one reads not only δίκαιον παρὰ θεῷ (I Thess. 1:6) but also δικαιοσύνη θεοῦ ἐν εὐαγγελίῳ ἀποκαλύπτεται (Rom. 1:17), οὐκ οἱ ἀκροαταὶ τοῦ νόμου δίκαιοι παρὰ τῷ θεῷ . . . ἀλλ' οἱ ποιηταὶ δικαιωθήσονται (Rom. 2:13), δικαιωθέντες ἐκ πίστεως (Rom. 5:1), οὐ δικαιοῦται ἄνθρωπος ἐξ ἔργων νόμου . . . ἀλλ' ἐκ πίστεως (Gal. 2:16; cf. 3:11), τὸ δικαίωμα τοῦ νόμου πληρωθῇ (Rom. 8:4), εἰς δικαιοσύνην παντὶ τῷ πιστεύοντι (Rom. 10:4), τί δὲ καὶ ἀφ' ἑαυτῶν οὐ κρίνετε τὸ δίκαιον (Luke 12:57), ἐκδίκησις of the good God (Luke 18:7), and δεδικαιομένος of the tax collector (Luke 18:14). [In these passages Marcion has followed our Greek text; the reader may consult an ET of these passages.] But the most instructive thing here is the fact that in Luke 13:28 Marcion has removed the reference to the patriarchs (for they are not to be seen in the kingdom of God), but without embarrassment has put "the righteous" in their place. From this it is evident that he was no more afraid of the designation "the righteous" for those who accepted the good God than he was of righteousness as a characteristic and a demand of this good God himself. This God is good and therefore just,[25] but the creator of the world is lacking in merciful goodness, and therefore his justice must necessarily become harshness, cruelty, and—in his exclusivist preference for his chosen people—injustice.[26] Moreover, this "justice" is evilly disfigured by "trivialities" and obnoxious fancies; for Marcion, the demand for circumcision was the most repugnant among these. Origen tells us that Marcion repeatedly derided it, and he has preserved for us an interesting criticism of this practice from Marcion's pen (see Appendix V). From that citation it appears that the critic reproved the tastelessness of the World-Creator for placing the sign of the convenant in a shameful part of the body and not only the contradiction involved in creating a part of the body and then at once requiring it to be removed but also the shedding of blood. On the other hand, he did not so detest an institution such as the Passover that he wished no longer to have it mentioned; instead he allowed to stand in I Corinthians 5:7 the phrase "Christ, our paschal lamb, has been sacrified."

Marcion did not reject prophecy as such (see I Thess. 5:20; I Cor. 11:5, 12:10) any more than he rejected righteousness and the law (in the sense of the command of love), but he wanted to hear nothing of the Old Testament prophets. This is shown by numerous passages in which he erased allusions to them. In his corpus of the apostle's writings they can be found only in I Thessalonians 2:15 ("who killed both the Lord Christ and their own prophets"). He also left standing in the gospel the reproach that the Jews had killed their own prophets (Luke 6:23; 11:47) in order to prove their wickedness, for although Moses and the prophets held exclusively to the Creator-God,[27] he still viewed them as morally superior to the mass of the murderous Jewish people who rejected them and then fell back into a pagan life. Like the law, so also the prophets have given instructions and teachings which the dissolute and the unmerciful should hear (see above: "they have Moses and the prophets"). The name "prophet" is a name of honor, and John the Baptist is highly esteemed by Jesus, who calls him the greatest prophet (7:28), in whom the law and the prophets found their culmination (Luke 16:16). Of course, one is to recognize precisely in this greatest of the prophets just how blind they all were, for he did not know the good God, took grave offense at Christ, and taught his disciples to pray to the creator of the world. This prayer, of course, was impossible for the disciples of Christ, and they had to request of Christ a prayer of their own (Marcion on Luke 11:11). But now a serious difficulty arises here: if John belongs entirely to the creator of the world, how could Marcion allow Luke 7:27 to stand,[28] where with the words "it is written" Jesus appeals to Malachi 3:1 and identifies the Baptist as his forcrunner? These appear intolerable to the mind of Marcion, both the appeal to the Old Testament (as affording a genuine prophecy) and the announcement that John the Baptist is the forerunner of Jesus!

The second difficulty may be eliminated by the reflection that the Baptist, as a great ascetic, could be recognized in this respect as the forerunner of Jesus. In this connection it is important that Marcion apparently excised 7:33,34 (the contrast of John as an ascetic and Jesus who came eating and drinking). But in order to remove the first difficulty, we must take a look at the passages in which Marcion allowed "it is written" to stand[29] or, without this formula, appealed to the Old Testament.

In Luke 6:1ff. Jesus appeals, in defense of the conduct of his disciples in response to the charges made by the Jews, to David and the shewbread;

In Luke 10:26 (see above) Jesus acknowledges the Old Testament commandment of the love of God;

(In Galatians 3:11 see above, the passage from Habakkuk is cited, but it is not said that it comes from the Old Testament);

In Galatians 3:13 Marcion has "it is written, 'cursed is everyone who hangs on a tree'," and he regarded this passage as having been fulfilled in Christ;

In Galatians 4:22 it is not altogether certain that the "it is written" was allowed by Marcion to stand, but it is quite certain that he had an explanation of the two sons of Abraham;

In Ephesians 5:31 Marcion allowed the quotation from Genesis 2:24 to stand; of course, it is not explicitly identified as such;

In Ephesians 6:2 (see above) Marcion preserved the words τίμα τὸν πατέρα σου taken from the Old Testament; they were not identified as a quotation and he excised verse 2b;

In I Corinthians 1:19 Marcion allowed to stand "For it is written, I will destroy the wisdom . . . ";

In I Corinthians 1:31 "As it is written, He that glories . . . " was allowed to stand;

Similarly, in I Corinthians 3:19, "For it is written, He takes the wise in their own craftiness" and also (verse 20) "The Lord knows the thoughts . . . " These, however, are clear expressions about the good God.

In I Corinthians 5:7 (see above) Christ is described as "our paschal lamb";

In I Corinthians 9:9 we read in Marcion, "For it is written in the law of Moses, you shall not muzzle . . . ," and even more: the following also was allowed to stand:[30] "Does He say it altogether for our sakes; for our sakes, indeed, it is written . . . ";

I Corinthians 10:1-6: This entire section is preserved, thus also the statement that Christ was the food and drink and the rock that followed. Preserved also is verse 11, but probably in the following form: ταῦτ᾽ ἀτύπως συνέβαινεν ἐκείνοις, ἐγράφη δὲ πρὸς νουθεσίαν ἡμῶν (or: ταῦτ᾽ καθὼς συνέβαινεν ἐκείνοις, ἐγράφη πρὸς νουθεσίαν ἡμῶν);

I Corinthians 14:21 preserved: "In the law it is written that in their tongues . . . ";

I Corinthians 15:54 preserved: "Then shall be brought to pass the word that is written . . . ";

Ephesians 5:31 retained the quotation of Genesis 2:24, which of course is not identified as such.[31]

Since it cannot be assumed that Marcion "overlooked" all these passages or intended only later to correct them—an assumption that is ruled out in the case of some of them because he has made some corrections in them—it follows that the observation that we have already made in connection with the "law" must be expanded. The following points are to be affirmed:

Marcion indeed rejected the Old Testament because it was the book of the World-Creator, but he taught that (as it indeed also is not a book of lies, and as in its laws it contains what is correct in the face of evil and of sin) *much in it is written for us "for our understanding."* Hence it also contains stories from which we can learn, however they may have happened,[32] and others which *the apostle* could explain in typological terms (we, on the other hand, are not justified in making allegorical expositions), and finally even some that Jesus Christ has fulfilled: a forerunner has gone before him, he is the paschal lamb, and through his resurrection the saying, "Death is swallowed up in victory," has come true. But now it is certain that the Creator-God simply was not aware of the good God and thus could not prophesy concerning him, then there remains only the assumption either that the good God already, before his appearance in Christ, secretly had a hand in the Old Testament documents and gently intervened in the formation of the book — but this view is highly awkward — or that the creator of the world unconsciously or presumptuously said things and used expressions that did not belong to him and that first took on their truth in connection with the good God. Even this assumption is unsatisfactory, for it disrupts the simple lines in which otherwise Marcion's views lie before us; only it is, in my judgment, unavoidable, and it has its analogy in the view of antiquity that even evil demons are able in some instances to utter true prophecies.

On the other hand, Marcion's view of the Jewish Messiah as distinguished from Jesus Christ was quite clear: the former is yet to come (not under the name Jesus, which is not predicted in the Old Testament [Tertullian III 15]), and therefore the Jews are perfectly correct in expecting him still. He will be a military hero — for this reason already he was objectionable to Marcion, who was outspokenly opposed to bloodshed and war — and will establish the visible kingdom of splendor for the Jews. Still, his activity can only be a temporally limited career, for Jesus Christ will bring the hoped-for consummation.[33]

These are the basic features of Marcion's views of the creator of the world as lawgiver and guide of history. If one misses a strict homogeneity here, it is to be remembered that the World-Creator is in fact said to be a contradictory being.[34] Besides, it should be remembered that Marcion did not set forth a doctrinal system; instead, as a strictly biblical theologian he only partly corrected given texts and partly provided explanatory expositions of them. Finally, it should not be forgotten that he undertook a reformatory work of revision which by its very nature did not admit a completion.

4. The Redeemer-God as the Alien and as the Higher God

The experience that Marcion had had with the gospel ("O wonder beyond all wonders, rapture, power, and amazement is it, that one can say nothing at all about the gospel, nor even conceive of it, nor compare it with anything") gave him the assurance that it is something utterly new, and he was conscious of being united most closely with the apostle Paul in this rapturous experience. But if this gospel is completely new in its message and in its effects ("a new creation"), then its originator must also be a God who is hitherto unknown ("novus utique agnitione," Tertullian I 9); "a new God . . ., unknown in the old world and in the old era and under the old God, whom Jesus Christ—he himself a new being under the old name—, and no one before him, has revealed" (Tertullian I 8). But this God was not only unknown but also *alien*; indeed, he is "*the* Alien," for world and history alike teach that before Christ he was never revealed, and experience teaches that no man by nature knows anything of him (Tertullian V 16: ". . . Marcion's God is *by nature* unknown and is revealed nowhere but in the gospel"), and that no natural bond connects him with men. This is explicitly confirmed by the revelation of this new God; for in solemn words he has proclaimed that no one knows his Father but himself, the Son, and he to whom he wills to reveal him (Luke 10:22). Moreover, he has said that one should love one's enemies, i.e., imitate the God who through his redemption ("a new and strange arrangement," Tertullian I 2) has bought and set free "strangers and enemies"—but one does not buy "one's own family and friends"; "Christ's love for man was all the greater since he redeemed one who belonged to another" (Tertullian, *De carne Christi* 4).[35] Through all the centuries of the existence of the Marcionite church and in all the languages that the Marcionites spoke, "the Alien" or "the good Alien" remained the proper name for their God. Conversely, from the standpoint of God men also were called "the aliens." That they nevertheless had come together and that the aliens had become the children of God was the confessedly great mystery of this religion.

But since this unknown God has entered into the world that is alien to him, as an alien visitor, and through an alien (because new and unprecedented) "dispositio," the God of this world had to be his sharpest antagonist, for the Alien was carrying off his children and was disrupting his providence and his guidance of the world. Just as surprised by the appearance of this alien God as were the Jewish people and indeed all mankind, he, the God of this world, had to fight the Alien God with every means at his disposal.

Although each of the two is, and is called, "God" and "Father" (even "the Alien," who has created the *invisible*, possessed his heaven and his world, which by virtue of their substance are inaccessible to eye and ear), still the struggle between them is a very unequal one, for "the Alien," because he has produced the greater work, is also "the Greater" and the Creator-God is the lesser deity. The former is the greater God, more sublime, and resides in his third heaven, high above the creator of the world from whom he is separated by an infinite distance. "The Alien" is free from all the limitations that the creator of the world exhibits; he knew the World-Creator from the very beginning, and he needed no material in order to be able to create. Only he is actually "above all things"; the World-Creator is "the God of this world," but "the Alien" is "the God who is above every principality and beginning and power."[36] Thus, the former is, by comparison with him, "in deminutione," that is, by no means do two *equal* deities stand over against each other. Instead, one is stronger and the other is weaker ("because of his greatness and because of his goodness the unknown God is superior to the creator," Tertullian I 8), and this weaker God is so much bound to his heaven and his earth that, when they vanish, he too must necessarily pass away.[37]

The proof of his weakness, however, is that "the Alien" descends unhindered from his heaven through that of the creator of the world down to earth and at once contests that dominion of the World-Creator, drawing his children away from him. "He has conquered the devil and has abolished the teachings of the world's creator" (Adamantius, *Dialogue* I 4); he is the stronger one, who overcomes the strong man (Tertullian IV 26); he governs even the elements of the World-Creator, the sea and the wind (IV 20); he himself descends into the underworld of his adversary and brings his redemption even there. At the end of all things his superiority will be definitively revealed, while at present it is still restrained (see the next section). In believing in *God* as the *Alien*, as the *lofty one*, and as the *redeemer*, Marcion sensed both the loftiness of God and his power to give aid — the comforting essence of the new religion, for the Alien God has come to us, and he is greater than the world together with its God, and greater than our heart.

In the "alienness" which exists between that deity who alone is truly God, on the one hand, and the world, on the other hand (thus also between *the* religion and all human striving and being), combined with "goodness," lies the distinctiveness of Marcion's view of religion and of the world. I know of no evidence that before him anyone in all religious history had taught anything similar to this.[38]

5. The Redeemer-God as the Good God,
His Manifestation in Jesus Christ, and the Work of Redemption.
The Call of the Apostle Paul

In his inner nature the higher God is *good* ("supremely good," Tertullian IV 36) and nothing but good. Indeed, he is *goodness* itself (Tertullian I 2: "simple and pure benevolence"; I 26: "solitary goodness"; I 23: "primary and perfect goodness"; Origen, *De princ.* II 5.4: "This word they declare is peculiar to the Father of Christ"; Tertullian I 25: "simple goodness, to the exclusion of all those other attributes, sensations, and affections", "good and excellent", etc.). By virtue of this goodness, this God is "blessedness and incorruptibility" which "brings no trouble upon itself or upon anything else"[39] (Tertullian I 25); he is *merciful love*. But this God is so utterly and completely goodness alone, that is, love (Tertullian I 24: "simply and perfectly good"; I 6: "both good and excellent"; Esnik, p. 179: "the benefactor") that no other qualities are to be expressed concerning him, or that his other qualities form a unity with love. He is spirit, but "beneficent Spirit" (Tertullian I 19); he is "tranquil," "mild," "placid"; he simply does not become angry, does not judge, does not condemn.

He is also "just," but the justice in him is the justice of love. He is "wise," and so on, but he is all of this because he is love, which as such incorporates all these qualities.[40] For just this reason, however, there can be no work for this God other than *self-revelation*, and this in turn can be nothing other than *redemption*[41] (Tertullian I 19, ANF III, 284: ". . . our God, say the Marcionites, although he did not manifest himself from the beginning and by means of the creation, has yet revealed himself in Christ Jesus"; I 17, ANF III, 283: "One work is sufficient for our god; he has delivered man by his supreme and most excellent goodness"; I 14: "Man, this work of the Creator-God, that better God loved, and for his sake took pains to descend from the third heaven to these impoverished elements and for this reason was even crucified in the cell of the Creator"; Adamantius I 3: "He who is good suffered with others as sinners; neither as good men nor as evil men did he suffer with them, but being moved with compassion he had pity on them"). Precisely in this redemption one recognizes that he is, and must be called, the "Father of mercy and the God of all comfort" (Tertullian V 11).

But because the good God intended to redeem sinners, he brought his redemption *to the whole of humanity*; for they are all sinners. He knows no partiality for *one* people but brings a universal redemption. However, he also recognized that along with the world and its creator it is the *law* from which mankind must be redeemed; but because it is the law, it is also the lawgiver, for the two belong together. The law is the power of sin. The law has intensified the comfortless state of mankind. The law is a fearful burden. The law has made the "righteous" slavish, fearful, and incapable of the truly good. Thus, it must be taken away, along with the entire book in which it is contained.[42] *The good God came in order to dissolve the law and the prophets*, not to fulfill them. He does this by means of the *gospel*, in order to redeem souls.

But just as the law is the lawgiver himself, so also the gospel is Jesus Christ (V 19: "Marcion separates the law and Christ, assigning one to one God and the other to another"). Who is this Jesus Christ? Marcion responds:

> The Son of the Father, by nature God,
> Became a stranger here on earth.
> He leads us out of the vale of woe
> And makes us heirs in his banquet hall.

Just as the World-Creator has a son whom he will soon send to the earth, so also the good God has a Son who has come ahead of that other son; but there is a difference between the two. The former is called "son" only figuratively, for he will be a man from the tribe of David who will be anointed with the spirit of his God. The latter also is called "Son" only figuratively, but he is distinguished from his Father only by name, for "in Christ, God was revealed by himself." The Father and the Son form an equation, just as do the Son and the Gospel.

Marcion was a Modalist like other early Christian teachers, but probably more consciously so than were they. He (like the author of the Fourth Gospel) placed great weight upon the fact that Christ had raised himself, and he made that correction in the text (though not consistently). When the Modalist question later became a burning issue in the church, the opponents of Modalistic Monarchianism put the Marcionites in the camp of its otherwise orthodox representatives in order to discredit the latter (see Appendix VI).[43]

The redeemer (Tertullian I 19: "salvific spirit"; Origen, *Fragm. in Gal.*, T. V, par. 266: "spiritual nature") was called Christ, as was the one promised by the creator of the world. This was incontestably an embarrassment for Marcion, only poorly concealed by the statement (Tertullian III 15) that only under this name could he find acceptance among the Jews.[44] It was all the more important to Marcion that the name Jesus was not prophesied in the Old Testament (Tertullian, loc. cit.). Jesus' self-designation as "the Son of Man" was also an embarrassment for him; he had to interpret it allegorically (see Megethius, *Dial.* I 7 on Luke 6:22).[45] It is understandable that he preferred the title "the stranger," as he then also liked to speak of the coming sojourn of the redeemer. Like the good God himself, so also his Christ was called "the Alien" among the Marcionites.

If the redeemer is not also the creator and if the way for his appearing is not prepared by the creation or by history or by prophecies,[46] then he could only appear suddenly and unexpectedly. Further, if the flesh, since it stems from matter, is basically evil, then the redeemer, since he had to remain pure, could not assume flesh and moreover could not be subject to the disgraceful order of procreation.[47] Finally, the invisible substance of the higher God cannot be manifested in this world of ours.[48] From this it follows by necessity that the history of Christ on earth only begins with his emergence as redeemer, i.e., in the fifteenth year of the emperor Tiberius, and that he appeared in a phantom body.[49]

In the ancient era "Docetism" did not mean the same thing it means today, because people did not draw the consequences that we believe must be drawn.[50] Compared with natural human bodies the body of Christ was an apparition; but just as the angels who visited Abraham were not phantoms but ate and acted as corporeal and actual men,[51] so also Christ was no phantom.[52] Instead, God was manifested in human form and put himself in a position to feel, to act, and *to suffer* as a man, although the identity with a naturally begotten body of flesh was only apparent since the substance of the flesh was absent. Thus it is utterly incorrect to think that according to Marcion Christ only apparently suffered, only apparently died, and so forth. This was the judgment of his opponents, but he himself connected the illusion only to the substance of the flesh.[53] Naturally, he did not assume that the deity had suffered; but to conclude from this that Christ's suffering and death were for him a mere shadow-play is incorrect. Of course one cannot blame the opponents when they, along with Origen, explained with reference to Marcion's teaching that Jesus acted out his fleshly presence by means of an apparition. Indeed, it is even possible that Marcion's very words were: "Christ seemed to have suffered," only then he referred the "seemed" exclusively to the body conceived of as a body of flesh. As a biblical theologian he held to the passage in Philippians: "he came in the likeness of a man." For him it was the basic passage for the solution to the problems that are found here, and for this reason he taught that Christ actually had suffered in and with the human form into which he had entered. For the salvation of men he descended hither. Can there be any greater love or compassion than that which impelled him to leave the vaults of heaven? The miscarried creation of a disagreeable God, miserable humanity—and indeed the most wretched of humans—he wishes to save, out of pure love! (See the compelling saying in *De carne Christi* 4.) It is his intention to redeem unto eternal life that which, by its origin and development, is rightly subject to death because it has nothing in it worthy of life. Moreover, he intends to put in the wrong that God who worsens and corrupts everything, precisely when and where he pursues what is his right.

In word and in deed ("new evidences of the new God") he at once showed the unprecedentedly new realities that he had brought ("a new kindness, a new and strange arrangement, a new patience, a new disposition, new life"). He preached the kingdom of God,[54] but one should also know that "in the gospel the kingdom of God is Christ himself" (Tertullian IV 33). Thus he brought himself, or his Father, which is to say the same thing. Everything is included in the new knowledge of God which the Son alone imparts.[55] Marcion even felt the form of Christ's speech to be a new thing, "when he sets forth parables and counters questions" (IV 11,19).[56] Thus Marcion possessed an ear and a mind for the originality of Jesus' speeches and sensed the contrast of their goodness, wisdom, and simplicity with the preemptory, rigid, and petty laws of the World-Creator—the "newness of spirit" (Tertullian V 1) enlightened him. But although according to Marcion Christ clearly stated that he had come to destroy the law and the prophets, and although all his actions obviously moved in this direction, still he had not, according to Marcion, unequivocally declared, "I am proclaiming a new God." Instead, he left his hearers to draw the inference. Tertullian stated this with amazement (IV 17), and it is indeed amazing. But the gospel as handed down did not allow for attributing to Christ the proclamation of two Gods. Marcion explained the reserve by saying that Christ had wanted to show his patience and long-suffering here, also; for this reason he even permitted the leper to show himself to the priest (IV 9), did not correct those who praised the creator of the world for his wonders (IV 18), and tolerated his disciples' misunderstandings, even Peter's colossal misapprehension in his confession (IV 21).

Above all, Marcion perceived in the Beatitudes the "proprietas" of Christ's preaching (IV 14) and placed them in the foreground as the Magna Charta of the new religion. In them there flowed for him the beneficent love of the redeemer God. With the gospel Christ brings blessedness to the poor, the hungry, the sorrowing, the hated, the despised, and the outcasts; that is, to the pariahs of the just God.[57] "In the laws of the just God happiness is given to the rich and misery to the poor, but in the gospel it is the other way around." To this must be added the prohibition of care about earthly things,[58] as well as the formal antitheses that Marcion composed with reference to the conduct of the Creator and of Christ. These contrasts must be considered if one is to perceive how exclusively he wanted to have recognized the love, goodness, patience, and super-worldiness of the new God who is manifest in Christ: "In the law is the curse, but in faith the blessing" (Tertullian V 3). In that same connection he also saw the newness of the gospel in its universality: "The Creator enjoined us to give to our brothers, but Christ enjoined us to give to all who ask"; "this is a new and different thing" (IV 16). It is manifested also in the boundlessness of forgiveness, which may never grow weary (IV 35,38). But beyond the universality and the unlimited forgiveness, the love of enemies is the characteristic note of Marcionite Christianity because it alone corresponds to the great deed of the love of God, who redeems the "strangers and foes," who moreover yearns to become the Father of those who are the refuse of humanity that is alien to him and wretched, who prays for his tormentors and has stretched forth his hands—not like Moses to slay multitudes but to redeem multitudes. To be sure, "righteous ones" do not accept salvation, for they are wholly swallowed up in the service of the inferior God and in the principle of "an eye for an eye, a tooth for a tooth." Anyone who follows this principle without mercy[59] is hardened and incapable of being redeemed.

The words and deeds of the redeemer,[60] however, were also accompanied by the clearest demonstrations of his power: he heals innumerable folk without needing any material means but solely by a word, indeed even without a word ("tacita potestate et sola voluntate" ["by his silent power and simple will"], Tertullian IV 9,15,35). He commands the wind and the waves;[61] he comes as the stronger one above the strong;[62] indeed he himself invades the underworld that belongs to the World-Creator and leads forth those who follow him, namely Cain and his kind, the Sodomites, the Egyptians and their kind, and in general all the heathen who wandered in every kind of wickedness but who hastened to the redeemer when he appeared among them.

Here one must pause, for here is the point that not only appeared to the church fathers to be the height of Marcion's blasphemous wickedness but even to us today still is offensive, and yet according to Marcion's principles is all quite in order.

First: the belief that Christ has to go into the underworld and carry his redemptive mission thence was an obvious piece of primitive faith-conviction that was generally held among Christians which Marcion could not dismiss. Most recently Carl Schmidt, in his work, *Gespräche Jesu mit seinen Jüngern nach der Auferstehung* (1919), has instructed us anew on this point in an illuminating and comprehensive way. The universality of redemption depends on the hearing of the gospel not only by the contemporaries of Jesus and the apostles and by those yet to be born but also by all of humanity from Adam onward. What is only a withered relic in the churches today was, in that time, not only *one* part but *the* major part of the redeemer's preaching.[63] According to Marcion, in the underworld were found the outcasts as well as the Creator's *righteous ones*, though in different categories and in different situations ("Both of the Creator's rewards, whether torment or comfort, have been reserved in the underworld for those who have obeyed the law and the prophets," Tertullian IV 34). But since Marcion had to bring his Christ into the underworld, it had to be decided which of the two viewpoints was for him the superior one: the view that the observance of morality is "good" as against sin and transgression (see above); or the view that this observance, if it serves as "the good," is the gravest hindrance to one's being found and captured by compassionate love. The decision could not be in doubt. Abel, Enoch, Abraham, Moses, *et aliis*, could not be saved, for their observance of morality was in the service of the God who with his standard of "an eye for an eye" is the worst adversary of the good God. They had surrendered themselves wholly to him in fear and trembling, belief and distrust. According to Irenaeus, Marcion emphasized as the reason for their rejection, their suspicion that their God, who had constantly tormented them with temptations, was once again laying a trap for them. In Epiphanius it is said simply that they did not want to follow Christ because they could no longer escape from their belief in their Jewish God. Hence, they had to remain in the underworld; however, the gross transgressors who for punishment were tortured by the World-Creator, and the godless heathen as well, all of whom indeed had already received double and triple retribution for their sins according to the cruel punitive code of the righteous God, yearningly hastened to welcome the new redeemer God. His compassionate love called them all, and they all came, and he saved them all; they trustingly leaped into arms, and he led them all out of the place of torment into his kingdom of the blessed. According to Irenaeus' account, one cannot doubt that Marcion simply taught an *apokatastasis* of all pre-Christian men who in this life had not yielded their allegiance to the God of the Jews,[64] however scarlet their sins were. Only the partriarchs, Moses, the prophets, and their followers remained behind in their miserable "refrigerium." What an exaggerated Paulinism! But at the same time, what a conviction, not retreating from any of its logical consequences, of the omnipotence and irresistibility of merciful love and of the inferiority of the merely moral which, where it alone rules, becomes the mortal enemy of the good.

There is no doubt—according to Marcion Christ as the superior has strength and power enough to snatch all the children of the world's creator, i.e., humanity, from their natural father and to draw them to himself. Hence, the church fathers also asserted that according to Marcion Christ had forcibly taken possession of the Creator's property, and this Christ is therefore a thief and a robber. Only it was far from Marcion's intention to teach this, for what he read in Paul about the death of Christ had to prompt him to connect the achievement of redemption with Christ, but therewith to rule out all violence, the use of which indeed is utterly unfitting for the good God.

Of course, Christ had already shown to the creator of the world in the course of his work that he, Christ, was the stronger. This was, so to speak, only a proof, and he did not intend to overcome his adversary with force and to snatch away from him his children. One must remember here what was earlier said about "righteous" and "righteousness": Marcion knows a righteousness that belongs to goodness and that is the true righteousness, while the "righteousness" of the World-Creator turns into wickedness. He also, as we have seen, respects the law against robbing and stealing as a self-evident standard. Under this presupposition not only has he been able to appropriate some of the apostle Paul's ideas about the death of Christ, but he seized in particular, and indeed with exclusiveness and with strong conviction, the idea *that by means of his death Christ purchased mankind from the creator of the world*.

"The death of the good one has become the salvation of men" (Adamantius, II 9). this was Marcion's fundamental confession and likewise that of his disciples. "He who hopes in the crucified one is blessed," says Apelles, and indeed this death was a purchase price paid to the Creator. Marcion not only put his finger on Galatians 3:13, but he also inserted "purchased" in 2:20 in place of "loved." Marcion especially welcomed the fact that Christ's death was by crucifixion, for the World-Creator had pronounced a curse upon this, and therefore he had not had it in view for *his* Christ (Tertullian III 18; V 3; I 11) — the clearest evidence that the Christ who has appeared does not belong to the World-Creator. But equally welcome to Marcion was the idea of a purchase, for one does not buy what is one's own property. Thus, men were alien to the good God, and he had to *acquire* them (See Appendix V).[65] At the same time, however, his love which goes beyond all reason is demonstrated in this act of purchasing what was alien to him. Finally, the "Placidum" of the Redeemer-God appears in a clear light. For although the World-Creator, or the earthly powers that he commanded, in their ignorance, blind injustice, and zeal brought him to the cross as a criminal (Tertullian V 6; III 23; Adamantius II 9), and he thus would have been justified in escaping the sufferings and in smiting his adversaries, nevertheless he chose the way of fairness. It cannot be said with certainty whether Marcion here shows a still deeper insight that he has acquired through other Pauline passages that were in his canon;[66] it is likely, however, that the infinite demonstration of love displayed in this death for effecting this purchase was sufficient for him.

But what is the scope of this purchase or redemption? Is it unconditional or conditional? Further, what is the state of those who are redeemed in the present? Finally, what is to be said about the final judgment and the future estate?

These three questions still have to be answered.

It was determined above that according to Marcion the redeemer has redeemed in their totality pre-Christian humanity who languished in the underworld, with the exception of the "righteous ones" who belonged to the World-Creator (see also Tertullian V 11: "He freed the human race"). But on earth his appearance does not meet with the same success, from the beginning on down to the present day. "For all are not put in a state of salvation by it, but the Creator's subjects, both Jew and Christian, are all excepted" (Tertullian I 24; ANF III, 289; cf. Irenaeus IV 27, 4ff.; and Clement, *Strom.* III 10.69: "With the many is the Demiurge, but with the one, the elect, is the savior").[67] Already with his disciples Christ has been compelled to undergo sorrowful experiences, and at last they fell back again entirely into the old ways, again held their Lord and Master to be the son of the creator of the world, or fell into poor halfway measures and abetted the Judaistic pseudoapostles whom the World-Creator now sent forth in opposition to the gospel (see above and Appendix V). The patchwork agreement with Paul in Jerusalem was the last flicker of better recollection in them, but even it was not an agreement of fellowship (Marcion excised "fellowship" in Galatians 2:9) but an unprincipled and fruitless, because only apparently amicable, settlement. The new apostle whom the redeemer now raised up in their place, Paul, indeed was perfectly suited for his task, but he had a frightfully difficult situation, for he had to fight not only against Jews and pagans but also against the false Judaistic Christians, and that was the most difficult battle of all. He was able therefore to win only relatively few, especially since even the "the wordiness of philosophy" ("by philosophy as empty deceit, according to the tradition of men, according to the rudiments of the world": thus Marcion read Colossians 2:8) was set in opposition to him. He had to learn that faith is not to every man's taste. But everything depends on faith in Christ; Marcion learned this from Paul and repeated it in his *Antitheses* or in his exegeses.[68] From this perspective he explained the stories of the woman who was a great sinner, of the woman with the issue of blood, of the ten lepers (Tertullian IV 18,20,35), etc. To believe, however, means to surrender oneself to the unmerited love of God in Christ and consequently to scorn and to thwart the law that is a hindrance to faith (Marcion in Irenaeus IV 2.7: "the law forbids belief in a son of God"), just as the woman with the issue of blood had done.[69] Because one owes eternal life solely to God's love (Tertullian IV 25: "Therefore your disciple, Marcion, will obtain his eternal life in consequence of loving your God"), the only condition here, but also the necessary condition, is faith. It stands in contrast to the slavish obedience and fear that the law demands. Marcion repeatedly stressed that in contrast to the creator of the world, who wishes to be feared, nothing can be offered to the good God but faith, and that all fear is eliminated ("The good God is not to be feared", Tertullian IV 8). "By delivering them from evil, by faith the good one changed men who were wicked and made those who believed on him good,"[70] "Through faith He also made the ones who believed in him good"[71] (Megethius, *Dial.* II 16), and "The One who is good saves those who believe on him" (Marcus, *Dial.* II 1f.).[72] In Marcion's complete excision of the motif of fear from faith (Philippians 2:12 certainly was not included in Marcion's Bible), he put himself at a distance from Paul but concurred with John. Only a few allow themselves to be saved; however, the number of those who are saved is limited to those who believe.[73] Tertullian's question addressed to Marcion, however, as to why he did not sin if his God were not to be feared and would not punish, was given the marvelously simple answer: "Absit, absit" ("God forbid, God forbid").[74] But this means only that Marcion felt no necessity for the believers expressly to offer a rationale for the "moral." Seized by compassionate love and devoted to it in faith, the redeemed person is elevated into a sphere to which the contamination of this material world and inferior legalism cannot reach. Therefore, he needs no standards of what is moral and no justification for it; therefore, it remains for that sphere that faith suffices, because God makes good people out of wicked ones by means of faith.[75] That "absit, absit" is a religio-historical document of the first rank (see below).[76]

The question of the scope of the redemption includes also the question of whether the whole man is saved or only his soul. According to what Marcion taught about matter and the flesh, the decision could not be in doubt for him: only the soul is saved, for the flesh, which indeed is not even a product of the world's creator but belongs to matter, contains nothing that is essentially human but is only a loathsome mixture. Hence, his opponents' complaint that according to Marcion man is only imperfectly redeemed does not accord with Marcion's view. After all, he did not imagine the redeemed person who had passed through death to be without substance. "For your God," says Tertullian (III 9), "promises to men the true substance of angels; 'For they shall be,' he says, 'like the angels.' "

The redemption that the believer experiences in faith is in sharp contrast to his actual situation in the present time, for, as Tertullian testifies: "Marcion thinks that he has been liberated from the kingdom of the Creator in the future, not the present" (I 24). Hence, it is in no way true that the triumphant working of the redeemer in the mighty acts performed during his life on earth—they were only examples—had already conquered the creator of the world or that the resurrection had done so. It is true that the redeemer has already purchased men from their creator, but that is an exchange payable in the future, even though absolutely certain, because as long as this *saeculum* stands the dominion of the God of this world[77] also continues. Hence, not only do the poor, hungry, abused, and persecuted remain as they are, but those who have followed God in faith experience greater woe than ever before. The heathen, Jews, and false Christians, spurred on by the lawgiver,[78] persecute them ruthlessly; hence, they are the community of "the wretched and despised" in the world, and all their comfort lies in their faith and in the future. Not a single ray of light falls upon their outward situation in the present. Only in *one* respect are they strengthened by this situation, namely, in the conviction that they are no longer children of the creator of the world but they belong to "the alien one," for the creator would not let his children suffer and bleed so (Adamantius, *Dial.* I 21).

But what is the shape of the end of things? Here a great difficulty was bound to develop for Marcion. He had vigorously declared that the good God is not to be feared; so also he used every opportunity offered by the Scriptures to testify *that the good God does not judge at all* (Adamantius, *Dial.* II 1f.: "The One who is good does not condemn those who do not believe on him"), and as a rule he excised or emended the passages where the traditional text has the good God appear as a judge. But how then is a distinction to be made, if indeed we are not to think of a restoration of all things? Here one must observe how Marcion handled the concept and the words "to judge," "judge," and "judgment" in his Bible where he could not relate them to the God who is the lawgiver (such as Luke 12:58 et al.). In Luke 11:42 he changed "judgment" into "calling"; in Romans 11:33 he excised "judgments"; but he did not always proceed in this way. Tertullian has reported to us (I 27) Marcion's important sentence: "The better God clearly *judges* evil by *not willing* it and *condemns* it by *prohibiting* it."[79] Thus in this sense Marcion could acknowledge the function of judging and condemning even on the part of the good God. Hence, he allowed Romans 2:2 to stand: "God's judgment is true," along with Galatians 5:10: "He who troubles you will bear his judgment." He even preserved the important clause in Romans 2:16: "In the day when God will judge the secrets of men, according to my gospel, by Jesus Christ," as well as a similar one in II Thessalonians 2:12: "so that all who do not believe the truth may be judged." He also preserved the stern warning in connection with the Supper: "He eats judgment upon himself" (I Corinthians 11:29; cf. verse 34), and presumably verse 32 as well.[80]

From his preservation of Romans 2:16 it follows that Marcion acknowledged a judgment day for the good God (Christ) at the end of all things, and this follows also from his preserving in Romans 14:10 (II Corinthians 5:10) the word about "the judgment seat of Christ."[81] According to this saying, on the judgment day Christ will judge *all* men—*thus at the end of time the good God appears as the Lord of all*—but, as we have just heard, he will judge *prohibendo*, that is, by mere *exclusion*. The children of God, having the substance of the angels, will possess "eternal life" and "spiritual abundance and enjoyment" (Tertullian IV 31).[82] What will be the consequence of this exclusion for sinners? Here again Tertullian (I 28) has handed down to us a valuable account: "When asked, 'What will happen to every sinner in that day?' the Marcionites reply, 'He will be cast away, as it were, out of sight.' " "But what is in store for him who has been cast away? 'He will be seized,' they say, 'by the fire of the Creator.' "

According to this, Marcion's teaching is clear: Christ (the good God) does not even punish at the final judgment, but by his barring sinners from his presence (*prohibendo, segregando, abiciendo*), they fall victim to the fire of the world's creator. But Marcion shares the Pauline teaching that *all* men, if they do not allow themselves to be redeemed by Christ, are sinners, and since there can no longer be righteous people in the sense of the World-Creator since Christ's crucial manifestation, all these sinners are under the same condemnation. But what becomes of the pre-Christian righteous ones of the Creator and of the Creator himself, who here at the end appears in the service of the good God, for in fact even he has announced in his law the condemnation of sinners?[83] The earliest sources give no direct answer here, but the pre-Christian righteous ones, even though they were in a tolerable situation, yet were *in the underworld, and the Creator cannot give them eternal life* and never even promised it to them. Thus, one will have to assume *that their days come to an end*, even though they are not destroyed by hellfire as are the sinners. Thus, the latter, like the former, will die; for since the Creator possesses nothing that is eternal, with him everything must end in death in the strictest sense, and we cannot speak of an eternal damnation. And he himself? Since Marcion assumed that heaven and earth will pass away, since he further frequently identified the world and the world's creator, and finally, since he preserved I Corinthians 15:22ff., it is very likely that according to his teaching even the creator of the world will disappear at the end of this *saeculum*. This is confirmed by Esnik's explicit testimony. He writes (see Appendix VI): "Moreover, they undermine the other saying of the apostle, which is truly spoken: 'When he has destroyed all principalities and powers, he must reign, until he has put all his enemies under his feet' [I Cor. 15:24ff.]. And the Marcionites say *that the lord of the world will destroy himself and his world forever.*"[84] Thus, Marcion assumed that for the creator of the world also, Christ has become or will become a sign of judgment, since in his appearing the disintegration of the world is being accomplished. The creator of the world himself is destroying it by destroying all his principalities and powers, only then to disintegrate and disappear along with them. By means of self-destruction he perishes along with the world that he has made, so that now the good God is the only God remaining.[85]

Here we have anticipated, but what was passed over has already been treated above in Chapters III and IV. The resurrection of the redeemer had virtually brought the cosmic drama to an end. The choice of the twelve disciples proved right away to be a failure, adduced by the forbearance and patience shown to them. They fell back more and more into their old ways.[86] Therefore, Jesus called Paul, through a special revelation, to be an apostle, and by this act the twelve were in fact divested of their status. In Paul the redeemer found *the* apostle,[87] and from that time onward he was to be the only one, attested only by Christ, and lifted up to the third heaven to hear unutterable words.[88] To him Jesus delivered *the* written gospel,[89] for the oral apostolic tradition was steadily deteriorating, placing the redeemer back in the legalistic context again. Like the apostle, the *one* gospel tolerates no rival alongside itself; Paul could call it "*my* gospel," for it was given to him, and he alone was authorized to explain it by means of his epistles and to defend it. These epistles, together with the gospel, are, according to Christ's provision, "the Holy Scripture"; they take the place of the Old Testament, and they establish and nourish the community of believers. In these documents the community has the complete presentation of the appearing and the works of the redeemer—a reenactment, as it were, in permanent literary form. *Hence true Christianity is objectively biblical theology and nothing else.*

The teaching of Paul is absolutely identical with the teaching of Christ. Therefore, the gospel writing also is to be explained in accordance with the epistles, and this is the way Marcion himself proceeded in his expositions. As to how he interpreted the epistles and used them to develop his doctrine after he had corrected them, see Appendix V. The prologues also must be taken into account (Appendix III). The expositions and the prologues show that Marcion was concerned about only a few major points in the epistles and paid little attention to the rest or else forced it into a connection with those major points of his concern. We have woven the most important elements into our presentation of Marcion's teaching.

Even Paul is not thoroughly saturated with "the truth of the gospel," but Marcion the reformer followed the apostle, who stands at the right hand of Christ in heaven. Clement, his great opponent, called him a *giant* and *theomach* (that is, one who fights against God). When his church looked toward heaven, it saw him, Marcion, standing at the left hand of Christ.

VII

THE HOLY CHURCH OF THE REDEEMED ONES
AND THE ORDERING OF THEIR LIFE
(CULTUS, ORGANIZATION, AND ETHICS)

Marcion learned from Paul the significance of the church; we may immediately acknowledge that he recognized and highly valued the apostle's original and grand conception. The clearest evidence of this is the fact that he preserved Ephesians 5:22–32 in his Bible. This passage in itself must have been highly uncongenial to him, and even offensive, for the relationship of man and woman and even that of a man to his own flesh must have disgusted him. Nevertheless, he did not excise these statements (after making an emendation) because he found no other passage in the Pauline epistles that made the church's close and intimate connection with Christ so clear: Christ the head of the church;[1] Christ deeply loving and cherishing the church;[1] the person who takes his stand within the church leaves father and mother and grows together with Christ into a unity. Marcion's way of thinking about the church also emerges from another passage. He (or one of his pupils?) so constructed Galatians 4:26 by means of emendation and addition that he contrasts the two dispensations thus: that of the World-Creator, aimed at the synagogue, over against that infinitely great dispensation of the good God, which is aimed "at the holy church which we have proclaimed, which is our mother." Thus, the church is the creation of God which has been produced by the work of redemption; she is holy (certainly in Paul's mind), and she is the mother of the redeemed. Even his opponents reluctantly acknowledged that Marcion had "churches" and not merely schools or formless fellowships.[2]

In this church baptisms were performed and the Supper was observed as among other Christians. Moreover, the baptismal rite was not at all different; otherwise Marcionite baptism could not have been regarded in Rome as valid (cf. Cyprian, ep. 73.4; 74.7; besides, Augustine explicitly confirms in *De bapt. c. Donat.* III 15 that it was administered in the same way).[3] The Supper also was observed in the traditional manner, yet with water along with the bread, but this is also found frequently elsewhere in that time.[4] Further, other rituals were not lacking; see Tertullian I 14: "Indeed, up to now he (Marcion's Christ) has disapproved neither of the water of the Creator, with which he washes his people;[5] nor of the oil, with which he anoints them;[6] nor of the combination of honey and milk with which he nurses them; nor of the bread by which he represents his own body, requiring the 'beggarly elements' of the Creator even in his own sacraments."[7] Likewise I 23: "I can think of no one more shameless than he who is baptized unto his God in water belonging to another, who reaches out to his God towards a heaven belonging to another, who prostrates himself before his God on ground belonging to another,[8] who offers thanks to his God over bread belonging to another, who in the name of almsgiving and charity gives for the sake of his God good things belonging to another." It is said in a general way in III 22: "The ascription of glory, and blessing, and praise, and hymns, and the sign on the forehead, and the sacraments of the church, and the purity of the sacrifices among you (scil., in your churches) are also observed." According to this, the Marcionite services of worship and sacral actions cannot have been essentially different from those of the great church.[9] Things cannot have taken a "Corinthian" turn in them, for even though Marcion may have asserted that speaking in tongues is a charismatic form peculiar to the new God (on I Corinthians 12:10, in Tertullian V 8; it is not entirely certain), still, several passages in Tertullian prove that nothing was known of any displays of enthusiasm in Marcion's worship services and elsewhere in his communities. In this passage Tertullian writes: "Let Marcion show forth the gifts of his God: some prophets . . .; let him bring forth some psalm, some vision, or some prayer that is of the Spirit, in an ecstasy . . .; let him also prove to me that any woman among them has prophesied," etc. Further, in V 15, on I Thessalonians 5:19–20: "It is then incumbent upon Marcion to show in his church the spirit of his God that must not be quenched and prophecies that must not be ill-considered. And if he has shown what he thinks [to be such], let him know that we shall challenge whatever it may be as to the nature of its spiritual and prophetic grace and power, . . . When he has produced and proven nothing of the sort, we will produce both the Spirit and the prophecies of the Creator, which speak forth in accordance with his will." Thus, as far as enthusiasm goes, the Marcionite communities were no rivals of the Montanists, and even Marcion himself no longer lived in the primitive Christian enthusiastic attitude. It is much to be regretted that none of Marcion's prayers are extant, for the picture of his piety would be complete only if we possessed such. They must have been quite distinctive, even unique, since major parts of the general Christian prayers would have been absent from them: praise of the Creator, thanks for his gifts, and trust in his providence and guidance of the world.

As to the organization of the communities, Marcion found in the Pauline epistles "bishops" and "deacons," and in the tradition he found "presbyters." These offices were accepted in the Marcionite communities and thus also the distinction between clergy and laity,[10] to which is added the further distinction between baptized and catechumens. We do not have any testimonies indicating that Marcion himself approved or introduced this organization, but it is very likely that he did so, for the testimonies for it begin as early as we could expect any (see the next chapter). Only on the other hand all the distinctions, which existed both here in the Marcionite communities as well as in those of the great church, appear not to have been so firmly fixed in the Marcionite communities as in the great church or to have been more freely treated than there. For this we possess a testimony of a documentary character from Marcion's *Antitheses* (the exposition of Galatians 6:6: "Let the one who is taught the word share all good things with the one who teaches") in Origen (as plagiarized by Jerome): "Marcion interpreted this passage as follows: he thinks that the believers and the catechumens ought to pray at the same time and that the teacher ought to participate in the prayer of the pupil, which is brought out especially in that which follows, 'in all good things.' " This report is in harmony with Tertullian's remark in *De praescriptio* 41, in his general portrayal of the "heretical conduct": "In the first place, it is not certain who is a catechumen and who a believer; they enter together, listen together, *pray* together, including the heathen, if any should attend. They cast what is holy to the dogs and their pearls (though not geniune) to the swine. They mean by simplicity the subversion of discipline, attention to which by us they call pandering." *Thus Marcion strove for simplicity in arrangements, rejected all idle nonsense involving mystery in the worship services* (i.e., the beginnings of the *disciplina arcana*),[11] and set himself against a hierarchical caste system and holy worldliness. If it now is certain that Tertullian's sentences just quoted refer to the Marcionites, then one can hardly doubt that his further account, which is indeed somewhat exaggerated but not fabricated, likewise refers to them, especially since this report presupposes actual communities and not schools like the Valentinian schools (loc. cit.): "Their ordinations are casual, frivolous, and changeable. At one time they will invest neophytes; at another, men who are involved in the world; at another, those who have apostasized from us. . . Consequently, one man is bishop today, another tomorrow; a deacon today is a reader tomorrow; a presbyter today is a layman tomorrow. For they impose priestly functions even upon the laity."[12] It would certainly be a mistake to take this portrayal literally, but it must be a reliable report that the functions of the individual positions and offices were not sharply distinguished, that Marcion wanted to hear nothing of any "grace of office" which allegedly pertained in varied kind and strength to each individual office, and that in a given case even laymen could temporarily assume spiritual functions in the communities. It is not easy to determine what else from Tertullian's portrayal refers to the Marcionites—probably the remark: "How bold are the heretical women themselves! They dare to teach, to dispute, to perform exorcisms, to promise healings in return, and perhaps even to baptize"—for Epiphanius (*Haer.* 42.3,4) reports that in the Marcionite church the women may baptize. Since among the redeemed sexuality may no longer play any role (see below), one can only marvel that Marcion did not also make all offices and functions accessible to women. We do not know what is meant by an obscure allusion of Tertullian (Marcion's "holier women"); obscure also is the fragmentary report that Marcion sent a woman to Rome ahead of him to prepare the way

(Jerome, ep. 131).

Reference was made not to Marcion alone but to all heretics by Tertullian's certainly justified lament (loc. cit., 42) that they did not win their following by converting the pagans but by leading astray the Christians.

The Marcionites could be entirely and unhesitatingly exonerated of Tertullian's description (loc. cit., 43) to the effect that the heretics especially frequently had commerce "with magicians, peddlers, astrologers, philosophers, namely with those given to curiosity," if he did not go on to say: "They deny that God is to be feared; therefore, to them all things are free and unrestrained," and if he did not assert (I 18): "The Marcionites are very much astrologers, not ashamed to make a living even off the very stars of the Creator." Hence one will be obliged to assume that some Marcionites actually concerned themselves with astronomical (and probably astrological) science, and that Tertullian therefore casually lumped them together with the worldly heretics. It is well known that Marcion wanted nothing to do with philosophy, which he regarded as "empty deceit," and he certainly was not a friend of astrology.

Marcion's *ethic* also lodges a protest here, for no Christian fellowship prescribed a more world-renouncing and severe ordering and conduct of life than did the Marcionite fellowship. Marcion absolutely forbade marriage[13] and all sexual intercourse among his believers, and therefore he baptized only such catechumens and admitted to the Supper only such as took the vow of remaining unmarried or such married people as pledged a complete separation from that time onward.[14] *Thus he staked the life and growth of his communities exclusively on the winning of new members, for the believers were not permitted to reproduce.*[15] Marriage not only is filthy and shameful, but it also brings forth death.[16]

The motivation given for this prescription was first of all the usual one, that of liberation from sinful flesh; however, not only does this demand appear here with an otherwise unprecedentedly strong disgust (see Appendix V), but there also appeared a second motive: one should not help to enlarge the realm of the World-Creator but one should rather restrict it, insofar as it lies within human capacity to do so. One should offend this evil god, irritate him, spite him, and thereby show him that one no longer is in his service but belongs to another Lord.[17] Thus the determined rejection of sexuality on Marcion's part is not only a protest against matter and the flesh,[18] but also a protest against the God of the world and the law. *It is a sign of deliberate abandonment of that God and withdrawal from his company.*

However, one is to spite the Creator not only by total sexual abstinence but likewise by the strictest abstinence in food and drink and by readiness to suffer martyrdom. "They abhor the enjoyment of food as dishonorable"; hence not only were meat and (probably) wine[19] forbidden (fish allowed; see Tertullian I 14; Esnik),[20] and hence not only was a particularly strict rule of fasting introduced which to spite the lawgiver applied even to the sabbath (Epiphanius, *Haer.* 42.3), but eating and drinking at all, as well as any contact with the created order, should be limited to the least possible measure "so as to destroy and defy and detest the works of the Creator." This is the "more complete rule of discipline" which Marcion prescribed, desecularizing and disembodying of life carried to extreme.

Those who so live *have become supermen*, for they regard man in himself as enemy;[21] but regarded in earthly perspective they dwell in utmost misery. They are to unite as "wretched and despised," indeed as "refuse,"[22] and they are not to flee martyrdom but accept it. Certainly, it is not accidental that beginning in Irenaeus' time we hear repeatedly of Marcionite martyrs;[23] there must have been great numbers of them, and it was obviously painful to their adversaries not to be able to overlook this fact or to hush it up.

His opponents tell only of Marcion's asceticism (Tertullian, *De praescr.* 30, scornfully: "Marcion was a most virtuous master").[24] They do not tell us with what vigor he proclaimed the positive commandment of love, but he certainly put it into operation in his communities, even though the love of God was the center of his piety. We possess a testimony *de silentio* with reference to the love of enemies that he practiced: his opponents were unable to reproach a single insulting word of Marcion against the church to which he had once belonged and which he condemned as false, in spite of his contending so sharply against the creator of the world and against the false apostles.

We hear nothing of communism in the Mariconite communities; but since according to Tertullian the Beatitudes were Marcion's "ordinary precepts" "by means of which he adapts the peculiarity of his doctrine," and Esnik (see Appendix VI) confirms that Marcion put his finger on the point, that according to Marcion the creator of the world promises happiness to the rich but Christ promises it to the poor. So he must have judged wealth and treated it in his communities even more unfavorably than was done in the great church. Perhaps the large gift of money that he contributed to the Roman church before the break is also to be understood from this perspective.

* * *

Marcion's organization of his church is not fully told in what has been said; in fact, the crucial point has not yet been touched. Marcion began with an historical criticism of all Christian tradition. One may say that at first he made a perfect *tabula rasa* by rejecting not only the Old Testament but also the entire popular apostolic tradition. Then he began to erect a new building and actually carried it through, though to be sure with great violence. First of all, he found it intolerable that Christianity possessed as *littera scripta* only a book that its greatest apostle himself had described as letters that kill, and alongside this book only oral traditions and books of still quite uncertain authority. Therefore he produced a document of absolute authority out of eleven writings and based

Christianity upon them. This document as such is wholly and entirely his work; *he is the creator of the Christian Holy Scripture*. Secondly, in place of the Old Testament he put a critical work (the *Antitheses*) which gave expression to the opposition between the new document and this Jewish book and which was to be preserved alongside the new document "in that most important instrument" and to be taken to heart by all believers. He did not forbid the continued reading of the Old Testament with the aid of the *Antitheses*, for it contains true and therefore instructive, though of course deplorable, history. Thus, before the main body of Christendom had followed Marcion's example and created the New Testament and thus possessed two purportedly harmonious Testaments, the Marcionite church already knew two *antithetical* written Testaments. Thirdly, Marcion did not give to his church a formulated body of doctrine; all philosophical dogmatics and all scholastic systems were obviously dubious in his sight. Still less did he arouse in the church any prophets and enthusiasts whose ideas would lead the church. Instead, he sought in the *Antitheses* to explain the contents of the biblical document *only by means of exegesis of the biblical word*. Christian doctrine was to be nothing other than biblical theology, and he did not doubt that in all major points this would allow only *one* interpretation and would guard against all error. Fourthly, through the belief in the alien God who had appeared in Christ as the redeemer, through his aversion to the Creator, through the submission to the new document, through a simple but definite local organization and order of worship, and through the strictest conduct of life, he bound the believers extremely closely together and could be assured that these forces were strong enough in the midst of the general confusion and uncertainty over what is Christian to stamp upon them a firm and unified character. In every other respect he could allow greater liberty to prevail in his communities — in doctrinal questions, in the matters of order, and in the cultus — than the communities of the great church allowed.

This is the firm foundation of the organization which Marcion gave to his church. It proves him to be a truly gifted organizer who as such also influenced the main body of Christendom through his conceptions. By means of his personal work and a simple scheme of organization, he brought into being a unified church which spanned the empire. The church of the bishops required several generations to get that far — only the development of the institution of the synod made it possible for it to reach the goal. As it appears, Marcion did not need these means.

VIII

THE HISTORY OF THE MARCIONITE CHURCH. ITS THEOLOGICAL SCHOOLS AND THE SECT OF APELLES

1. The External History[1]

We know little of the external history of the Marcionite church. Justin's statement that Marcion himself had already disseminated his teaching "throughout the whole human race" is confirmed by the testimonies that we possess with reference to the second half of the second century for Asia, Lydia, Bithynia, Corinth, Crete, Antioch, Alexandria, Rome, Lyons, and Carthage (Tertullian V 19: "Marcion's heretical tradition is flooding the entire world"). Everywhere people were writing against the dreadful devilish sect which already in the second century was proclaiming its teaching even in the Latin language and by the beginning of the third century at the latest in the Syriac language as well.[2] Celsus, the Greek Roman who was the first to display a thorough knowledge of Christianity, studied the Marcionite church as well as its opponent, the catholic church. In the following period one meets the former everywhere Christianity has spread; hence the enumeration in Epiphanius (*Haer.* 42.1: Marcionites in Rome, Italy, Egypt, Palestine, Arabia, Syria, Cyprus, Thebais, Persia, and other areas) is incomplete. Far from segregating themselves, sectlike, from the great church, the Marcionites constantly sought to exert a missionary influence upon that church and to absorb the whole of Christendom. With reference to no other heretical fellowship do we hear so much of personal contacts with people who believe differently. Just as Marcion himself confronted Polycarp and the Roman presbyters, so also are personal contacts reported by tradition or to be inferred with Rhodon in Rome, Tertullian, Origen, Bardesanes, Adamantius, Ephraem, an unknown Syrian, Jerome, Chrysostom, and Esnik. Their community's worship services were open to everyone, even to pagans, and one could see their church buildings in the cities and in the country. Origen speaks of these buildings (*Fragm. XIII in Jerem.*, p. 204); in the year 318 one stood in the village of Lebaba near Damascus, and Bishop Cyril of Jerusalem warns the believers that when in a city they innocently ask about the "church," they should take care not to get into a Marcionite church by mistake. In organization and worship the Marcionite fellowships were so similar to the catholic that an uninformed person could

easily be deceived. Here one meets a Marcionite bishop, and there a presbyter;[3] nowhere could Jesus Christ and Paul be spoken of and preached with
greater devotion than here, and the Sunday cultus in Marcion's congregations
appears not to have been significantly different from that in the great church.[4]
But in this the Marcionites were not, as was the practice of so many Gnostics,
concealing their true identity; they were and wished to be called Marcionites.
Numerous opponents charged them with calling themselves after their human
founder and made this a serious accusation against them. But they remained
loyal to the name they had assumed at the very beginning and even placed it
on their church buildings (see the inscription of Lebaba, Appendix VI).

The danger that this church presented to Christianity was greatest in the
generation between 150 and 190. *In this period it and it alone was actually a
counterchurch*: this observation is evident from the abundance of opposing
writings, and it can be read from the nature of the opposition offered by Justin
and from the work of Celsus as well. Justin counted Marcion among the
demonic new founders of religions with a Christian adornment. Celsus often
spoke as though there were only the two churches, the "great church" and the
Marcionite, and alongside them only Gnostic underbrush. When Irenaeus,
Clement, Tertullian, and Hippolytus took up the pen, the situation for the
church was indeed still extremely perilous—Irenaeus, who intended to write
primarily against the Valentinians, in fact wrote more against the Marcionites
in Books II–V, and Tertullian's work against Marcion is, next to his *Apology*, the
major work of the zealous polemicist. But the danger of being overrun by the
Marcionites, which must once have existed, is no longer present. This is already
shown by the way in which, beginning with Irenaeus, they were arranged in the
list of heretics alongside and among the Gnostics, Valentinians, Ebionites, etc.,
while Justin had condemned all heretics as offspring of Simon Magus,
Menander, and Marcion. But Origen still saw in Marcion the chief adversary
of the church and threw himself with all diligence and with full force into the
battle against the "doctrina Marcionis," which he sharply distinguished from the
"longa fabulositas" of Basilides and the "traditiones" of Valentinus.[5] In addition
to the ancient and newly shaped authorities that they brought into the battle, he
and the great old catholic theologians before him also forged the spiritual
weapons with which they met Marcionitism. The ecclesiastical theology they
developed and which still today is the doctrinal foundation of the great confessions is in much greater measure an anti-Marcionite theology than an anti-
Valentinian or anti-Ebionite theology. One may also unhesitatingly assume that
this theology had a great part in the suppression of the Marcionite church.[6]

After the middle of the third century, at the latest, the movement began to
recede in the West. It is true that still in the controversy over heretical baptism
it appears that Marcionite baptism was actually the point under dispute.
Cyprian's attitude alone allows us to conclude that the Marcionite danger in
Africa for a long time had not been as great as it was in Tertullian's time and

as perhaps it still was in Rome (cf. Novatian's work *De trinitate*; the Roman bishop Dionysius also refers in a prominent passage to the Marcionites). Then after only a hundred years more had passed, Marcionitism in the West had run its course. According to the testimony of Optatus, in Africa even the name was forgotten, and even in Rome, according to Ambrosiaster's testimony, only scattered remains of the movement still existed.[7] After the year 400, whatever was stirred to move against it either knew it only through the literature – indeed, in the struggle against the new heresies (Manichaeans, Priscillianists, etc.) people liked to come back to the old ones – or felt moved to do battle by an unusual flaring up again of the old sect (pseudo-Tertullian's *Carmen adversus Marcionem*?).[8] In the West Manichaeism certainly appropriated the remnants of the Marcionite movement, after having drained it, and the short-lived movement of Patricius in Rome, a kind of neo-Marcionite movement, may also have contributed to its disappearance.[9]

But in the Orient, whence it came and where it belongs in spite of its agnosticism, Marcionitism still had a long history. Oppressed and submissive as the founder demanded[10] and confirmed by martyrdoms in the times of the great persecutions,[11] Marcion's church there entered into the Constantinian age as a large and strong fellowship which still was producing significant propaganda.[12] Nevertheless, one notes that in the course of the fourth century it was gradually suppressed in Egypt and in western Asia Minor and soon thereafter in Greek-speaking Syria, particularly through the efforts of Chrysostom, who incidentally tells (see Appendix VI) that in Antioch in his time a high official and his wife were Marcionites. On the other hand, the Marcionites held on longer in Cyprus and Palestine, and in the Syriac-speaking part of Syria (all the way to Armenia and Persia) the movement apparently continued to grow in significance. In Cyprus it was especially strong (see Appendix VI; the city of Salamis there was simply besieged by Marcionites), and no less so in Palestine (Cyril of Jerusalem). In the Syrian city of Laodicea even around the middle of the fourth century it was felt necessary to incorporate into the first article of the confession of faith the words "the God of the law and the gospel, just and good" (Appendix VI), and the great bishops of Antioch down to Nestorius waged an unceasing war against the dangerous sect. But the threat to these regions of the church still appears small – in spite of the amount of concern that confronts us in Epiphanius' extensive chapter against the Marcionites – when compared with that in the Syrian national territory which had its center in Edessa. From the works of Ephraem and others one gains the impression that the Marcionite danger there was not at all less than that of the Manichaean, and indeed that it exceeded the latter. Marcionites, who worshipped "the Alien God," and Manichaeans – first connected by Eusebius (see Appendix VI) – have for many generations marched separately in the Orient in that the former group remained fully conscious of their peculiarity, but to the catholic church they were very closely related brothers. Only after the middle of the fifth century did Marcionitism recede there also, particularly after Rabbulas undertook to oppose it (see Appendix VI), and, in his diocese of Cyrus, Theodoret as well. The latter triumphantly reports in his epistles that he has converted eight Marcionite *villages* and, in all, *thousands, indeed, tens of thousands* of Marcionites (Appendix VI).

Marcionite *villages* — this statement must not be overlooked, and it leads us to the attitude of the civil authorities with reference to the heretics. Up to the time of Constantine the authorities, as is known, made no distinction among the Christians, and hence the Edict of Milan and that of Nicomedia were beneficial to the heresies as well. The church inscription of Lebaba (see Appendix VI) in the territory of Licinius shows us that in the year 318/319 the Marcionite community there could erect a church building with an inscription on which the owner of the building was announced to everyone. But the rejoicing was not long-lived. Constantine began to forbid heretical assemblies and to destroy the meetinghouses, and even to forbid worship services in private homes, to expropriate the tracts of land, and to confiscate the heretical books. Although for a half-century these decisions were only incompletely carried out, they did not remain entirely without effect. The process of retreat of the heretics from the West to the East and from the cities to the country must already have begun rather vigorously in that time in specific areas. But with the edicts of Gratian and Theodosius, the unrelenting persecution by the civil authority, incited by the great bishops, began. State and church in league had decided on the total suppression of the heresies, and they took appropriate measures. Now there followed the migration to the country on a large scale — for in the countryside the civil authority was more lenient towards the pagans and the heretics — insofar as the unfortunate ones had not already abjured their faith in great throngs under the redoubled pressure: "God sent them *fear* of the holy Rabbulas, and they accepted the truth in faith, by renouncing their error." Not only Saint Rabbulas but the other great bishops as well had convenient weapons at their disposal, and now they pressed into the rural districts, also. When Theodoret was able to convert eight Marcionite villages in his diocese, this shows the social grouping of the heresy as it had been achieved for a century, its still-existing outward strength, but at the same time its lack of powers of resistance. The retreat to the country must already have begun in the pre-Constantinian period. This is indicated not only by the existence of a Marcionite community in Lebaba in Hauran but still more by the fact that it had set up an inscription *in the Greek language*. Greek was not the language there; thus, the Marcionites there were Greek settlers who had withdrawn into this remote region. In fact, it is very well possible that *the entire village* was Marcionite (see Appendix VI). This was the case in the eight villages that Theodoret converted. Thus, not only was there a retreat to the country but the Marcionites also formed there *closed settlements*. Their unsociable attitude towards the world explains this very well, even if one does not think of the desired protection from persecution: they were thus better able to preserve their peculiarity. Only any religious sect that felt obliged to leave the cities necessarily had to become "countrified," and even though they thereby acquired a certain tenacity in the assertion of their traditions, yet they forfeited some intellectual powers of resistance and must ultimately succumb. This is how it went with the Marcionite churches in the East also. Incidentally, here they also maintained for a long time a remarkable independence in relation to Manichaeism,[13] but after the middle of the fifth century they probably were able to play only an insignificant role as compared with the latter group. The fact that the Marcionites drew closer to the Manichaeans is shown primarily (according to the *Fihrist*) by the quite close kinship of their special written characters (modelled after the Persian and Syriac letters) with the peculiar letters developed by Mani (or by the Manichaeans) out of these same alphabets (see Appendix VI).[14]

What can be ascertained about the demise of Marcionitism in the East (in particular about the relationship to the Paulicians) is collected in the Appendices. In the year 987/988 the author of the *Fihrist* was able to observe Marcionites only in the Far East, that is to say, in the area between the Caspian Sea and the Oxus: "they creep behind Christianity." But his reports on the sect and its teaching perhaps are not based on contemporary knowledge but rather on a literary tradition.

2. The Internal History

Marcion, the founder of churches, as a fundamental biblicist and opponent of all philosophy, did not set forth a philosophical-theological system, and he did not teach "principles" as a systematician. Instead, he proclaimed the good God in Christ, preached redemption, and unmasked the just God of the world and the law. We are to believe in the one, the Alien God, and to deny obedience to the other, who is sufficiently well known.[15] Certainly both are Gods in Marcion's view, but quite unequal Gods, since the latter will pass away along with his heaven and his earth, and thus he possesses no eternity. Hence, it is only conditionally correct to say that Marcion taught two "principles." In a certain sense this is to say too much and at the same time too little; for only *one* is *eternal* God, and according to Marcion there are *three* uncreated beings, since matter also, from which the just God has shaped the world, is uncreated. It is true that in his purely biblical expositions it plays no role at all as an active principle; but insofar as everything material and corporeal comes from it and has rendered the creation of the Creator still worse, in the whole of creation it, as "nature" ($\varphi \upsilon \sigma \iota \varsigma$), does possess great significance.

From this one can understand that even those opponents who had in mind Marcion's own teaching and not that of later Marcionites could be uncertain about whether in summary they should attribute to him two or three "principles."

But this uncertainty must be intensified by a look at the development of the Marcionite church.

That is to say, the most important thing in this development was that the Marcionite church indeed strictly and faithfully maintained the character and spirit that the founder gave to it, and, with *one* exception (Apelles) allowed no division to arise in its midst. However, soon after the death of the master, theological *schools* began to take root in its soil. This shows again that Marcionitism was a phenomenon on a par with the great church; for in fact in the latter also, beginning with the second half of the second century, schools were formed (the earliest known to us is that of Justin), which soon began to fight among themselves but whose members did not thereby cease to be faithful children of the great church.[16]

The unity of the Marcionite schools was evident in (1) the acknowledgment of the Bible that had been assembled by the founder (including the *Antitheses*), (2) the rejection of the Creator and the Old Testament, (3) the proclamation of the *alien* God who has appeared redemptively in Christ, (4) strict asceticism,[17] as well as (5) the high esteem in which the master was held.[18] In these aspects no variation and no uncertainty can be detected in the Marcionite church as long as it existed. On the other hand, as soon as the attempt was made to construct a systematic theology out of Marcion's biblically expressionistic preaching, differences had to appear. It was bound to be seen immediately that the founder had left behind a legacy of some gaps and some unsolved problems. These are connected with the number of principles and their mutual relationship, the nature of the God of this world, the origin of sin, and the person of Christ. In the final analysis, this proclamation of religion could no more endure a theology, in the sense of a rational philosophy of religion, than could the so-called apostolic religion, although as a religion the former was far more compact and unitary than the latter; hence the differences had to show up as soon as theological schools began to arise.

Rhodon in Rome, toward the end of the second century and thus two or three decades after Marcion's death, is the first to tell us of the Marcionite schools and the schism of Apelles. He himself had had a dispute with Apelles. He had also become personally acquainted with followers of Marcion's pupil Synerus and had received the account of the peculiar opinions of their teacher directly from them. The account first confirms what is also known from other sources and then gives the following picture: *one* "untenable opinion" dominates all Marcionites and holds their company together. Since this is not to be sought in their teaching about the principles, it must lie in the other aspects (named above), that is, primarily in the conviction about the *redemption* that is wrought by the Alien God. But on this ground theological differences of opinion arose— Rhodon says that the correct division was not recognized[19]—and this led to the forming of schools on the basis of a two-principles doctrine (Potitus and Basilicus) and a "still worse" doctrine of three principles or three natures

(Synerus). Unfortunately, Rhodon does not give anything more specific. It cannot be determined whether the former school taught precisely as did the Marcionite Marcus (in Adamantius), and the latter as did the Marcionite Megethius (ibid.).

As to the sources, Justin, Irenaeus, Tertullian, Clement, Hippolytus (*Ref.* X 19 init.), Origen, and Ephraem relate Marcion's genuine teaching. The Marcionite Marcus teaches a two-principles doctrine, but it is no longer the genuine doctrine. It is true that he distinguishes the two Gods, one as the Redeemer and the other as the Creator/Judge, and he also properly says that men have transgressed the laws of this latter God, but the Redeemer on the other hand brings them amnesty and remission.[20] Yet he does not characterize the Creator as just but as evil,[21] and he further asserts, setting himself at a great distance from Marcion and adopting a major *Gnostic* dogma, that at the creation of man the spirit in man had been placed in him by the good God and that this spirit is all of man that is saved (the salvation even of the soul is explicitly rejected, since it is created by the demiurge).[22] Therewith the basic idea of Marcion's view, that man is not bound to the Creator by any natural tie, is eliminated; yet Marcus does maintain the view that no one had previously had a presentiment of Christ (Adamantius, *Dial.* II 13–14: "Christ (was) a stranger and there had never been an intimation of him in anyone's mind"). That alleged emendation is quite easily comprehensible on rational grounds, and it also comes at the two weak points in Marcion's preaching to make the point that the good God does not save the *whole* man, although the psychic-spiritual aspect stands no nearer to him than does the corporeal, and that with Marcion the demiurge is a being who vacillates between being just and being troublesome (as a nuisance). The Marcionite Megethius (*Dial.* I 3–4) distinguishes three principles: the good God, the demiurge (= the just one), and the evil god (= the devil), and he assigns the three ἀρχαί to Christians, Jews, and pagans. Marcion knew nothing of an evil god alongside the just God (Megethius substitutes the former in the place of matter). According to Marcion, the pagans do not belong to a god but are sinners who have fallen from the Creator and have sunk into the material realm and hence into the service of idols. But according to Megethius the three ἀρχαί are by no means "equal" but "that of the good is strongest" (this is genuinely Marcionite). "The weaker principles are subject to the strongest one," nevertheless they did *not* do what they did "in accordance with the will of the better." Yet Megethius puts the "middle one" (the demiurge) much closer to the good principle than does Marcion himself when he remarks on II Thessalonians 1:6–7 (*Dial.* II 6): "The middle principle, in obeying the good, grants forgiveness, but in obeying the evil, it bestows affliction." This can only refer to the end of things. But here also for Marcion himself this teaching is false and is based on the idea that there is only *one* remission, while Marcion sharply distinguished the temporary and imperfect *refrigerium* of the World-Creator from the blessedness that only the good God can guarantee. According to

Megethius the creation proceeded as follows (*Dial.* II 6–7): the demiurge created men according to his own will, but since they turned out badly, he regretted it and intended to judge and destroy them; more precisely said, even the soul of man, which the demiurge has bestowed upon him, in Paradise refused to obey its Creator, and he rejected it; *the evil god now drew it to himself*, but then the good God came and, filled with compassion, redeemed the souls "and liberated the men who had become evil from the evil god and changed them by means of faith and made these his believers into good people." *This version of doctrine shows that for Megethius, the major interest was in the pagans*, and he paid less attention to the Jews (the biblicist Marcion otherwise). But in spite of this, Megethius remained loyal to Marcion's teaching in that he had the purchasing act in redemption, which he relates in detail, take place not between the good God and the evil one but between the good God and the just one, who thus continues to be recognized as the rightful owner of men. He says explicitly that according to Paul, Christ has not bought us from sin (or from the evil god) but from the demiurge.

Three principles, or gods, are attributed to the Marcionites by the following authors: *Dionysius of Rome* ("three separate beings and deities"; see Appendix VI); *Athanasius* (see Appendix VI); *Cyril of Jerusalem* (See Catech. 16.3; but in 16.6 he speaks only of the contrast between the good God and the creator of the world; see Appendix VI); *Gregory of Nazianzus* (properly: the two Gods of the Old and New Testaments, nevertheless three natures[23] so that, as with Megethius, the Old Testament God appears as the Lord of the "middle" φύσις; *Basil* also is probably to be understood thus, although he only gives expression to the opposition between the Old Testament God and the New Testament God in Marcion; see Appendix VI); *Maruta* ("one good, one evil, and one just, the middle one between them," see Appendix VI); and *Abulfaraj* (properly: "The just God, good God, and evil God; the just God, however, performed his works upon the evil God, i.e., Matter, and out of him established the world"; see Appendix VI). These accounts contain a certain muddying of the teaching of the founder, and they go back to diffused opinions of schools when they roundly assume *three* gods and explain that the just god is the "middle one." Through this latter process of making more precise,[24] Marcionite Christianity is gravely injured or rather loses its edge and becomes a vulgarized version of the original. As soon as the just God appears as the *middle* one, as has already occurred in Megethius, and is not seen as the most profound contrast to the good God, Marcionitism loses something of its peculiarity and approaches Gnosticism and Manichaeism, regardless of how people may have continued the master's teachings in words.[25] This deterioration must actually have taken place in broad areas of the church, for it is inconceivable that the authorities cited above would have invented their reports.

Megethius' doctrine of the three principles (good, just, evil) is also found in Marcion's Assyrian pupil *Prepon* (who in Hippolytus' time defended

Marcionitism against Bardesanes; see Appendix VI). Here, however, it is found with the curious statement, based on the saying that "There is only one who is good," that Christ as "the mediator" ("the middle one"), as Paul identifies him, indeed was free "from the entire nature of the evil one" but also from the nature of the good one. According to this, Christ would be the son of the middle god or rather the middle one himself. On this see below.

We hear from Hippolytus (*Ref.* X 19) that some pupils advanced to a doctrine of four principles (good, just, matter, and evil): in fact, the differentiation between matter and the evil god was obvious, since the sequence of "the good God, the Creator, and Matter" could appear awkward. The same author also tells of the uncertainty shown in the fact that some Marcionites call the just one only just, while others call him both just and evil.[26]

It is clear that the doctrine of the three principles afforded a certain footing against Manichaeism; but this footing threatened to disappear when the good and evil gods were distinguished as the gods of light and darkness. (This was not Marcion's view; on this see Appendix V). But later Marcionites taught thus; this is shown by the accounts given in the *Fihrist* and by *Shahrastani*: "They assert that the two eternal principles are light and darkness and that there is a third essence which has been mixed in with them." "They assume two eternal, mutually hostile fundamental beings, the light and the darkness, but also a third fundamental being, namely the just mediator, the one that unites; he is said to be the cause of the mixing; for the two that are in conflict with each other and are set opposite to each other in hostility are mixed only by means of one who unites them. They say that the mediator is on the level beneath the light and above the darkness, and this world has emerged through the uniting and mixing. There are among them those who say that the mixing took place only between the darkness and the just one, since the latter stands closer to the darkness (i.e., than to the light), but that it was mixed with him so that through him it might be made better and might be diverted by his amusements . . .; but they say, 'We accept the just one only because the light, which is the most high God, cannot be mixed with Satan; how could it be possible that the two adversaries, which by nature are at war with each other and by virtue of their inner being are excluded from each other, be united and mix? Thus a mediator is necessary, who stands beneath the light and above the darkness and with whom (through whom) the mediation takes place' " (See Appendix VI).

Here the materialistic-Manichaean basic outlook has had a bad influence on Marcionitism, and the evaluation of the mediating principle, the Marcionite demiurge, now becomes a totally different one, more or less favorable; but thereby Marcion's entire teaching is corrupted. This Marcionitism is nothing but a milder form of Manichaeism and as such may have possessed a certain power of attraction.

From the author of the pseudo-Augustinian Quaestione (see Appendix VI) we learn that according to Marcion Satan made the world and even the body of man, but that the soul fell "by a certain error" and thus slipped into this world of darkness. Here also is a Gnostic-Manichaean influence, if the report is reliable. On the other hand, Theodoret reports (see Appendix VI) that according to the teaching of the Marcionites the serpent is better than the creator of the world, because the latter forbade the eating of the tree of knowledge but the serpent urged it. Marcion certainly did not teach this; but it perhaps is not an invention of Theodoret, since he reports that some Marcionites are serpent-worshippers, and he himself had found among them a brass serpent in a box, which was used in their mysteries. It is possible that Ophitism is exerting an influence here; but one will do better to leave this story aside.

The Marcionite doctrine of principles and the cosmology, as Esnik portrays them, still are in essence genuine (the good God, the creator of the world, matter; man a product of the creator of the world with the help of matter), and the character of the World-Creator, as Marcion pictured him, is maintained. But the spinning-out of the cosmology, the compact between the Creator and matter, the Creator's deception of matter, and the latter's revenge are of later origin, for no one who had read the *Antitheses* was acquainted with these stories, and the biblicist Marcion would have rejected them (see Appendix VI). But still Esnik's presentation here and in its continuation (the doctrine of redemption) shows that in the fifth century there was among the Marcionites a group loyal to the founder with respect to the doctrine of principles.[27]

With reference to Christology there are a couple of remarkable theories in the history of the sect. It was related above that according to Hippolytus, the Assyrian Marcionite Prepon taught that Christ belonged neither to the good nor to the evil principle but was *the middle one*, since in fact God alone is good and Paul identifies Christ as "the mediator." In light of this, one could at first be induced to assume that here Hippolytus has made a bad mistake in identifying the just God as the middle and Christ as the $\mu\alpha\acute{\epsilon}\sigma\sigma$ (but in an entirely different sense). But this appears not to be the case, for Epiphanius reports (chapter 14; see Appendix VI) that some Marcionites say that Christ is the son of the evil God, and others that he is the son of the just one; since he was compassionate and good, he had left his own father, had ascended to the higher God, joined himself to him, and was sent by this God for redemption into the world and to contend with his own father, to destroy all that the one who by nature is his father had established (whether this is the just God of the law or the evil God). Following this, one may no longer assert that Hippolytus has committed an error; instead, one must believe that in Marcionitism — strangely enough — there were already fairly early some teachings according to which Christ from the first did not belong to the supreme good God. Here the account in the *Fihrist* also comes into consideration. It says that the Marcionites were of differing opinions as to what the third being was: "Some say that it is the Life, i.e., Isa (Jesus), and others assert that Isa is the emissary of this third being, who created things according to the command and by the power of this being."[28] These three accounts do not give the impression that they are derived from a *single* motif; unfortunately they are all too fragmentary and brief to allow us to draw assured conclusions. Prepon and the *Fihrist* probably belong together. Even Prepon appears to have framed his dualism so strictly that he used a third principle from which he derived the *creation and redemption* of this world,[29] and certain Marcionites, of whom the *Fihrist* gives an account, may have taught something similar. It is evident that therewith the entirety of real Marcionitism is annulled. But the Marcionites of whom Epiphanius had heard perhaps had been under the influence of adoptionism intended especially to honor Christ by predicating for him a great moral achievement. Of course this theologoumenon also is anti-Marcionite. Again, it appears in Esnik that the Marcionites to whom his account refers also strictly held to the master's teaching in the matter of Christology; only they spun it out, particularly in the narrative of Christ's death and its effect with respect to the creator of the world: after the resurrection and ascension Jesus descends a second time, in the form of his deity, to the creator of the world and judges him because of his own death. Only now does the creator realize that there is another God besides himself; Jesus places the creator's own law at the basis of the proceedings. Because the creator himself had written that one who shed the blood of the righteous should die, he must put his own life and death in the hands of Jesus, who says to him, "I am rightly more just than you, and I have bestowed great benefits on your creatures." Now the creator begs for his life and says, "Because I have sinned and have unwittingly killed you, because I did not know that you were God, as satisfaction I give to you all those who will believe on you." Jesus accepts this proposal.[30] Marcion did not relate this; but the spirit of the account does not conflict with his teaching.

Leaving aside Apelles, whose peculiar significance must be presented separately, after Marcion the Marcionite church possessed only *one* head of a school who appeared as an author and remained faithful to the master but was so significant that the heresiologists, following Tertullian's, Hippolytus', and Origen's procedure, have provided a special place for him: that was Lucan. Of course it is only very little that we know about him. He appears to have led a school in the West (Rome?), and, occupying himself with Aristotle,[31] to have affirmed that there is in man an element even higher than the soul, and this element alone can share in the resurrection.[32] He continued the master's work in textual criticism and introduced his pupils to it and, according to the report of Epiphanius (Hippolytus), as a follower of the three-principles doctrine developed the scriptural evidence against the Creator-God. He also appeared as a strict defender of Marcionite asceticism. One gets the impression that he was the most significant Marcionite after the death of Marcion (see Appendix VI).

Only in recent times, thanks to two discoveries, have we gained an important insight into the history of the church after Marcion's death (but still in the second century). Through the discovery made by de Bruyne and Corssen we have learned that the Vulgate prologues to Paul's epistles, which have long been in circulation, are of Marcionite origin. Through the evidence that I have presented it has become clear that the false Laodicean epistle, widely disseminated in the biblical manuscripts of the West, is a Marcionite forgery (see Appendix III). Those prologues, which define the content and aim of Paul's epistles solely in terms of Paul's battles with the Judaizers, show how strictly the Marcionite church felt itself bound to the chief interest of its master. But this false epistle, which is very closely related to the spirit of the prologues, shows that some had also advanced to the point of producing forgeries, which the master certainly would have stoutly rejected. Moreover, unfortunately we cannot make one single Marcionite responsible for the forgery, for—apart from the fact that we also hear of a second forgery, a forged Alexandrian epistle of Paul—it could not have been so widely disseminated if it had not had a propagandist authority standing behind it. But on the other hand, it is important that none of our reporters was acquainted with a Marcionite Bible containing the forged epistle, neither Tertullian nor Origen nor Epiphanius, etc. It appears to have been an article for export and, paradoxically enough, to have made greater inroads into the catholic "apostolos" than into the Marcionite one. But the fact that these Marcionite pieces so frequently made their way into the catholic Bible at all is evidence that (1) the distribution of catholic copies of Paul's epistles in the second century must still have been quite limited, and (2) in this very century there must have been possibilities, not visible to us, for Marcion's church to exert an influence upon the catholic church. This is further confirmed when one looks at the history of the text.

Alterations were constantly being made to Marcion's text by the Marcionites; for the master had not forbidden this, but rather had perhaps encouraged it. Not only the educated pupil Lucan made changes, but also nameless emendators, as is directly attested (Tertullian IV 5, ANF III, 351: "They are daily retouching their work, as daily they are convicted by us"; Celsus, in Origen II 27; Origen himself; Ephraem, *Hymn* 24.1). Examples are not lacking; see, e.g., Adamantius, *Dial.* II 25 (according to this, later Marcionites inserted "spirit" in place of "body" in I Corinthians 15:38); Esnik (Appendix VI; here, in I Corinthians 15:25, $\theta \hat{\eta}$ is changed into the passive form); above all one should compare the various textual traditions in Tertullian and Epiphanius, which at least in part go back to later Marcionite emendations. But additions to the Bible are also made from other New Testament books. Johannine passages are quoted by the Marcionite Marcus (*Dial.* II 16,20: John 13:34 and 15:19); according to Isidore of Pelusium (see Appendix VI), the saying, "I have come to destroy the law and the prophets," was inserted into the gospel. According to Epiphanius (*Haer.* 42.3) one must assume that Mark 10:37–38 (or the Matthean parallel) was found in a Marcionite copy of the gospel, and according to Origen also this seems likely (see Appendix IV). Ephraem appears to have read Matthew 23:8 in the Marcionite literature (see Appendix VI), and Syrian Marcionites perhaps again accepted the baptism of Jesus by John (Appendix VI). The Pastoral Epistles also were read among some Marcionites, as the prologues prove and as appears from a passage in Chrysostom (Appendix VI): "From the words, 'the Lord grant . . . from the Lord,' the Marcionites conclude that there are two Lords." (If this is actually Marcionite, then underlying this explanation is a view of the relationship of the two Gods that is no longer the authentic one.) Explanations of the gospel that are not Marcion's but come from later Marcionites also can be recognized; thus, one of the two different expositions of the command of Jesus to show oneself to the priests (Luke 5:14 and 17:14; see Tertullian IV 9,35) may be a later one; thus also Tertullian distinguishes two expositions of Luke 6:24, one (genuinely Marcionite) which takes the "woe" not as a curse (*maledictio*) but as a warning (*admonitio*), and another according to which Christ here is speaking of what the demiurge will do (Tertullian IV 15, ANF III, 368: "Others, again, admit that the woe implies a curse; but they will have it that Christ pronounce the woe, not as if it were His own genuine feeling, but because the woe is from the Creator, and He wanted to set forth to them the severity of the Creator"). It is possible also that in IV 30 Tertullian had two expositions of Luke 13:19 before him. In the *Dialogues* of Adamantius there are numerous expositions which probably come not from Marcion himself but from later Marcionites; but when they are good Marcionite explanations, there is no profit in attempting the not very promising task of tracing out the criteria of distinction.

What is otherwise known to us from the later history of the Marcionite church with reference to its writings and its belief is little enough. Its relationships with other sects are unclear to us, even though we possess a few fragmentary reports from the Muratorian Fragment onward, and we know that even outside Marcion's church the *Antitheses* were read by those who had freed themselves from the Old Testament. Manichaeism in particular made use of them for its purposes, as did Patricius and others. Thus, it is uncertain whether pagan polemics made use of them (Porphyry), as, conversely, is the relationship of the *Antitheses* to Jewish anti-Christian polemics, yet in both cases some dependence is probable.

An anecdote in Theodoret (see Appendix VI) shows how seriously the asceticism which spites the Creator was still maintained in this church even in the fifth century. He tells that he knew a ninety-year-old Marcionite who always washed himself in the morning with his own saliva in order, as he explained it, to have nothing to do with the works of the Creator and thus even with water; he would have preferred even to avoid food and drink, etc., but unfortunately one cannot live without these things nor perform the mysteries without them.

As to the mysteries, Esnik asserts (Appendix VI) that the most precise exposition of the nature of the redemption (a purchasing by means of Christ's death as a price) was kept secret in the Marcionite church and was not handed on to all — and even to the few only orally. It was communicated to all that we are redeemed by an act of purchase, but "not all know how and by what means Christ made the purchase." Is this report, which is not supported by a second testimony, reliable? If it is, then the original openness by which the Marcionite church once distinguished itself has here been restricted. This is possible; external or internal influences could have been decisive, and Esnik is after all a reliable witness.[33]

Concerning baptism, Epiphanius asserts that Marcion permitted it to be repeated (*Haer.* 42.3) even the third time ("thus I have heard from many"). Since Esnik, who says the same thing, is dependent here upon Epiphanius, the latter is our only witness on this point. But now Esnik reports, where he is speaking on the basis of his own knowledge (see Appendix VI): "The Marcionites falsify the [baptismal] vows; for because they do not resist appetite, they subject [sinners] to repentance again . . . The true believers (the catholics) are not like those who boast that 'from baptism onward, we are pledged to refrain from eating meat and from marriage,' and then dissolve the vow and engage in penance." Since the biblicist Marcion cannot possibly have permitted a repeated baptism, since Epiphanius, the only witness, appeals only to hearsay, and finally since Esnik speaks of a repentance among the Marcionites by means of which the *restitutio* can be achieved, Epiphanius' authorities most probably have been deceived or have given their report out of malice. Those Marcionites had regarded repentance as repeated baptism, and since they applied to it Luke 12:50 and Mark 10:38 ("the new baptism"), it was easy either to misunderstand or to construct the calumny that the Marcionites allowed baptism to be repeated.[34] But of course all this comes out of the reports of Epiphanius and Esnik that even the Marcionites must have modified their strictness and introduced the possibility of repentance for *all* sins, which coincided with the later catholic position and was hardly in keeping with the intention of their master. The catholic sacrament of penance also is nothing but a repetition of baptism.

There is a report in the tradition of still another peculiar practice. Tertullian (V 10) comments on I Corinthians 15:29 (baptism for the dead): "Do not immediately think that the apostle is designating a new author and supporter [of this practice]. Rather, he is establishing the resurrection of the flesh as firmly as those who in vain were baptized for the dead practice their faith in this resurrection." One cannot deduce from this anything about a peculiar Marcionite custom, but on this passage Marcion only commented that since there is nothing in the gospel about a baptism for the dead, Paul's acknowledgment of this custom proves his position as one who can lay down law for the church. It is also impossible to infer anything about Marcion from Tertullian's *De carne* 48. But Chrysostom reports on I Corinthians 15:29 that when a Marcionite catechumen died, he was asked whether he desired baptism; a brother who had crawled under the bed then would give an affirmative answer, and the baptism would then be performed (see Appendix VI). This account, confirmed by Esnik (see Appendix VI; was he dependent on Chrysostom?), only shows that a custom of the apostolic age was maintained longer in the Marcionite church than in the catholic church, and hence it offers nothing special for us.[35]

3. Apelles and His Sect[36]

Apelles was won as a pupil by Marcion (presumably in Rome). He left his teacher (*De praescr.* 30: "he withdrew from the view of his most sacred master") and went to Alexandria,[37] whence he returned as an independent teacher who had separated from his master. Since he now rejected Marcion's dualism and taught the monarchy of God as well as the preexistence of souls, it is probable that the theological speculations in Alexandria, to which the teachers of Clement and Origen paid homage, had gained an influence over him. In Rome he founded a school outside the Marcionite church. To it belonged a virgin given to ecstasies, Philumene,[38] a prophetess with whom he collaborated as a devoted adept by expressing his ideas to her and receiving from her her revelations and predictions. On the basis of these he wrote the lost work entitled *Phaneroseis*.[39] A clear picture cannot be gained of this woman who was able to captivate so highly educated a man as Apelles; she told of her visions in which a young man appeared to her, identifying himself sometimes as Christ and sometimes as Paul, and in the role of an oracle gave answers which Apelles then repeated to inquirers. She is said also to have performed miracles and to have lived exclusively on a large loaf of bread which she daily slipped undamaged into a very narrow-necked bottle and then extracted undamaged with her fingertips.[40]

In association with this woman Apelles combined a romantic-religious activity with a critical-theological activity. His former master had written the *Antitheses* and in them had demonstrated the religious worthlessness of the Old Testament (but in so doing still held it to be a thoroughly reliable book). Apelles wrote a large work of at least thirty-eight volumes, to which he gave the title of *Syllogisms* and in which he demonstrated the fables and contradictions – in short, the unreliability of the law and the prophets, to say nothing of their spirit which was alien to Christianity. The remnants of this work show that he proceeded in a boldly rationalist fashion.[41] Although he remained true to his teacher on the main points, he spoke plainly against him: "Marcion lies," he wrote, "when he speaks of (multiple) principles."[42]

Apelles carried on a very successful activity in Rome and out from Rome. It is true that Irenaeus still had not taken note of it (nor did Clement); but already in the early writing of Tertullian, *De praescriptione haereticorum*, the sect of Apelles appears as the most significant heretical sect next to those of Marcion and Valentinus.[43] This trio, which is often found in Tertullian, is also brought together by Origen in many passages for polemical purposes, also with the other trio of "Marcion, Valentinus, and Basilides," and sometimes they are intermingled – evidence that the sect of Apelles[44] had taken root in Palestine and elsewhere in the East[45] and was in competition with the most significant heresies. Still, it was granted a much briefer life-span than was the church of Marcion. We have no assurance that it continued long after the age of Origen, who was its untiring adversary; he even undertook journeys in order to combat it in lectures in various cities.[46] The judgment of Firmilian, that Apelles agreed with Marcion's blasphemy but added to it much that was even more inimical to the faith and to truth,[47] probably was generally held in the church in spite of Apelles' doctrine of the one principle, and this incited particularly vigorous battles against the heretic who dissolved the Old Testament into legends and fables.

Just as we have reports of disputes of Marcion and the Marcionites with the catholics, so also there are such reports about Apelles. In the *Syntagma* Hippolytus tells that Apelles asserted in a conversation about the faith: "I do not need to learn from Marcion, in order to assert with him two co-eternal principles; I preach *one* principle." More important is the religious discussion that Rhodon had with the already aged[48] Apelles.[49] *In fact, this is the most significant religious discussion that we possess from earliest church history at all.* It must have taken place toward the end of Marcus Aurelius' reign.

"The aged Apelles," writes Rhodon, "engaged in a discussion with us,[50] and in it was convicted of having made many false statements. Hence he also said that it was not necessary thoroughly to investigate the word (of someone), but *each one should remain as he had once believed, for he asserted that those who had placed their hope in the crucified one would be saved, if they only were found doing good works*. But the most obscure matter of all that he said, as we have already noted,[51] was that about God, for he repeatedly said '*one* principle,' as our doctrine also holds."

Eusebius then continues with his excerpt thus: Rhodon expounds all of Apelles' opinions and then adds the following:

> But when I said to him, "Where is your proof, or how can you say that there is *one* principle? Tell us," he countered saying that the prophecies refute themselves because they have told nothing true at all, for they are inconsistent and false and in conflict with themselves; but as to how there is *one* principle, he said, *he did not know, but was only inclined to that opinion*. When I adjured him to speak the truth,[52] he swore that he was being completely honest, in saying that he did not know how an unbegotten God could be, but he believed it. But I laughed him to scorn, that he claimed to be a teacher, and yet could not prove what he was teaching.

Rhodon presents the results as though the final utterances of the heretic, that is, those to which Eusebius' quotation unfortunately is limited, are an expression of the doubt of an old man who has been driven into a corner. Eusebius understood them in this way, and he cited the words in order to expose Apelles. But this is not the only case in his "Church History" in which by means of his quotations he achieved an end in later ages quite different from that which he had intended. The words also by no means arose out of a momentary embarrassment—they are much too important for that—but they represent the well-considered conviction of Apelles, indeed its very essence. Only, it is not immediately clear whether they are to be understood as a note of resignation or whether it was Rhodon who introduced this note of resignation. Still open also is the question whether Apelles as a teacher had always expressed himself thus or only when he was an old man.

In the sentence, "Salvation is certain for those who have placed their hope in the crucified one, if only they are found doing good works," Apelles, like his former master Marcion, unequivocally confessed a Pauline Christianity. This is attested even by the formulation, as is shown by the absolute form "the crucified one," [53] a form which so far as I know does not appear anywhere else in all the postapostolic literature and which gives a special weight to the idea. The essence of Christianity is summed up here as in a motto.[54]

But only from the ideas that follow does one discern what import going beyond Paul this confession holds for Apelles. According to Paul, to place hope in Christ and to believe in one God are equally important, equally necessary, and inseparable; he would not even have been able to imagine that this connection could be severed. Not so Apelles. Instead, according to him the *only* thing absolutely necessary for salvation is hope in the crucified one, i.e., in God's act of redemption which is set forth in Christ's death on the cross.[55] It is true that with Apelles himself this believing hope is connected with the acceptance of only *one* principle, the one unbegotten God;[56] but he knows that other Christians think differently about this matter, and *this does not disturb him*. Instead, he thinks that where that hope in the crucified one is found (together with a holy life), *as far as the problem of God is concerned*, everyone should be left in the belief that he has once adopted.[57] According to Apelles, even the question of how many eternal principles there are does not determine one's status as a Christian, for the crucified one alone is the Alpha and the Omega.[58] The whole of "theoretical" theology here is simply expelled from the Christian religion and every investigation of the word is categorically forbidden. The Christian religion is an assured hope and it has to do exclusively with salvation and the crucified redeemer. Thus proclaimed this Christian thinker in the age of Platonism and of the all-dominating religious intellectualism!

But how does Apelles justify his attitude with reference to theoretical theology? He does so by means of two interrelated judgments, one negative and the other positive. The former runs thus: the matter concerning God is the most obscure of all problems;[59] indeed, there is no Gnosis and no knowing at all about God ("I do not know, I have not learned"). *Therewith any knowledge of God from the world is rejected*, but in addition, it is explicitly emphasized that no such knowledge is to be gained from the Old Testament,[60] for in this book one will find nothing real and true; what it contains is absurd, false, and full of contradictions in itself. With reference to God the "how can it be?"[61] remains closed to *knowledge*, and therefore any proof likewise is impossible here. But the second judgment is created out of the self-observation: "I for myself indeed hold the belief in the *one* principle (the one unbegotten God),[62] but I am not able to communicate this belief by means of proof; for it is not a rational knowledge, nor one that is based on any authorities, but a matter of an inner certainty ('thus I am moved') for which I can give no further account."

Thus, Apelles is no skeptic;[63] he rather is certain of God—indeed of God as the sole principle, but for him this certainty is *not a saving faith*. Further, it is not based upon an insight, but exclusively upon being moved, a stimulus.

This "thus I am moved" unquestionably is, next to the plain Pauline confession of the crucified one, the most valuable thing in the entire statement. Κινεῖσθαι ("to be moved"), a Stoic concept, is a psychic stimulus in the sense of the internal arrival at certainty.[64] Does not Apelles deserve a distinguished place in the history of the psychology of religion for the statement that the question of God (in the sense of the existence and the unity of God) is not a matter of knowing (neither of logical nor of historical knowing), but exclusively a matter of a psychic state of assurance? Who before him expressed this so surely? Indeed, who expressed it at all? Who before him eliminated all *knowing* about God and from the standpoint of theoretical knowledge interpreted the question of God as the most obscure of all things without ending up in materialism or skepticism, but simply declaring for himself that in this context to believe = to be moved and that for him this κινεῖσθαι takes the place of the answer to the question "how can there be one principle?", that is, "how can there be one unbegotten God?". If this is not Kant's distinction between the "theoretical" and the "practical" reason, the difference is that here in place of the ambiguous concept of the practical reason there appears the unambiguous concept of a psychical fact that cannot as such be proved but that also cannot be transmitted. Apelles, like another of Marcion's pupils, Lucan, had studied philosophy—his terminology shows this—and had thoroughly worked through the Old Testament, but he rejected both as sources of the knowledge of God. He rejected these totally, but for them he substituted the *subjective awareness of God*—indeed, the monotheistic awareness—and, using the tools of the Stoa but going beyond them, he described it as an inward state of being impelled and constrained. His κινοῦμαι ("I am moved") corresponds to Augustine's "ad te," and it is psychologically more precisely observed than Schleiermacher's "feeling of absolute dependence" with which it is akin in the strong emphasis upon the one principle. For Apelles, God is and remains unknown (in the simple sense of the word), but this is not the final word, for by means of an inward certainty for him God is subjectively required as being and as *one*, and therefore he believes in him.

But now this single warning must be uttered: one must not overlook the fact that the kinship with Schleiermacher and Kant is only a conditional one. Why? *Because for Apelles the question of God does not play the decisive role in religion—not even in the answering of the question by the* κινεῖσθαι. Here he means rather to allow the validity of every experience and to tolerate even such Christians as those who hold a belief in two or three principles and who thus know nothing of the unequivocal κινεῖσθαι. He wills, indeed he demands, that each one remain with his own subjective metaphysical belief, because for redemption and salvation only the hope in the crucified one comes into consideration. *Thus Apelles has completely detached this hope not only from knowing but also from monotheistic belief.*

But then what is the basis of the hope itself? Is it necessary for everyone and yet it neither can be demonstrated nor has its foundation in the metaphysical monotheistic faith? The answer can only be: either here a second κινεῖσθαι comes into play, which as distinguished from the first one is not solely subjective—for everyone can and should hope in the crucified one—*or the fact of the crucified one simply speaks for itself* and the gospel creates for itself those who hope. Apelles can only have thought the latter; for a κινεῖσθαι is and remains subjective. Thus Apelles' ideas arrange themselves in this way: there is (1) a beneficent hope in the crucified one which arises out of the fact itself or from preaching; anyone who has gained this hope is certain of salvation, *because the knowledge of the merciful (good) God arises only from one's laying hold upon the crucified one.* It is true that Apelles has not said that here explicitly, but it follows from the context and is assured in keeping with his Marcionite tradition.[65] The κινεῖσθαι has no reference to God as the merciful one (the redeemer).[66] There is (2) an inward κινεῖσθαι, which leads one and another to the metaphysical belief in *one* unitary ground of the world and thus in one God; but since not everyone experiences this, the recognition of the one principle cannot be necessary to salvation.[67] Moreover, the question, "how can there be one God?", perpetually remains, scientifically speaking, without an answer. There is (3) a rational knowledge that is capable of demonstration, but it relates exclusively to the world; the question of God, as metaphysical and as beatific, remains for him a closed one.

Apelles has torn apart the hope in the crucified one (and thus the hope in a good, redeeming principle) and the belief in one unbegotten God, which is based on a κινεῖσθαι, and in addition has separated both from perceiving and knowing! *Thus he has based the Christian religion exclusively on the impact of its historical content.* Did he himself sense the tremendous act of resignation which is implied in this? We may assume that he did, for alongside the κινεῖσθαι stands a significant μόνον [only, alone] which belongs all the more to saving faith. In addition, there is the fact that we know (see above) that he earlier had declared the two-principles doctrine of his teacher to be error and a lie, and thus at that time he cannot possibly have held to the principle that everyone can and should remain with the belief that he has regarding the principles. Thus, what he earlier had adjudged a matter of knowing the *aged* Apelles now describes as a subjective certainty that lies beyond knowledge, from which saving faith is completely independent. Such a change cannot have occurred without an act of resignation.[68]

Because of his sharp distinction of the three entities (a rational knowledge of the world which cannot arrive at a certain knowledge of God; a psychologically-subjectively conditioned belief in God as the *sole* ground of the world; and a hopeful Christian belief, grounded in history, in God the redeemer), Apelles deserves an eminent place in the history of religions. He is the only theologian before Augustine with whom we today are able to come to an understanding without some laborious processes of accommodation.[69]

Apelles' teaching in its divergences from Marcion is still discernible and comprehensible from the extant fragments of his writings; in every place it begins with obvious logical difficulties in Marcion's teachings. In the divergence, however, the actual superiority is by no means always on the side of Apelles.

(1) Marcion assumed two principles, but since he did not see them as equal but rather was obliged to see the good God as superior to the just God and moreover was obliged to teach that in the consummation the just God would meet his end, Marcion's affirmation of the two principles appeared to be logically untenable. Apelles therefore affirmed, in harmony with the general Christian teaching, only *one* divine principle; this deity is supposed to have created, besides the angels, a special "virtus" which Apelles called "the renowned angel," and indeed in a broader sense, the ἀρχή; for it is the creator of the world.

(2) Marcion had condemned the creation (including mankind) in its totality and in particular as a worthless and miserable product, similar to its creator. However, he saw in the "flesh" something especially reprehensible; it had developed out of the material that the creator was obliged to use. Apelles was unable to approve this condemnation of the world (with respect to the flesh he shared Marcion's view), because it did not do justice to the obvious state of affairs. Here he began with the perspective that he had learned from the religious philosophers of Alexandria: the world, regardless of how bad it is, does contain some things that are relatively exalted and good; this good is best accounted for if one interprets the world as the unsuccessful copy of a higher, better world, *in which therefore there also is found a tragic note of regret and repentance.*[70] Thus, its creator must have combined the best of intentions with a weakness. To this is added an observation that unmistakably betrays its Platonic source but also is completely dissociated from Marcion's view: in this imperfect world there is something that in spite of its lamentable circumstances yet must have a heavenly origin, namely, the human soul; it can only spring from the μία ἀρχή itself. How could Marcion deny its lofty nature? But how did it come into this world?

(3) Marcion simply assigned the same qualitative value to the creation and the Old Testament. To him, the two are alike in their nature and are equally deplorable. But he utterly neglected to test the Old Testament with respect to its credibility and trustworthiness and was satisfied with engaging in a purely religious criticism of it. Apelles began here. He studied the book thoroughly and concluded that it is a book of fables and falsehoods, but if Moses and the prophets are nothing but a great lying legend, then they are far worse than the creation. Hence, there must stand behind them a power other than the creator

of the world. A second "angel" must be involved here, one who has fallen, and it can only be that fiery lying spirit that had spoken to Moses in the burning bush. He, the "superintendent of evil," is the God of Israel and the God of the Christians as well, who follow the God of Israel; it was he, also, who had lured the souls by means of base seduction ("terrenis escis") out of the upper regions of the good God in order to clothe them here with sinful flesh.

(4) Marcion was not willing to acknowledge that the body of Christ was really born, and he explained it as only an apparent body. Apelles also accepted the first of these points, but he perceived that Marcion's Docetism would be difficult to defend because he attributed an act of deception to the Redeemer and because he called in question the actuality of the work of Christ on which everything hinged. Therefore Apelles attributed to Jesus a real body, though one formed out of pure elements, with which he was clothed in his descent as he passed through the starry worlds.

These are the most important points of divergence from Marcion's teaching that underlie a new teaching. *The first and second of these abandon the idea of God as an alien God; this is the main point of difference between Marcion and Apelles.*

Thus Apelles' catechism went thus:

(i) The Christian Bible, on which alone doctrine is to be established, was rightly defined by Marcion; thus, it consists of the (abridged and adulterated) gospel of Luke and the (abridged and adulterated) epistles of Paul; the Old Testament is to be rejected.[71] The "revelations" of the prophetess Philumene also are to be read (see above).

(ii) There is *one good God* ("there is one good God and one fundamental principle and one nameless power");[72] this God has created angelic powers and a higher world as well as the souls of men, which originally were with him in the upper regions,[73] but he did not create the world and, furthermore, he is not concerned about it.[74] His Christ, the Son, has been with him from all eternity.[75]

(iii) The highest of the created angels ("inclytus," "gloriosus") – so high that he is to be characterized as "virtus," a second fundamental principle, another God, a second God and Lord and thus very closely approximates the Logos, though Apelles appears to have avoided using this name[76] – obeys the warnings, commandments, and directions of the supreme God in all matters. This supreme God entrusted to him the creation of the world, which he was to accomplish after the pattern of the higher world to the honor ("gloria") of the One God, and Christ supported him in this work with his spirit and will and power. But since this angel could not be "good," because this attribute is reserved to the supreme God alone, the world (heaven, earth, and all that is in the cosmos, including the visible stars) became imperfect, and its creator mingled with it a sense of remorse about it; in fact, in this remorse he ashamedly removed himself completely from the good God, so that he is to be compared with the lost sheep in the gospel.[77]

(iv) But things now went from bad to worse with the world, or with men, for a second angel fell away completely from the supreme God, became the "superintendent of evil" ("praeses mali"), and lured to itself the souls out of the higher world by means of earthly food in order to clothe them in sinful flesh. But he was not satisfied with this. As a fiery angel (and thus a consuming one) he spoke to Moses out of the burning bush and led astray the Jewish people to the creator of the world; he also led astray those Christians who, like the Jews, worship him as their God.[78]

(v) The same fiery angel, the gainsayer and lying spirit, is the source of the book of lies, the Old Testament, which is full of fables, absurdities, contradictions, and logical and factual impossibilities. The law and the prophets have utterly led astray the Jews and the common Christian people and have put them in bondage. Anyone can read in the *Syllogisms* how matters stand with this book. Yet there are some things contained in the Old Testament that were inspired by Christ.[79]

(vi) The good God had mercy upon humanity and *at the request of the World-Creator* in this last time sent his Son for the redemption of humanity.[80] Before him no emissary from this God had appeared.[81] With this Son came also the Holy Spirit.

(vii) The Son, Christ, upon his descent formed a body for himself out of the four elements that were also found in the starry world belonging to the cosmos, and thus he appeared upon earth in an *actual* body. In this body he *actually* did all that he did and suffered. The most important element of doctrine ran thus:[82] "Upon descending from the supra-celestial realm he came upon earth and shaped for himself a body out of the four elements; for from the dry he took the dry and from the warm he took the warm," et cetera. Then in this same body he submitted to suffering and was truly crucified and truly buried, and he truly rose again and showed his flesh to his disciples. Then once again he dissolved his humanness and returned to the individual elements that which belonged to each of them; then he took up again his σῶμα ἔνσαρχον and flew back to the heavens whence he had come.[83] His redemptive work consisted in the crucifixion that he actually suffered.[84]

(viii) The redemption has to do only with the soul,[85] for just as the assumption of sinful flesh would have stained the Christ so also the perfected believer must put it off.

(ix) Marriage is utterly to be rejected.[86]

The teaching of Apelles — leaving aside the position that he adopted at the very last — is an interesting combination of Marcionitism and Gnosticism at the cost of the former.[87] It stands close to Valentinianism[88] (and to Clement of Alexandria), but closest, it appears, to Tatian,[89] and is more moderate and more "reasonable" than Marcion's teaching. It is also, to the same degree, weaker and duller.[90] It is a corrective to Marcionitism by means of speculation that is akin to the Valentinian speculation. But it undoubtedly also comes closer, because of its one-principle doctrine, to the theology of popular Christianity than does the teaching of Marcion. However, that Apelles wanted to make concessions to that popular Christianity is an assumption that is indeed cherished but unprovable, and none of the church fathers ever had any notion that such was true. At the end of his life Apelles once more shook off Gnosticism, assumed as a thinker a wholly unique and broad-minded position, and as a Christian was rescued on the plank of Pauline saving faith, tolerant toward all who seized that plank with him. But even in this last phase of his life he still held firm to the view that the Old Testament is, in its major portion, a book of fables. With this view he took the side of the educated Greeks who fought against Christianity,[91] and this fatal alliance would not have been conducive to the spread of his school.

IX

MARCION'S HISTORICAL POSITION AND HIS HISTORICAL SIGNIFICANCE FOR THE EMERGENCE OF THE CATHOLIC CHURCH

The historical orientation that we placed at the beginning of this study must now be taken up again:

The lifework of a man is determined by the struggle that he has waged. Marcion fought against only *one* adversary, the "pseudoapostoli et Judaici evangelizatores" ["false apostles and Jewish evangelists"]. We do not know a single word of his that attacks the heathen; he simply pushed aside the "deceitfulness" and "the wordy eloquence" of their philosophers. About the Jewish Christians in the national sense of the term he was utterly silent; he does not mention the Gnostics,[1] and he fights the Jews because he fights the Judaizing Christians.

But his understanding of this group, those who are led astray and deceived by the "pseudoapostoli et Judaici evangelizatores," is that it includes "*the whole of the main body of Christendom.*" To convince it of its error and to bring it back by means of reformation to true Christianity was his only struggle.

Wherein did he perceive that error? Essentially in *one* element from which, as from a corrupt root, an entire tree of error had grown: *Christendom had poured the new wine into the old wineskins and had transposed the gospel into the Old Testament.*

He did not see this transposition in details and minutiae—it was true that Christianity had not taken over the Jewish circumcision, the ordinances concerning feast days, the dietary laws, and so on, but this did not make the slightest impression upon him and could not afford him the slightest comfort, for in his view the trouble lay much deeper: this Christianity considered *law and gospel as a unity and thus denied the essence of the gospel.* Where *separation* was essential,[2] it had bound things together! And he was not satisfied even with the fact that, like himself, Christianity regarded the present age as at enmity with God, wanted to be free from it, and was assured of possessing in the redemption by Christ the earnest money of blessedness, for how could that be the true faith that recognized in the creator of the world the father of Jesus Christ?

However Marcion understood the contrast between faith and works, gospel and law, and whatever conclusions he drew from this contrast for religious doctrine, he actually was what he intended to be: a pupil of Paul who took up again, as an actual reformer, the work and the struggle of the apostle.[3] It is understandable that Neander could call him the first Protestant.

But we may go a step further. He not only took up again the work and the struggle of Paul, but he also did this in the apostle's *understanding and consciousness of faith*; for it was his intention to know nothing save Christ the crucified one. In Christ alone he perceived the face of the gracious God, and he knew himself to be inseparably bound to this God of goodness and mercy in faith and love, because he was conscious of having been bought and redeemed by Christ. Sin and world, law and commandment, lay far behind him.

And if Paul had reappeared three generations later, would he not have pronounced the sharpest kind of judgment upon the Christianity that he now would find and indeed have accused it of apostasy? What would he likely have said if one had laid before him the Shepherd of Hermas and offered him Christianity according to this book as authentic revelation? What would have been his judgment about these visions, mandates, and parables? and, again, about the self-righteousness and self-approval of the author and the dull penitential mentality that is expressed by this book in which the name of Christ hardly appears at all? Or what judgment would he have pronounced upon the works of Justin? Certainly he would have read much in them with pleasure, but how would he have taken Justin's doctrines of freedom and virtue? What would he have said about the discussion with philosophy, about the recognition of Socrates' and Plato's philosophy? and about the new legalism that he would encounter in every postapostolic writing?

No doubt Paul would have taken note of the development of Christian syncretism with pain and dismay, would have joined in the Marcionite criticism of Christianity on the most important points, would also have condemned this Christianity as a flock that had been led astray, and would have seen in the man who here appeared as a reformer his own authentic pupil.

But Marcion cut the bond between the law and the gospel, rejected the Old Testament, attributed it to another God, proclaimed Jesus Christ as the son of an alien God, and denied the birth of Christ and the genuineness of his flesh. No doubt Paul would have turned away in horror from this blasphemous teacher and would have delivered him up to Satan; and certainly he would never have considered even remotely the question whether he himself was not responsible, with his own teachings, for these earthshaking errors of Marcion.

And yet this is a very necessary question, and it is not difficult to show that Marcion's extreme teaching, whereby he became the founder of a new religion on the basis of the Christian tradition, grew out of Paulinism or out of an extension of it. Moreover, Marcion was not the first continuator, but he only carried this continuation to its conclusion.

First of all, one must comprehend here what extension of primitive Christianity is signified in the teaching of Paul himself. In this process we may leave aside the question of Christ's teaching, for it is not necessary in the present context for us to go back that far.[4]

Paul abolished the validity of the Old Testament law and thereby set aside the Old Testament as the obvious foundation of religion for the Gentiles who should be converted. In place of the messianic faith he placed the Kyrios Christos with his saving work of death and resurrection, and he strictly identified religion with the belief in the Father of Christ, the God of love and redemption. Something entirely new—even in Paul's mind—was given therewith: the old has passed away, and *behold, all things are become new*.[5] But in order to be able to maintain the inner connection with the God of the law and the prophets, which was so obvious to him that no doubt could ever emerge at this point, he was obliged to offer instead of *one* means or instrument a whole series, for each one served only imperfectly and had narrowly defined limitations. But instead of being stumped in the face of the inadequacy of each individual means of clarifying the problem, Paul saw in their abundance only the richness and the wisdom of God and, when every means failed, withdrew at last to take refuge in God's unsearchableness. The means that he propounded were: (1) a distinctive dialectical consideration of the education of the human race in connection with the Adam-Christ antithesis; (2) a special and peculiar dialectic with respect to sin and grace, sin and law, guilt and redemption, and life and death; and (3) the allegorical exposition of passages of Scripture. *If one rejected these means or if one was unable to derive from them any understanding at all, then one had to understand Paul in a strictly dualistic sense (a fundamental opposition of the God of the law to the God of the gospel), and then consequently must declare anything that contradicted this interpretation to be an interpolation.*[6]

Marcion took this position. As far as the substance, namely religion, is concerned, he thereby took a step away from the given basis of Paulinism, a step that in itself was no greater than the step Paul himself had taken.[7] For according to Paul, the old order of religion of the Jewish God to which Christianity both before him and after him held was abolished, and the Old Testament is no longer the divine document from which one now has to perceive God's salvific intention and his nature. *But a document, particularly a divine one, that had only conditional validity is in principle set aside together with its originator.* Thus Paulinism signified an immense revolution in the Jewish-Christian religious history. The fact that the church stopped at the halfway house of Paulinism and that it in fact soon even took a revisionist step backwards is astounding and can be understood solely in terms of the great inward and outward authority of the Old Testament in connection with Christianity's historical origin in Judaism. But it is by no means true that Marcion was the only one to sense the Pauline half-heartedness; there are rather several attempts of various kinds in non-Gnostic Christianity of the postapostolic period that have been related to us, attempts to go beyond this halfway house. When the author of the epistle to the Hebrews with reference to the Old Testament acknowledges the validity only of a view that it is something shadowy (10:1) and now anti-

quated (8:13), in his evaluation of the Old Testament he goes farther than Paul
and denies any validity to that book for the present. Furthermore, the author
of the epistle of Barnabas, unequivocally and in full awareness that he is dealing
with a most important matter, declares that a literal interpretation of the Old
Testament is always and everywhere a dreadful misunderstanding on the part of
the Jews, introduced by the devil. Anyone who follows this misunderstanding in
faith, doctrine, cultus, manner of life, and so forth is a child of Satan. In making
this interpretation, he is simply and literally making of the Old Testament a second book; *only this book has validity for Christians!* Here too the identity of
the God of the law and the God of the gospel is maintained, as it is in Paul,
but at what a price! Marcion had no intention of getting into that kind of
sophistry. It is also highly noteworthy that in his epistle to the Philadelphians
(chapter 8) Ignatius opposed the thesis of the Jewish Christians that said "If I
do not find something in the archives (in the Old Testament), I do not believe
it, even if it is found in the gospel." His answer was, "To me the archives are
Jesus Christ, his cross, his death, his resurrection, and the faith that he has
founded." This comes very close to an abrogation of the Old Testament, because
it is replaced by the gospel and is no longer needed. Marcion actually created
"the archives" out of Paul's letters and the gospel, because they contained the
crucifixion and the resurrection. We may also refer to the author of the epistle
to Diognetus, who in his apology leaves the Old Testament aside altogether, has
Christ appear as the *only* one sent from God, and emphasizes in God only his
love and goodness.[8]

But the most important phenomenon along the line leading from Paul to
Marcion is the gospel of John together with the Johannine epistles. It is true that
with reference to the law and the prophets the author stands theoretically on the
same ground as does Paul: he has Jesus declare that salvation comes from the
Jews and that the Old Testament bears witness to him. He has no idea of
distinguishing between two Gods,[9] but in his lively religious thinking with
respect to the concept of God and the related questions he goes beyond Paul and
in the direction of Marcion. We have already indicated to what extent he is kin
to Marcion with respect to the undertaking of setting forth a new gospel,
because the gospel writings that were then in circulation were not satisfactory
to him. Both are characterized by a lofty and superior attitude toward tradition
and indeed in some cases a disregard for it, and the motives in the two are very
similar: both John and Marcion want to form, out of the variety of materials
that those writings afford, a presentation that is focused by means of *major
ideas*; they want to bring out clearly the newness of the phenomenon of Christ
and his gospel; they want to demonstrate the absolute worth of his person and
his work, plainly to present his utter supra-worldliness and with it his full deity,
and solely to declare the new reassuring knowledge of God that is illumined
through him and in him.

The affinity is exhibited in the substance and in the historical material.

With respect to this material we may refer to the fact that for John, too, God (he is "spirit," as with Marcion, "spiritus salutaris") is *love*, which drives out *fear*,[10] and he should be conceived of exclusively as love – of course, according to Marcion God did not love the *world* but men. Further, the Son appears as one who himself has the power to sacrifice his life and to take it up again (10:18). According to Marcion, he raised himself, and numerous Johannine utterances are in harmony with the Marcionite Modalism. The entire Johannine dialectic about God's "judging" has as its presupposition the idea that the Father does not judge but has given judgment over to the Son, but even the Son says (12:47) that he will not judge the unbelievers, "for I did not come to judge the world, but to save the world." Thus he too is only love and redemption. This is altogether in keeping with Marcion's thought. And, as with Marcion, in *one* of John's trains of thought the cosmos stands over against God as a dark, alien, hostile power; men belong to this cosmos, which (I John 5:19) wholly and entirely lies in the evil one, and they must be redeemed from it and out of it. Even what John says of the "Jews" approaches Marcion's view of them, for regardless of other views that John harbors concerning them, they are the real enemies of Christ, the cosmos-men, *whose father is the devil*. This and much else that is related to it is admittedly then subordinated in John to a different perspective, according to which these elements do not contain this religious thinker's final and conclusive word, but they are still there and one must not disregard them. For Marcion they are the final word. For him, the Jews, as the chosen people of the creator of the world, are the enemies of Christ, and their patriarchs, prophets, and leaders cannot be redeemed. But the qualities that, according to Marcion, render the Jews incapable of redemption – their boasting of Moses, their blind failure to perceive what is truly good, and their fleshly self-righteousness – are, according to John who in the Apocalypse calls them "the synagogue of Satan," characteristic of them.

This already brings us to the *historical* consideration that both of these men pursued. Going beyond Paul, John, in Jesus' conversation with the Samaritan woman, sets Jewish and pagan worship, as similar to each other and equally wrong, over against the new worship in spirit and in truth. Like Marcion, he can have Jesus say that all who came before him are thieves and murderers; like Marcion, he excludes from the Old Testament the proclamation of grace and truth – Moses had proclaimed nothing but the law. But further: it is on the way toward Marcion when John, although Matthew and Luke had already composed their gospels, considered it unnecessary and superfluous to speak of the birth of Christ, when he further reduced the significance of Christ's baptism to a sign that was supposed to have been given to the Baptist, and when he indeed proclaimed the message that "the Word became flesh" but held the human element in Christ in suspension.

These features, which could easily be multiplied, may suffice to show that Marcionite doctrine did not come as a bolt out of the blue. To be sure, John did not prepare the way for it, but the way was prepared by a development that by an inner necessity had to attach itself to Paulinism in the Gentile Christian realm and whose strongest elements we find in John. Of course, he himself, as a born Jew, knew how to avoid the ultimate consequences in favor of the general tradition and to maintain the authority of the Jewish God along with his book.

Marcion and numerous Christians along with him or concurrently with him took the decisive step[11] and, in the interest of the newness of Christianity, its unambiguous nature, and its power, separated the gospel from the Old Testament and its God. However, it is only of Marcion that we know that he gave an *historical* accounting of why he did it and how the violent procedure was to be justified. While John with his pneumatic sovereignty and certainty offered his crucial emendations and sublimations of the tradition as historical facts, Marcion—and this gives him a unique place in the entire history of the early church—possessed a clear awareness of his obligation as a critic to give historical justification for his position. In this connection it will always be worthy of note that with a sure grasp he selected the Galatian epistle as his basis, as have Semler and F. C. Baur in recent times. *Moreover, even that early there could not have been still existing generally recognized documents or reliable traditions alongside this epistle and the other epistles of Paul that would have ruled out such exaggerated conclusions as he and, later, Semler and Baur have drawn.*[12] From the Galatian epistle Marcion drew the conclusion that Paul preached a gospel totally different from that of the original apostles, namely, the genuine gospel of Christ, which those original apostles had adulterated in a Jewish fashion, and further, that in all his epistles Paul had only *one* task and *one* battle, the battle against the Judaizers. In his exposition of the Pauline epistles he brought this to light, and now it was possible for him to distinguish between the genuine and the inauthentic elements in them and to extend this distinction then to include the gospel as well. The parallels with the work of the Tübingen school are here everywhere so striking that they do not require any singling out. Of course, there is the difference that this school did not go so far as to deny that Paul recognized the Old Testament and the God of the Old Testament, and that the representatives of this school possessed means that Marcion did not have for separating those materials that were genuinely Pauline from "Deutero-Paulinism." But this difference is, in the final analysis, not so great, for according to Baur Paul too had surrendered "in idea" the Old Testament God, and in a certain sense he was correct in this assertion (see above).[13]

But when Marcion compared the purported discovery in the genuine epistles of Paul with the current situation in Christianity in general, he was bound to see that the apostle had labored in vain and that in spite of his indescribable efforts everything had remained the same as it had been. As a consequence of the recognition of the Old Testament, everything had been crystallized in legalistic forms, and Marcion perceived with distress that Christianity had once again become a version of Judaism. Next to his religious ideas, the most remarkable thing about him was the energy and vigor of the organization that he now instituted in order once again to take up the work of Paul, to create a reformed and definitive Christianity, and to call back all the brethren who had fallen away, and his successes were amazing. In the seventh and eighth chapters, above, we have set forth what he intended and accomplished as an organizer; here this achievement must once again be set in the context of the history of the development of primitive Christianity into catholicism.

The Christianity of the church at large was "catholic" by virtue of the abundance of religious motifs (syncretism) that it embraced, and it was "catholic" by virtue of the universality of its mission. But since it only possessed the same book as did the synagogue, its proclamation of "two covenants" upon which, following the apostle, it took its stand (see Justin's *Dialogue with Trypho*) had to remain incomplete and questionable. *For the second and more important of these convenants it had no documents!* But it also had *no centralized, catholic doctrine.* There existed in Rome at least a brief and pregnant baptismal confession and perhaps one in Asia Minor as well. But as important as that was, still even this confession did not yet enjoy any "catholic" dissemination and standing, and alongside it, every Christian teacher built, taught, and speculated on his own authority and in his own right. Finally, this *concordia discors* of doctrine, which was held together only very insecurely by the appeal to the unformulated "apostolic tradition," was matched by and corresponded to the *loose connection between and among the churches.* Bishops and teachers strove to make up for the missing inner connection by means of personal admonitory writings and injunctions, but they were far from perfect in their effect. Already in that time it was only *the Roman church* that spoke and acted as a *congregation moving in the direction of establishing a whole church.*

It was upon this diffuse set of circumstances, so perilous for the survival of Christianity, that Marcion's reformation broke in. The first necessity that confronted him, since he rejected the old documents and recognized only *one* convenant, was the production of a *littera scripta* of this same single convenant. He, and no one else, did it! The second necessity that pressed upon him, because from his standpoint it was self-evident, was the connection of the gospel with the epistles of Paul and therewith the division of the new canon into two parts, which was so rich in blessing and at the same time so fateful. He, and no one else conceived of this! The third necessity that he perceived was to put an end to the dominant syncretism of religious knowledge and motifs as well as to prophetism, to allegorizing, to pervasive philosophical speculation, to rationalism and Gnosticism, and in short to all subjective elements, and to put in their place not a humanly devised "doctrine" but a clear and unequivocal biblical theology. This he did, by means of his *Antitheses*, that is, his biblical commentary, which in its uniformity was extremely powerful. Finally, he saw the necessity of using these newly created instruments to produce an actual *unity* of Christianity in the form of a great *church* and thereby to give to this same

Christianity both strength and durability. He himself was his own missionary, and according to the testimony of his contemporary, Justin, he spread his creation "throughout the whole human race," i.e., through the entire empire. [14]

The objections that say that in all these points he was not the first but that he copied ideas already at hand are, on the whole, invalid. Some have attempted in vain to prove that the conception and creation of a second body of holy writ, the New Testament, had already been achieved in Christianity at large even before Marcion. Justin's *Dialogue with Trypho*, to say nothing of other negative witnesses, argues against this assertion. [15] It is true that in Christianity at large since the time of Paul people had been aware of two testaments, or convenants, but in the form of *Scripture* there was only *one,* the Old Testament, and there was no thought of doubling the number. Whence would a person have been supposed to derive the authority for the creation of a New Testament? [16] Further, it is true that in Marcion's time some leading communities already possessed the four Gospels and read them in the worship services alongside the Old Testament. However, neither was the collection already generally distributed nor was it regarded as the body of documents corresponding to and formally of equal value to the Old Testament. [17] Moreover, the idea of placing the epistles of Paul alongside the gospel with equal status could not arise where the apostle stood in the shadow of the original apostles; but he stood in this shadow in Christianity at large, corresponding to the distinctive content of the "apostolic tradition" which placed all the emphasis upon eye-witness accounts. Hence if Christianity at large on its own initiative wanted to combine the gospel and the epistles of Paul, this could have happened only by means of an original apostolic medium; however, the witnesses for such a formed canon are all post-Marcionite. [18] Besides, it was Marcion who first recognized the necessity of setting the doctrinal content of Christianity in opposition to all the syncretism and subjectivism, however crude or refined and from whatever source it was derived, within specific bounds and of creating it as biblical theology solely from the sacred documents, but at the same time developing this theology not cosmologically but soteriologically; and he carried this through with the most consistent thoroughness. Finally, it was also Marcion as an individual who with admirable energy first undertook to unite the scattered communities into a unity *by means of this understanding of Christianity* into an actual church and thereby to protect it against becoming dissolved in the contemporary currents and in Judaism.

What did the bishops and teachers of the great church do when this "wolf," as they called him, invaded the flock, when this "ungodly mouth" commenced to speak and this "monster" began the battle against the Creator-God? What did they do when there arose in the very midst of the scattered individual congregations the completed building of the Marcionite catholic church, like something conjured up out of nowhere? We have already related how they acted with the most intense zeal, and we know from the abundance of counterliterature that was composed *everywhere* in the period between 150 and 200 that the new church had spread throughout all the provinces of the empire. There was no doubt that this church was to be condemned; but *in order to guard itself against this new church, the great church had to accept and did accept from Marcion everything that he had created with the exception of the basic religious idea*. The church itself now for the first time also produced a *written* New Testament; in this New Testament it combined "Gospel" and "Apostle" (expanding the "Apostle," in keeping with the tradition) *on the same level*. It learned from Marcion forthwith that it was necessary to guard doctrine against its being dissolved and against influences from without, but seeing doctrine as *theology of the New Testament*, and it also began to learn from him that *soteriology* must be given a higher rank than *cosmology*.[19]

Marcion's priority over the church, as a cause is prior to an effect, is demonstrated not only by the fact that all these items showed up in Marcion earlier than in the church[20] but even more surely by the observations (see Appendices III and IV) of what a powerful influence the Marcionite Bible *as such* had upon the catholic Bible. This is most eloquently attested by the vigorous incursion of the Marcionite prologues to the Pauline epistles into the Latin Bible of the church.[21] How often in the early days must the Marcionite collection of epistles have come into the hand of catholics without their at first being recognized for what they were! For decades, copies of Paul's epistles were lacking in catholic churches (see above). But furthermore, it is both obvious and highly important that Irenaeus, the founder of the church's soteriological doctrine, as well as Tertullian and Origen, developed their *biblical* teachings about goodness and righteousness, about the creator God and the redeemer God, and so on, in the struggle against Marcion and *in that process learned from him*.[22] Finally, it was through Marcion also that Paul was recovered for the great church, Paul who, for example, had been altogether pushed aside by such a teacher as Justin and whom the Roman Christian Hermas had utterly ignored. But above all, the attitude of Christianity in general toward the Old Testament became, as a result of the dispute with Marcion, something essentially different from what it had been earlier. Previously there had been a burning danger that the Old Testament would be explained, in part literally, in part allegorically, as the Christians' basic document and that it would be recognized and the church would be satisfied with it. Now, to be sure, this danger still was not entirely eliminated and a satisfactory clarity had not yet been achieved, but the conviction that in the Old Testament "the ore still lies in the ground" and that it is the submission to servitude over against the New Testament's submission to freedom gained a place and recognition for itself. Indeed, we now hear from prominent ecclesiastical teachers some expressions about the Old Testament that even go beyond Paul. This the church owes to Marcion.

It must be added that only after Marcion did those in the great church begin the purposeful work of deriving from heaven the holy church, the bride of Christ, the spiritual Eve, and the aeon from beyond, and of combining the congregations here on earth into an actual community and unity on the basis of a fixed doctrine that is rooted in the New Testament, just as Marcion did. *This demonstrates that by means of his organizational and theological conceptions and by his activity Marcion gave the decisive impetus towards the creation of the old catholic church and provided the pattern for it. Moreover, he deserves the credit for having first grasped and actualized the idea of a canonical collection of Christian writings. Finally, he was the first one in the church after Paul to make soteriology the center of doctrine, while the church's apologists contemporary with him were grounding Christian doctrine in cosmology.*[23]

X

MARCION'S CHRISTIANITY
IN LIGHT OF CHURCH HISTORY AND
THE PHILOSOPHY OF RELIGION

1. Antinomianism and the Rejection of the Old Testament

Marcion was led to the rejection of the Old Testament by his renunciation of the Creator-God and by his rejection of the law as well, yet the latter alone would have impelled him to this conclusion. To him anything legal in religion appeared to be a perversion of it. Apelles, certainly in harmony with his master, thought that in comparison with the creation the law was even worse. If one carefully thinks through with Paul and Marcion the contrast between "the righteousness that is by faith" and "the righteousness that is by works" and is persuaded also of the inadequacy of the means by which Paul thought that he could maintain the *canonical* recognition of the Old Testament, consistent thinking will not be able to tolerate the validity of the Old Testament as canonical documents in the Christian church. It may also be stated as an assured fact that the church maintained the Old Testament not so much for reasons of content and substance as for reasons of history. Among the historical reasons must be included the fact, crucially important for the church of the early period, that Jesus himself, as well as Paul, had stood on the soil of the Old Testament. As a child of his time, even Marcion would not have been able to get around this argument. For this very reason, therefore, he set it aside by a *tour de force* by declaring the tradition concerning this position of Jesus and his apostle to have been falsified.

But what, after all, was intended to be said in those times by using the word "proofs" with reference to religious matters? They were inadequate, mistaken, and sophistic, and indeed they frequently were nothing but sparkling soap bubbles. And what does it mean in any and all times to speak of the common logic of consistency or coherence when speaking of religion, since religion has its own logic? Only the matters themselves possess an interest and deserve serious evaluation; for they contain that which is unalterable and inescapable.

Marcion wanted to free Christianity from the Old Testament, but the church preserved it. He did not forbid his followers to pick up the book but even recognized that it contained material that was useful for reading. But he saw in it a spirit different from that of the gospel, and he wanted nothing to do with two different spirits in religion. Was he right or was the church, which did not detach itself from the book, right? The question must be posed, for we are confronted not by some theologian without following or influence but by the man who established the New Testament and created a great church that flourished for centuries. He may rightly lay claim to the honor of deserving to be taken seriously even today. There is not yet universal recognition of that philosophy of history that does justice in all circumstances to what has happened.

The thesis that is to be argued in the following may be stated thus: *the rejection of the Old Testament in the second century was a mistake which the great church rightly avoided; to maintain it in the sixteenth century was a fate from which the Reformation was not yet able to escape; but still to preserve it in Protestantism as a canonical document since the nineteenth century is the consequence of a religious and ecclesiastical crippling.*

It is easy to provide proof for the perception that the rejection of the Old Testament in the second century (and throughout the early history of the church and in the Middle Ages) was a mistake. At that time, because the historical development was concealed from the eye, it was simply impossible to reject the Old Testament without severing any and all connection of the Christian religion with it and declaring it to be the book of a false God.[1] This is what Marcion did. But this assertion is so unhistorical and so earth-shaking—but at the same time so confusing, religiously speaking—that the church instinctively and rightly accepted over against this assertion of Marcion all the difficulties, all the fateful consequences, and all the sophisms that maintaining and preserving the Old Testament brought with it. Certainly, one will not deny recognition to the man who, because he held the gospel and the law to be irreconcilable, vigorously rejected the most powerful tradition and gave up the Old Testament. But—quite apart from the spiritual vacuum that now developed behind the Christian religion as a result, and apart from the violence that was done to the preaching of Jesus and of Paul—what indescribable confusion had to arise when people were compelled to condemn the piety of the psalmists and the profound utterances of the prophets as the works of a reprehensible deity! Any religion can tolerate, to a certain extent, the necessity of something that is not holy as holy, but the treatment of good as evil, or what is holy as abhorrent, calls for retribution. The Old Testament brought Christianity into a tragic conflict; it was not to be resolved, in the second century and beyond that time, as Marcion would resolve it but rather as the church resolved it. From the close of the second century onward the church managed to cope with this problem and eliminated at least some of the oppressive difficulties and the sophisms with which people had been blinding themselves. Now it was permissible to distinguish *levels* and to place the Old Testament on the lower level; of course, this distinction continued to be threatened, for—this seemed self-evident—there can be only *one* inspiration and only one law of truth that is established by that inspiration.

It was Luther[2] who once again gave a central position to the Pauline-Marcionite recognition of the distinction between law and gospel; this recognition became the lever of the Reformation as a spiritual movement. His thesis, which was set above all the other faith-perspectives, stated in negative terms reads thus: "the law is unable to show us the true God." The law is "The Jews' 'Sachsenspiegel' " (i.e., Code of the Saxons). It is "carnal law" which the Christians no longer need; in its place they have the royal code, the law of the emperor. The righteousness that comes from the law, even from its totality, is fictitious and servile. The entire sphere of the law as earthly is subordinate to the Christian, not he to it,[3] but as religious it belongs to a level or stage that has been superseded, and anyone who does not recognize this must remain a Jew. But since the law pervades the entire Old Testament, including the prophets, the entire book as a unity lies below the level of Christianity.

Agricola saw it even more clearly: he assessed the law as a failed attempt on God's part to lead mankind by means of threats. But can God make a mistake or fail?[4] From here it was hardly more than a step to the prudent explanation that Luther also actually gave with respect to the Alexandrian components of the Old Testament, that the Old Testament books are "good and useful to read," but they do not belong alongside the New Testament because they are not a canonical guide. What an unburdening of Christianity and its doctrine it would have been if Luther had taken this step! Would it have required any more Christian courage and boldness than the step that he took in relation to the sacraments in his writing "On the Babylonian Captivity of the Church," and was not his critical historical perception already awakened? Had not Luther himself, ever since the Leipzig debate and all the way down to his writing concerning the councils and churches, pronounced one critical judgment after another upon the church's historical tradition? And with respect to the Old Testament, were not all the premises at hand for finally withdrawing from it its *canonical recognition* in Christianity and assigning to it the *high historical position* that it deserves?

The premises were at hand, but their conclusions and consequences could not yet be drawn, for on this point tradition and custom were still even stronger than the just-dawning historical criticism the Bible was more firmly entrenched than the church's teaching, which was still dominated by allegorical interpretation, and the Psalms were as dear to Luther as were Paul's epistles—and even if he had had the courage and the strength to go counter to a mere tradition, still *on this point he was religiously restricted*. This was the decisive thing. While Agricola, like Marcion, preached that God's goodness alone achieves repentance and therewith proclaimed the superfluity of the law for the *ordo salutis*, Luther believed that the law was indispensable for the awakening of the conscience, and he also found other perspectives according to which the preaching of the law as the clear expression of God's holy will must not be allowed to cease. It is true that in taking this stand he came into conflict with concepts of faith that were precious to him, and this caused him great inward disquiet, but his conservative stance in relation to the Old Testament was firm. Hence the canonical authority of the Old Testament remained fateful for Protestant Christianity; the opposing powers were too weak, and the awareness that "the law is not able to show us the true God," when applied to the Old Testament, fell powerless to the ground. But still more must be said. Through the Reformation, biblicism, which even earlier was growing, received extraordinary strengthening, and this benefited the Old Testament, too. It is true that in the Lutheran territories its dubious effects were less strongly felt, but they were all the more powerful in the Anabaptist churches, in those churches formed by a mixture of Anabaptism and the Reformation, among which were the Calvinist churches. Here the Old Testament that was placed on a fully equal footing with the New Testament had an unhealthy effect on dogmatics, on piety, and on the practice of the Christian life. In some groups it even produced an Islamic zeal, while in others it called forth a new kind of Judaism and promoted everywhere a legalistic entity. The gradual disappearance of the allegorical method of exegesis worsened these effects, for it had in large measure rendered ineffective the most inferior and dubious features of the Old Testament. If Marcion had reappeared in the time of the Huguenots and Cromwell, he would once again have encountered the warlike God of Israel whom he abhorred, right in the very middle of Christendom. A reaction was bound to come, and it arose in the very same territories of that Christianity—Calvinist Christianity—in which the spirit of the Old Testament had so unthinkingly been granted room.

At the transition from the seventeenth to the eighteenth century, the question of the rightful place of the Old Testament in the church once again arose, first of all in the English Enlightenment, but this time it appeared as a *general* religious and historical question. Even where the question was answered in dependence upon Paul, his profound antinomianism did not enter into the issue. Thomas Morgan, following Tindal, went further than any others, and in the results of his historical and philosophical speculation he exhibits the most striking parallels to Marcion, though without actually being inwardly close to Marcion. Even the title of his famous dialogue between a Christian Deist and a Christian Jew (1737) has a Marcionite ring to it. The God of the Old Testament is pictured, approximately as Marcion had done, as a limited, petty, and contradictory national deity who also does immoral things; the Mosaic legislation is a wholly unsatisfactory, particularly limited and offensive work, a distortion of the *lex naturae*, very little different from the pagan religions. The nation of Israel, of bad character from the outset, runs aground on this law. Jesus brings the *lex naturae* that is clarified by means of revelation; Paul was his only true disciple; all the other apostles misunderstood Jesus and fell back into the Jewish way; along with them, the church also fell, and thus, even though some improvements through the influence of Paul were not lacking,[5] down to the present time it is halfway snared in Judaism. It is understandable that this interpretation, in spite of the fact that it contains a great deal that is correct and valuable, with all its audacious exaggerations could not make any impression upon the official churches. For the emergence of a universal and positive-critical philosophy of history it has become immeasurably significant.

Such a philosophy was developed in the early part of the nineteenth century on the basis, but also with sharp correction, of the religio-historical knowledge of the English Enlightenment. It received its meaning and significance for the nature and worth of the Christian religion from Schleiermacher and Hegel as well as from the entire company of thinkers who arose out of Pietism. As to form, the major result (besides the schooling in observation of reality in all its manifestations) was the recognition of *the immanence of ideas in actuality and of the development of truth in the course of history*. As to matter, one may, with regard to Christianity, consider the major result to have been *the recognition of the nature of its concept of God subspecie Christi*. On the historical-critical and religious grounds, then, it follows from this with inescapable necessity—particularly since the concept of inspiration in its old sense was dissolved—that any sort of equation of the Old Testament with the New Testament and any authority for the Old Testament in Christianity cannot be maintained. Schleiermacher, and others along with him, clearly recognized this: Marcion was given his due, though in part for another reason. For a hundred years the Protestant churches have known this, and according to their principles they have the obligation to acknowledge the consequence, that is, to place the Old Testament indeed at the head of the list of books "which are good and useful to be read" and to maintain in force the knowledge of those parts that are actually edifying but to leave the churches in no doubt about the fact that the Old Testament is *not* a canonical book. But these churches are crippled. They have not been able to create an instrument whereby they can free themselves from outdated traditions, and they do not find the strength or the courage to give to truth the place of honor. They have been fearful about a break with tradition, while they do not see, or else they wrongly estimate, the far more fateful consequences that will continue to develop more and more from the maintenance of the Old Testament as a sacred and therefore infallible document. Yet the greatest number of objections that "the people" raise against Christianity and against the truthfulness of the church arise out of the recognition that the church still accords to the Old Testament. To clear the table here and to give the place of honor in confession and instruction—that is the great deed that is being demanded today, already almost too late, of Protestantism. The objection offered by the know-it-alls and the crafty, wily ones, however, who say that the authority of the Old Testament is in fact dissolved by the destruction of the dogma of inspiration and that therefore one can leave both testaments undisturbed side by side, is only subterfuge. To be sure, the authority even of the New Testament has become something different from what it was, and this should be acknowledged unequivocally; but it still remains the *canon* for the church not for formal reasons and not with the formal authority of the letter—we now know how it came into being as a collection: Marcion laid the groundwork—but because it is not possible to create a better collection of documents for the definition of what is Christian. The Old Testament cannot be placed in this canon, for it is not possible to perceive from the Old Testament what is Christian. But the other two objections—that one must accord to the Old Testament its old position and esteem because Jesus recognized it as sacred Scripture and because it is the great document for the pre-history of Christianity—likewise must be denied any weight. For Jesus himself, in his most solemn saying to his disciples, said that thence forward all knowledge of God would come through him, and the scholarly point of view that would combine the documents of the pre-history of Christianity and Christianity's own documents *on the same plane* is not a religious perspective but a secular one.

Thus the question of the Old Testament, which Marcion once posed and answered, still today confronts and challenges Protestant Christianity. The rest of Christianity must ignore the question, for it is not in a position to give the correct answer. Protestantism, however, can do so, and it can do so all the more because the frightful dilemma under which Marcion once stood has long since been removed. He was obliged to *reject* the Old Testament as a false, anti-godly book in order to be able to preserve the gospel in its purity, but rejection is not in the picture today at all. Rather, this book will be everywhere esteemed and treasured in its distinctiveness and its significance (the prophets) only when the *canonical authority* to which it is not entitled is withdrawn from it.[6]

2. The Gospel of the Alien God and Pan-Christism

The Scriptures are to be understood in their literal sense. All allegorism is to be banned—the gospel stands on its own. It requires no attestation by external authorities and proofs from prophecy,[7] no foundation provided by philosophy, no transfiguration by means of an aesthetic perspective, and no enlivening by means of syncretism or by fanaticism, mysticism, and pneumatic perspective—such as "the Old Testament is the book of the less-worthy Jewish God." For an historical understanding of ecclesiastical Christianity with its legalism, one must refer back to the struggle between Paul and the Judaizing Christians. In order to insure the future of the essence of Christianity, there is needed over against the Old Testament and its modern writings a canonical collection of its genuine documents. This collection must be in two parts; that is, it must include Christ and Paul, for the latter, and only he, is the authentic interpreter of the former. The church is to be united and grounded in unity, not only in faith but in reality as well; not, however, upon any sort of philosophical dogmatics but upon the principles of faith and life found in the gospel. If Marcion had only implemented these affirmations and, as he did, powerfully represented them, that would have been enough to secure for him a unique and eminent place in church history as an equally sharp and profound spirit, equally realistic and religious.

Yet there is given in what he rejected and in what he demanded a wholly definite and characteristic type of the Christian religion, namely, a type in which the Christian religion is simply nothing but *faith* (in the sense of *fides historica* and *fiducia*) *in God's revelation in Christ*. Since in this context there is no recourse to any religious system (in the sense of the prologue to Augustine's *Confessions*), and man thus is in relation to the (alien) message of salvation "a stock or a stone," *Luther's concept of faith actually is the one that stands nearest to the Marcionite concept as Neander has already seen*.

But Marcion went far beyond Luther, carrying to an extreme the contrast between the Savior God and the world, between the miracle of redemption and the human—even the loftiest human quality—and this is what constitutes his singular characteristic. He experienced the gospel—that is, Christ—in such a way that he simply condemned *every* religious revelation and awakening outside Christ as false and inimical.

From this he was obliged to draw the conclusion, which though wrenching was at the same time liberating in its simplicity, that made him the founder of a religion upon the soil of Christianity: the acknowledged God of this world is a reprehensible being, *but the gospel is the message of the alien God*; he calls us, not out of an alien existence in which we have gone astray and into our true home but out of the dreadful homeland to which we belong into a blessed alien land.

Only insofar as it is soteriologically oriented does this religious institution bear the stamp of its time.[8] Otherwise it is utterly un-Jewish and un-Hellenistic. Can there be anything more un-Hellenistic than this utter rejection of cosmology, metaphysics, and the aesthetic?[9] And when any harmonizing with the higher levels of humanity, with the inspired, the prophetic, and the speculative, is just as stoutly excluded as a harmonizing with moralism, legalism, and the merely authoritarian—what a reversal of values and what a dissolution of culture must be the consequence! In the new light of the gospel Marcion proclaimed to the entire ancient world and its glittering ideals the twilight of the gods: "Hold up to scorn those would-be gods; a new Lord is now our God!"[10]

In order fully to understand Marcion, one must attempt to dismantle the scaffolding that belongs to the history of those times. This can be done without modernizing him in any respect. In the following this attempt is undertaken:

In this evil world to which we belong and in ourselves, two realms are intertwined: one of them is the realm of matter and of flesh and the other is that of "spirit," of morality and righteousness. They are joined and intertwined even though they stand in opposition to each other. This very fact points back to the lamentable weakness of the one who is responsible for this creation: He, although "spirit" and a moral power, was unable to create anything better than this abominable world, for the forming of which he had to take the materials from the "matter" which he abhorred as evil. Man stands in this world; coming into being out of fleshly lust and of unutterably base copulation, burdened with a body and chained to it, he is dragged down by it into the natural drives, and the great mass of humanity conduct themselves in all sorts of shameful behavior and vice, living in animal self-centeredness, wickedly, shamelessly, and as "heathen." The God who created them does not will them to be as they are. He wants them to be "righteous," and he planted in them a sense of what is righteous and good and seeks to lead them to this. But what is this "righteous and good," and what is the highest ideal? And how does he lead them? One can read the answer to these questions from "the world" and history, from "the law" and morality themselves, for "the world" and "the law" are in fact nothing other than the God of this world and the God of the law.[11]

The objective state of things therefore exhibits a contradictory interweaving that holds up to derision any attempted justification. On the one hand one sees a stringent and painstaking righteousness that strives to prevail in the physical and the moral realms; it works with prohibitions, rewards, and punishments, and strives thus to overcome what is natural and common; one perceives the spirit of the Ten Commandments, of authority, of demand for obedience, of the slavishly "good," and of an irksome, purportedly moral world order. But this "righteous" cluster is so inextricably bound up with senselessness, harshness, and cruelty, and again with frailty, weakness, and pettiness, that it all becomes a miserable spectacle. And even this does not tell the worst about it: This righteousness itself is most profoundly immoral, and that precisely where it appears the purest and has more or less brought what is natural under control; for it is devoid of love, it places everything under constraint, precisely thereby it lures one to sin, and *it does not provide a way out of the world*.

This God (that is, this world) is the fate and destiny of man. Man is left with only a fearful choice: either he withholds his obedience from his creator through libertinism, shameful behavior, and vice, and thereupon as a runaway slave falls victim to the creator's wrath and judgment—this is the lot of the great majority—or he follows him and his capricious will with slavish obedience and becomes a righteousness-, law-, and culture-man. Then he does indeed overcome what is base and common, but things become worse with him, for in principle the evil is not the enemy of the good—they are not commensurable, and evil is capable of being remedied. What is the enemy of the good is that compulsory, acquired, and self-satisfied "righteousness" that knows no more of love than it knows of exaltation into the supraterrestrial realm and that oscillates between fear and a haughtily virtuous behavior, never arriving at genuine freedom.

That is the fearful tragedy of human destiny. The virtues of man are not splendid vices, but they render one hopelessly insensitive to the higher. How much more deeply Marcion saw into human characteristics than did the average Christian of his day:[12] the means of salvation that was offered, the heteronomous law, is worse in its effect—so he taught—than the basic evil itself! It is true that it sets one free from this evil, but it brings on a worse evil, the hardening of one in self-righteousness and incurable mediocrity. Therefore, away with any theodicy, and away with any teleological cosmology; there is nothing about this world, together with its ideals and its God, that is worthy of justifying, and its "righteous ones" are slaves! Here not only is it proper to say, "I will bid you farewell, you wretched, false world," but equally proper is a holy pride toward the "heavenly powers" that bring one into this life, cause him to become guilty, and rule him with their outrageous "righteousness"—one should feel a rejection, even to the point of physical revulsion, toward all that the masses call "God" and that really is "world."[13]

But to feel this revulsion is possible only for one for whom the "Wholly Other," the "Alien," has become manifest—manifest as *the power of love*, and not only as something subjectively but *also as objectively new*. Here even those who, like Paul and his disciples, have spoken in moving confessions of the "new creature" and the "new condition of the soul" remain far behind Marcion,[14] for they have thought only of a *new kind* of revelation of God, but such a half-hearted idea with reference to God was an abomination to Marcion. Hence he proclaimed the *Alien* God with an entirely new "dispositio." He had experienced this God in Christ and only in him; therefore *he elevated the historical realism of the Christian experience to the level of the transcendent* and caught sight, beyond the dark and gloomy sphere of the world and its creator, of the sphere of a new reality, that is, of a new deity.[15]

That new reality is *love*, and nothing but love; absolutely no other feature is intermingled with this. And it is *incomprehensible* love, for out of pure mercy it accepts an entity wholly foreign to itself and, *by driving out fear*, brings to it the new, eternal life. Now there is something in this world that is not of this world and is superior to it! It is proclaimed and imparted by the gospel as an incomprehensible gift: "O miracle of miracles, rapture, marvel, and wonder, that one cannot say anything at all about the gospel, nor think of it, nor compare it with anything!" It is only received in humble faith by the poor and by those who hunger and thirst.

In the idea that God is nothing but love, the concept of God is at once brought to the loftiest and the most unequivocal formulation. One must indeed ask whether the Holy as the *mysterium fascinosum et tremendum* can exist where the "wrath" of God is rejected, where there can be no more "fear," where the praise that "the heavens declare the glory of God" falls silent, and where love is not bound up with any law. But only a glance at the words of Marcion quoted above ("O miracle of miracles" and so on) is required in order to recognize that for this man the exalted and the mysterious, the great and the holy of religion actually are all included in *love*; for to him this love was incomprehensible, *almighty* love. It is true that at present this alien God, who deeply stirs one's innermost being, "cannot move anything outwardly." Therefore, his believers must still endure this dreadful world as miserable and hated people, but in Christ this world is already overcome, and at the end of the world's course it will be demonstrated that the one who is in us now is greater than the one who

is in the world. The world, together with its righteousness, its civilization, and
its God, will pass away, but the new kingdom of love will abide. And in the certainty that nothing can separate us from the love of God that has appeared in
Christ, the wretched and despised ones are also, even now, the triumphant ones.
Ruled by the spirit of love and bound together in a bond of brotherhood in the
holy church, even now they are already exalted above the sufferings of this age.
They have patience, and they can wait.

But all of this is no pale and subtle speculation concocted out of the pride
of doubt concerning the world but it is rather *Christian* experience, for in the
person of Christ this new reality is a bodily reality. It is experienced in him.
Love is He, and He is Love; he is compassion, and he is the manifestation of
the supraterrestrial God and of the supraterrestrial life. The kingdom of the
Good and of Love is Pan-Christism. Through Christ and only through him is
the transmutation of values achieved. Of course, he too rejects that which is
common and base in its very nature, the mind of the flesh, just as the creator
of the world does — *this moral disdain is always self-explanatory* — but it is only
the sinners that he is able to redeem; for those who have fled from sin into the
"righteousness" of this world, into its law and its culture, are, as hardened
"righteous ones," no longer capable of redemption. Is this an exaggerated
assertion?

* * *

Was not Marcion right in his relationship to Christianity at large, both then
and in the present time? Does he not provide the final consistent link in the
chain that is characterized by the prophets, Jesus, and Paul in spite of the great
differences? Is the paradoxical distinction between the prophets and Jesus then
somewhat reduced when Jesus indeed confirms and affirms the prophets but
declares, "No one knows the Father but the Son"? and again, is the paradoxical
distinction between Jesus and Paul lessened when Paul indeed proposes in every
respect to maintain the Lord's word, but against this word describes him as the
end of the law and develops an antinomian concept of faith that is not actually
covered by any single saying of Jesus? Further, is there a rational theodicy that
does not expose itself to ridicule? Is it not always a failed undertaking when one
strives to harmonize the essence and nature of faith, its ground and its hope,
with the "world" — that is, to comprehend faith from the perspective of reason
and of the course of the world? And is it not true that the spirit only becomes
spirit, the soul becomes soul, and freedom becomes freedom, when that incomprehensible love which is not of this world is given to them? And are
"righteousness," morality, and civilization actual means of salvation for the man
who is bound to the senses? Are they not palliatives that ultimately make evil
still worse when the selfless, higher will to love is lacking? Do "the starry
heavens above and the moral law within" actually engender the turn to the

aeterna veritas and *vera aeternitas* that is given in love for God and for one's brothers, or are they not powers that fail in any great test? Are there not actually three kingdoms, two of which are inextricably interwined in spite of their contradictions, and only the third represents a new sphere? And is not Christ—what actually does the living man have to do with the question of the Absolute?—the initiator and the perfecter of the new and liberating power of God?

In all these questions, which are not here arbitrarily attributed to Marcion but in which his faith lived, his decision is clear. The Christian and the philosopher of religion, however, still may consider the following:

Marcion proclaimed with a splendid assurance that *the loving will of Jesus (and, that is, of God) does not judge, but comes to our aid,* and he intends that nothing else at all is to be said of him. Moreover, he so fully relied upon this gospel that he excluded the motive of fear in any sense, and therefore even in connection with sin he admitted only the one motive: "Absit, absit." That is to say, the only turning away from sin is that turning away from it that arises out of abhorrence for it. It is no sophism when he explains that at the end God will not judge, and yet he concedes that the great mass of humanity will not be redeemed; for, as he expresses it, they are removed from the sight of God because they have already definitively removed themselves from him. For the rest, here as on other points of his discussion of the world and religion he comes very close to a healthy agnosticism. In fact, it is correct also to say that in principle he has no fundamental teaching—he must have left such matters free, as is shown by the various schools that he admitted (see above). Instead, the highly diverse fashion in which he treats the good God, the creator of the world, and matter shows that his placing them alongside each other was not intended to mean and cannot mean that they are similar entities in any formal sense. His thoughts must be interpreted to mean that in his reflections upon sensuality, the world (as cosmos and law), and pure love, he arrived at the ultimate, irreducible, and irreconcilable entities, consistently stopped with them, and described their realms by means of the integrals—Matter, World-Creator (Lawgiver), and "Alien God."[16]

All this is thought out in such pure terms and—precisely because further speculations are excluded (although Apelles differed here)—is so free of contradictions that one finds intellectual delight in his ideas which disarm dozens of objections to which the church's teaching is exposed. Moreover, it may be noted in passing that his way of proclaiming the gospel remarkably addresses the needs of the present day, perhaps for the very reason that the circumstances of his time are akin to those of our time. Those who are most profoundly acquainted with the soul of the people, as that soul resides today in those who hold ecclesiastical Christianity in contempt, assure us that only the proclamation of hopeful, nonjudgmental love now has any prospect of being heard. Here Tolstoy sides with Marcion, as does Gorky. The former is a Marcionite Christian through and through. He too could have written what we have by way of direct religious utterances of Marcion. Conversely, Marcion would have recognized himself in Tolstoy's "wretched and despised ones," in the latter's exposition of the Sermon on the Mount (which for Marcion also "were the thoughts of Jesus in which he expressed the distinctiveness of his teaching"), and in his zeal against common Christianity. Gorky's gripping piece, *The Lower Depths*, can simply be described as a Marcionite play, for "the Alien" who appears here is the Marcionite Christ, and his "lower depths" are the world.

This much is certain—that in church history and in the philosophy of religion the Marcionite gospel has hardly ever again been proclaimed, or at least as a rule has not been the result of a deeper and richer religious experience, but rather a sign of religious dullness and stagnant dependence upon tradition. It is true that flashes of Marcionite summer lightning flash through the entire history of the church and of dogma, from Augustine's sense of grace and freedom onward; it is not difficult to see Marcionite teaching underlying the theoretical interpretation of that Augustinian sense, but that still can only be called another flash of that summer lightning. There is only one religio-philosophical work that is strictly Marcionite, even though Marcion's name is not cited in it: I refer to *Das Evangelium der armen Seele* (*The Gospel of the Poor Soul*, with a foreword by H. Lotze, 1871).[17] The anonymous author (Julius Baumann), however, did not undertake his task in strictly scientific fashion, and he wrote in a broad and diffuse style. Thus, his highly noteworthy book fell to the ground without any long-lasting effect. In the present day it should be taken up again, for the Marcionitism that it represents has something more profound to say than the phenomena of the philosophy of "As If" and of agnosticism.

For both the philosophy of religion and Christian dogmatics the serious question is raised whether Marcionitism as it must be understood today—how readily can its time-bound trappings be laid aside!—is not actually the sought-for solution of the greatest problem, namely, whether the line of "the prophets, Jesus, and Paul" is not appropriately continued only in Marcion. Equally serious is the question whether the philosophy of religion must not sense itself compelled to recognize as the last word the antithesis of "grace" (the new spirit and freedom) versus the world (including conventional morality). What objection can be raised against Marcion? To give an exhaustive answer here, which in the final analysis could only be a negative one but would maintain the major motifs of Marcion, would mean opening up the entire range of questions of the philosophy of religion; hence, I shall restrict myself to a few statements:

First of all, there is something expressionistic in the Marcionite discussion of God and the world; one could even say that there is a certain avoidance of thinking. For a keen thinker, in antiquity and in the present time, it must be difficult to be comfortable with this. Moreover, there is the threat that this interpetation of the actual leads to mythology, for it is characteristic of our thinking that as thinking persons we can be monists or pluralists, but not dualists, without becoming mythologues, that is, without losing ourselves in fantasies. Hence, one cannot help regarding the emphatic judgment upon the world, in spite of the justifiable distaste for the way of the world, as somewhat audacious. Is it man's task to pronounce condemnation upon the whole of reality in nature and history insofar as it is not a matter of grace and freedom? And are "morality" and freedom in the good that is bestowed really to be understood only as opposites and not as stages as well? Moreover, it is true that Marcion cannot be accused of recognizing no such thing as providence—he denies it only in connection with the course of the world but nevertheless is sure that nothing can separate the redeemed person from the love of God, and therefore he calls for an unshakable patience. However, he severely restricts the life of piety when that piety may no longer regard the cross and suffering as provisions of the same God who bestows salvation. Further, is it not a mistaken kind of inwardness, and indeed lovelessness, when one demands that the entire world be abandoned as incapable of salvation, limits oneself to the *preaching* of the gospel, and strives for nothing more in *works and deeds*?[18] Does not all activity presuppose the possibility of reform of the actual state of things and thus something originally good in it? And ultimately all of this has still another connection: A view of God and the world that, when it draws up the balance sheet, must carry asceticism so far as to forbid propagation of the human race cannot be right, for it would take away the basic presupposition of all positive thinking, namely, that life itself must somehow be valuable. And if love not only bears all things but also *hopes* all things, may one surrender the hope that its mystery and its power, even against all appearance, embrace from the very foundations even the world and its history, with their wretchedness and their sin, with the aim of reforming them in a better character?

This may signify the most important objection that one must maintain in opposition to Marcion. He might indeed have had something to say in response to all this, but I doubt whether it would have been persuasive. The church's teaching, along with its Old Testament, of course is far from being redeemed by this objection, but this does reclaim the first article of the church's faith, which was rejected by all Marcionites: "I believe in God the Father Almighty." Nevertheless, one can only wish that in the chaotic chorus of those who seek after God even Marcionites might once again be found today, for "it is easier for truth to be brought out of error than out of confusion!"

NOTES

I. INTRODUCTION

1. On these, see the penetrating analysis by Norden (*Agnostos Theos*, 1913, pp. 1ff.).

2. It is noteworthy, however, that Marcion's greatest opponent, Tertullian, once (in *Apol.* 1) voiced a sentiment concerning "the truth" similar to that expressed by Marcion concerning God: "The truth knows that she is but a sojourner on the earth, and that among strangers she naturally finds foes; and more than this, that her origin, her dwelling-place, her hope, her recompense, and her honors are above" (ANF III, 17). Though the connection is also tenuous, one may recall here the line by Goethe: "Every idea makes its appearance as an *alien* guest."

3. Since one's view can be distorted by a wide variety of speculative myths used by the Gnostics, what is overlooked is that Gnosticism represents, negatively, the rejection of late Jewish syncretism of disparate religious motifs and, positively, the attempt to work out one *clear* religious motif on the basis of the Christian kerygma. The myths were used only to provide a foundation for a basically religious faith, in the belief that one could see in them the philosophical and historical expression of the main theological idea intended.

4. The "Apologists" must be excluded here because it is characteristic of them that their attempts at systematization, though underlying the efforts of the old catholic fathers, merely served the defense of the Christian religion and the task of missions and did not proceed from the inner urge to get a grasp on the religion intellectually. So far as such an intention *is* discernible in them, it fell short of the Gnostics in depth of insight into the essence of the religion. Perhaps we would take a different view of this in the case of Justin Martyr, however, if we had his lost works in our possession.

II. MARCION'S LIFE AND CAREER

1. On this see Appendix I, "Investigations into the Person and Life History of Marcion."

2. Tertullian knew only about Pontus, not Sinope. In their frugality Marcion and Diogenes were two of a kind. The opponents of the latter called him "the mad Socrates"; those ill-disposed toward the former could say something similar about his relation to Paul.

3. That both Aquilas were from Pontus seems to me beyond suspicion (contra Schuerer, *A History of the Jewish People*, III, 169). One may let it stand that Sinope was the home town of the Bible translator, even if other statements by Epiphanius (Aquila a relative of Hadrian, first a Christian, excommunicated as an astrologer, then a Jew) must remain doubtful.

4. According to Epiphanius (loc. cit., 17f.; cf. *Chron. Pasch.* I, 491), the other Jewish Bible translator, Theodotian, is also supposed to have come from Pontus—from Sinope, in fact. Originally a Marcionite, he was converted to Judaism and was active during the reign of Commodus. So far as one is able to test them, however, Epiphanius' statements do not hold up. According to Irenaeus (loc. cit.), Theodotion was an Ephesian and, like Aquila, a proselyte. Strong objections can be raised also against Epiphanius' chronology.

5. He is familiar with their contemporary interpretations, takes the entire Old Testament as *real* history, and trusts its literal meaning. Which Gnostics, which doctors of the church normally did that? The former make distinctions or take the Old Testament as lies or as fraud; the latter

allegorize. Marcion, however, sides with the Jews! One recalls here that Tertullian's polemic against Marcion is, to a large extent, virtually identical to his polemic against the Jews.

6. See Wilcken in *Hermes*, 49 (1914), 120ff.

7. Even if the anecdote were sufficiently documented, it would be questionable to consider the story likely on the grounds that the strict sexual asceticism demanded by Marcion later on could be understood as a resentment of his past.

8. We know nothing about his education, but his work in textual criticism shows that he was an educated man and thus possessed at least the usual philosophical knowledge. His strong aversion to philosophy (see below) does not contradict this. "A man glowing with genius and most learned" is what Jerome called him, certainly echoing Origen (Jerome refers to a tradition), *Comm. in Osee*, Book II on 10:1. That the church fathers claim every possible important Greek philosopher as his teacher is not of concern here. But a man whom Origen called "most learned" must, first of all, have been well informed about the Bible, and, second, have also possessed a good secular education.

9. Perhaps Marcion's trip to Rome was also determined by the consideration that there the church's break with Judaism was more complete than in Asia. People did not fast on the Sabbath or celebrate the Passover together with the Jews. Marcion could hope to find more favorable soil for his teaching there.

10. Tertullian repeatedly uses Marcion's secular profession to ridicule him.

11. He did become angry with the original apostles and Judaistic evangelists but looked upon the great church of his day as the victim of a seduction.

12. Marcion did not speak to the Romans about the Gods of Light and of Darkness, about the opposition between spirit and matter, or anything similar, but about the opposition between the Old Testament and the Gospel, which demanded the acceptance of two Gods.

13. The letter could, however, also belong to a much later time.

14. Like the wicked legend of his seduction of a virgin, it likely represents the kind of polemical-confessional material still in vogue today.

15. See Appendix II, "Cerdo and Marcion."

16. Next to nothing is known about Cerdo's personal relationships. As far as the presuppositions of his doctrine are concerned, Irenaeus connects him with the Simonians ("from the followers of Simon," *Adv. haer.* I 27, ANF I, 352), which tells us nothing, and identifies Marcion as his successor. Hippolytus calls him Marcion's teacher and says that he came to Rome from Syria. Epiphanius links him, among others, with Saturninus, of whom he does, in fact, seem to have been an adherent. But Irenaeus states on the basis of good information that Cerdo, like Valentinus, came to Rome during the time of Bishop Hyginus and that his (negative) relationship to the church only gradually became clear (he "entered the Church . . . and made confession, and continued in this way, now teaching in secret, now making confession again, and now denounced for corrupt doctrine and withdrawing from the assembly of the brethren." Eus., HE IV 11, NPNF[2]I, 183). This is the most valuable information we possess with respect to the difficulties in the pre-catholic era concerning the removal of heretics, and it also sheds light on Marcion's relationship to the church until the definitive break occurred in Rome. Both heretics, apparently, wished to remain in the great church.

III. MARCION'S POINT OF DEPARTURE

1. For a certain qualification that holds true here — since the moral law is valid in relation to the carnal man — see our later discussion.

2. To the question, from what has Christ freed us? — from demons, from death, from sin, from guilt, from the flesh (all of these answers can be found already very early) — Marcion gives a radical answer: He has redeemed us from the *creation* (and thus from ourselves) *and from its God*, in order to make us children of a new and alien God.

3. Marcion was, to our knowledge, the first to call a *book* "the Gospel" and to identify a book with the gospel. Before Marcion, the gospel was seen as a message, which, along with other things, was recorded in books.

IV. THE CRITIC AND RESTORER: MARCION'S BIBLE

1. One has to conclude from this fact that already around the year 140 there were no more reliable sources for geniune historical knowledge of early Christianity than we have today, even in the main centers of Christendom. People will continue to wonder and investigate whether Marcion's critique of the apostles' relation to Paul was not determined by a living, albeit tendentious, tradition. But all such studies surely will lead to a negative conclusion. His critique was purely a material and linguistic one, lacking any historical basis.

2. On this, cf. Tert. *De praescr.* 22f. (ANF III, 253f): "Now, with the view of branding the apostles with some *mark of ignorance*, they put forth the case of Peter and them that were with him having been rebuked by Paul. 'Something, therefore,' they say, "*was wanting in them*' 'Paul added yet another form of the gospel besides that which Peter and the rest had previously set forth' . . . for the set purpose of bringing the earlier doctrine *into suspicion*."

3. Considering his low opinion of the original apostles, Marcion could have had no basis for denying that Matthew and John wrote the Gospels that bear their names. Nevertheless, his negative judgment about the authors of these Gospels is not without value even today and may not be overlooked.

4. Marcion does not explicitly say that this is true also of Mark, but when he considers the names of the other three authors to be falsifications, Mark is never mentioned as an exception.

5. On Marcion's handling of and dispute with the other gospels, see Appendix IV, C, 2. It is certain that he expressly attacked the saying, "I have not come to destroy but to fulfill," and thus was familiar with the Gospel of Matthew.

6. See Iren. III 14.3 (ANF I, 439): " . . . for, curtailing [the Gospel] according to Luke . . . they boast in having the Gospel [in what remains]." Tert. IV 2 (ANF III, 347): "Of the author whom we possess, Marcion seems *to have singled out* Luke"; IV 4 (ANF III, 349): " . . . the Gospel, said to be Luke's which is current amongst us . . ., Marcion argues in his *Antitheses* was *interpolated by the defenders of Judaism*, for the purpose of a conglomeration with it of the law and the prophets . . ." Other witnesses also could be cited.

7. The forgery of an Epistle to the Laodiceans is quite another matter and does not lie in the critical line of the founder.

8. If Marcion had always proceeded consistently in his textual criticism, quite a few of the passages and verses passed over by Tertullian would *ex analogia* have to have been missing in the original canon. These conclusions are doubtful, however, since Marcion was not always consistent. This can be shown from a number of passages that are clearly unfavorable to him but that he leaves standing. Perhaps he had reserved to himself *curae repetitae* also.

9. Did he himself also make additions? Can they not all perhaps be credited to his disciples?

10. Not unimportant is the substitution of "who bought" for "who loved" in Galatians 2:20 and the placement of Peter before James in Galatians 2:9.

11. The addition of "as the temple for God and God for the temple" in I Corinthians 6:13 is not tendentious; its origin is puzzling. On the other hand, the addition of "and wisdom" after "power" in 1:18 is quite deliberate: "power" by itself does not seem a sufficient antithesis to "foolishness."

12. Here one could conclude that Marcion, like the Gnostics, regarded the human spirit as undefiled. But he probably substitutes "blood" for "spirit" because he was thinking about the received Spirit of God, who cannot be defiled.

13. In Galatians 3:11 Marcion leaves standing the words, "The just shall live by faith."

14. Tertullian remarks (IV 43, on Luke 24:38f.; ANF III, 422), "Now Marcion was unwilling to expunge from his Gospel some statements which even made against him—I suspect, on purpose, to have it in his power from the passages which he did not suppress, when he could have done so, either to deny that he had expunged anything, or else to justify his suppressions, if he made any. But he spares only such passages as he can subvert quite as well by explaining them away as by expunging them from the text." As the "I suspect" clearly shows, this is an insinuation. Quite correct, however, albeit sneering in tone, is the remark in V 4 (on Gal. 4:22ff.; ibid., 436): "But as in the case of thieves, something of the stolen goods is apt to drop by the way, as a clue to their detection, so, as it seems to me, it has happened to Marcion: the last mention of Abraham's name he has left untouched."

15. In Luke 4:16 Marcion has deleted "brought up" and "his," begins with "and coming," and, along with still other deletions, thus gives the sentence another meaning.

16. The most drastic is the deletion of the "in" in Ephesians 3:9. Cf. the same fatal deletion of "in" in Ephesians 2:15, as well as the serious deletions of "being made" and "as" in Philippians 2:7. The deletion of the "new" next to "convenant" in Luke 22:20 is also very significant, as are the deletions of "father" and "and earth" in Luke 10:21, "eternal" next to "life" in Luke 10:25 (however, it is left standing in 18:18), "of fellowship" in Galatians 2:9, and "in this" in Galatians 5:14.

17. It is reasonable to assume that all the additions originated in Marcion's disciples (see above), and grounds for this assumption can be provided. It cannot, however, be proven. It is also possible that several "additions" were pre-Marcionite.

18. On the addition in I Corinthians 6:13, see above.

19. No definite statements by Marcion exist concerning the grounds for proceeding as he does in his critique of individual passages from the Gospel or Apostles.

20. Marcion's restrictions on this basic assumption will be discussed later.

21. It is most critical and regrettable that there are a very great many passages where it is uncertain whether Marcion deleted them or they were overlooked by his adversaries. The older critics engaged in more or less extensive reflection on these instances in order to reach some decision, and even Zahn joined them, however cautiously. With very few exceptions I have stayed clear of these passages since they cannot contribute to any real expansion of our knowledge of Marcion's teaching. Judgments about these passages must be made on the basis of what is known, and given Marcion's notorious inconsistencies, such judgments can almost never be completely certain (see above).

22. With good reason Tertullian (III 5) upbraids Marcion for allegorizing, too, and for approving the allegories of Paul: "But why enlarge on such a subject? When the very apostle whom our heretics adopt, interprets the law which allows an unmuzzled mouth to the oxen that tread out the corn, not of cattle, but of ourselves (I Cor. 9:9f.); and also alleges that the rock which followed (the Israelites) and supplied them with drink was Christ (I Cor. 10:4); teaching the Galatians, moreover, that the two narratives of the sons of Abraham had an allegorical meaning in their course (Gal. 4:22ff.); and to the Ephesians giving an intimation that, when it was declared in the beginning that a man should leave his father and mother and become one flesh with his wife, he applied this to Christ and the Church (Eph. 5:31f.)" (ANF III, 324). Tertullian could have added that Marcion's *locus classicus* for the distinction between the two Gods ("the bad and the good tree") is based on an arbitrary allegorical interpretation of a parable.

23. There is a respect manifested in this attitude that is hardly understandable unless Marcion grew up with the Old Testament (see above). The influence of Jewish exegesis is likely.

24. The inner relationship between "John" and Marcion, so far as it existed, will be treated later.

25. See my essay, *Die Entstehung des Neuen Testaments,* Beitraege zur Einleitung in das Neuen Testament, sixth part. (1914).

26. My assumption that Tatian published his *Diatessaron* in Greek has not been shaken by the work of Plooij on the Dutch-Latin Tatian (1923). His evidence for the dependence of the German (Latin) *Diatessaron* on the Syriac is no more compelling than Harvey's earlier "evidence" for the

dependence of Irenaeus' biblical text on the Syrian. The use of microscopes in this area of tempting illusions can come to no good. Only carefully weighed evidence is of value and such evidence is lacking here.

27. I will not demonstrate once again that originally the selection and combination of the four Gospels could only have been for the purpose of fitting them together into a *single* work. The execution of this plan had to be abandoned by the leading churches (i.e., those leading the struggle against the heresies), since they soon had to place all their emphasis on possessing authentic writings by John and Matthew. In this way the texts of Mark and Luke were also saved.

V. MARCION'S *ANTITHESES*

1. The presumptuous title *Antitheses* — a rhetorical concept — is, to the best of my knowledge, unique in Greek literature. Apelles, Marcion's disciple, published a book under the title *Reckonings*, and Tatian, who was of a kindred mind with Marcion, published a work entitled *Problems*. One is reminded also of the work of Stephanus Gobarus and of Abelard's *Sic et Non*.

2. The only attempt — and an unsatisfactory one — to restore Marcion's *Antitheses* can be found in Hahn's *Antitheses Marcionis gnostici* (Koenigsberg, 1823).

3. Only Tertullian mentions also a letter by Marcion (see above, and Appendix I; on whether there were several letters, see below). Epiphanius, it is true, speaks (*Haer.* 42.9) of "constitutions" that Marcion wrote for those whom he had seduced, but that is merely an echo of the *Antitheses*. Irenaeus announces (I 27) that he will refute Marcion out of his own writings ("scriptis"), but that too does not take us beyond the *Antitheses*. Ephraem likewise speaks of Marcion's writings. Since he was familiar with the *Antitheses*, one must regard this as his reference. On Maruta's statements see, in connection with Marcion's *Apostolikon*, Appendix VI. An unknown early Syrian author (Schaefers, *Eine altsyrische, antimarcionitische Erklaerung von Parabeln des Herrn* usw., 1917, pp. 3f.) attributes to Marcion a writing entitled "Proevangelium," enlarges upon this title, and cites an encomium concerning the gospel from the beginning of this book. This citation fits perfectly as the beginning of the *Antitheses*; it may therefore be regarded as genuine. The name "Proevangelium," however, need not mean, as that author believed, that what follows in this book is earlier than the gospel; it can very well be understood as "introduction" to the gospel. In that case, one can without hesitation recognize in the "Proevangelium" the *Antitheses* which, as Tertullian notes, Marcion had attached to the gospel as a "dowry" and "protection." R. Harris ("Marcion's Book of Contradictions," *Bulletin of the John Rylands Library*, VI, 3, [1921], 289ff.) regards it as inconceivable that the encomium concerning the gospel stood at the beginning of the *Antitheses*. On the other hand, he does think it probable (following Tertullian I ?) that reflections on the origin of evil did stand there. However, if Tertullian had read an introduction or a foreword to the gospel that had been composed by Marcion, he would have dealt with it. And how would Marcion have dared to give an introduction to the gospel!

4. Tertullian I 19 (ANF III, 285): "Marcion's special and principal work is the separation of the law and the gospel; and his disciples will not deny that in this point they have their very best pretext for initiating and confirming themselves in his heresy. These are Marcion's *Antitheses*, or contradictory propositions, which aim at committing the gospel to a variance with the law, in order that from the diversity of the two documents which contain them, they may contend for a diversity of gods also." IV 6 (ANF III, 351): " . . . and challenge (as we promised to do) the very Gospel of Marcion, with the intention of thus proving that it has been adulterated. For it is certain that the whole aim at which he has strenuously laboured even in the drawing up of his *Antitheses* centres in this, that he may establish a diversity between the Old and New Testaments, so that his own Christ may be separate from the Creator, as belonging to this rival god, *and* as alien from the law and the prophets. It is certain, also, that with this view he has erased everything that was contrary to his own opinion and made for the Creator, as if it had been interpolated by His advocates, whilst

everything which agreed with his own opinion he has retained." IV 1 (ANF III, 345): "To encourage a belief *of this Gospel* he has actually devised for it a sort of dower, in a work composed of contrary statements set in opposition, then entitled *Antitheses*, and compiled with a view to such a severance of the law from the gospel as should divide the Deity into two, nay, diverse, gods—one for each Instrument, or Testament, as it is more usual to call it; that by such means he might also patronize belief in 'the Gospel according to the *Antitheses.*' These, however, I would have attacked in special combat, hand to hand; that is to say, I would have encountered singly the several devices of the Pontic heretic, if it were not much more convenient to refute them in and with that very gospel to which they contributed their support." IV 4 (ANF III, 349): "For if the Gospel, said to be Luke's which is current amongst us (we shall see whether it be also current with Marcion), is the very one which, as Marcion argues in his *Antitheses*, was interpolated by the defenders of Judaism, for the purposes of such a conglomeration with it of the law and the prophets as should enable them out of it to fashion their Christ, surely he could not have so argued about it, unless he had found it (in such a form)." II 29 (ANF III, 320): " . . . his *Antitheses*, which aim at drawing distinctions out of the qualities of the (Creator's) artifices, or of His laws, or of His great works; and thus sundering Christ from the Creator, as the most Good from the Judge, as One who is merciful from Him who is ruthless, and One who brings salvation from Him who causes ruin."

5. One observes here the expression "in summo instrumento." (*Instrumentum* can also mean Holy Scripture in Tertullian, but the *summum* weakens rather than strengthens the term here. For if the *Antitheses* had exactly the same authority for Marcion as the Gospel and apostolic writings, Tertullian would have written simply "in instrumento." One may presume, however, that Tertullian is slanting his report and exaggerating.) Cf. Tertullian IV 4 (ANF III, 349): "They, at any rate, receive his *Antitheses*; and more than that, they make ostentatious use of them."

6. Other testimony concerning the content and character of the *Antitheses* can be found in Tertullian II 28 (they contain a summary of the "weaknesses and malignities and the other [alleged] notes" of the World-Creator [ANF III, 319]); II 29 (after refuting individual antitheses in the first two books of his *Against Marcion*, Tertullian considers a "more elaborate demolition" unnecessary [ANF III, 320]); IV 9 ("We have indeed already laid it down, in opposition to his *Antitheses*, that the position of Marcion derives no advantage from the diversity which he supposes to exist between the Law and the Gospel, inasmuch as even this was ordained by the Creator" [ANF III, 355]); IV 36 (on Luke 18:42: "And so he will remain blind, falling into *Antithesis* after *Antithesis*. . ." [ANF III, 411]). The *Antitheses* acquired simply an important, not an inspired, authority in Marcion's church. According to Maruta, whose reference is perhaps not entirely correct, the work is supposed to have possessed canonical status as a "Summa" among the Marcionites. What they learned about the Old Testament, they learned from the negative references in Marcion's book.

7. "Contrasts" (Hippolytus, *Ref.* VII 30) is an allusion to the title. Cf. also the "e contrario opponentes" ["out of a totally different set of opinions"] of the Presbyter in Irenaeus I 28.1, referring to the Marcionites, and Origen, *Comm. V in Joh.*, p. 105: "If we were to remain silent, not contrasting."

8. Esnik's representation of Marcion's doctrine is based upon a later Marcionite writing; indirectly, it too would have been heavily influenced by the *Antitheses*.

9. Cf. Justin, *Apology, Address* (ANF I, 163). He says that he is espousing the cause of those "of all nations who are unjustly hated and wantonly abused." Their term "sharing in misery" can probably be explained from Romans 7:24.

10. In Tertullian IV 34 (ANF III, 404) there is a literally rendered commentary of Marcion's on Luke 16:18: "*You see*, therefore, that there is a difference between the law and the gospel—between Moses and Christ."

11. The Greek words that Tertullian quotes from the *Antitheses* indirectly confirm the observation that he had before him only a Latin version of Marcion's Bible, *for he never quotes from Marcion's Bible in Greek*. It is probable, though not completely certain, that the *Antitheses* were already translated into Latin also, considering the close relationship between them and Marcion's Bible.

Among the numerous citations from the *Antitheses* in all five of Tertullian's books, there is only *one* expression which might point to a Greek original (the designation of Christ as "the stranger" Tertullian IV 23,24). He need not necessarily have gotten it from the *Antitheses*, however; it could have come from a letter by Marcion and thus have had absolutely nothing to do with the *Antitheses*. Hilgenfeld (*Ketzergeschicht*, p. 525) even regards this as certain, inferring from *De carne Christi* 2 that Tertullian must have known several of Marcion's letters, since there he uses the expression "in quadam epistula" ["in a certain letter of yours"]. This argument is anything but certain, however. The assumption that Tertullian means the *Antitheses* there, is, in my judgment, much more likely.

12. From Tertullian IV 1 it might appear that by contrasting Old Testament and Gospel passages exclusively and in scrupulous fashion, the *Antitheses* served only to prove that the God of the Gospel is a new God, who stands in opposition to the God of the Old Testament. For Tertullian believes that the whole work is refuted by the bit of evidence he furnishes here that the Old Testament God himself announced a New Testament beforehand, that his creation is full of antitheses, and that one therefore may not infer a difference in Gods from the difference in words and deeds. He concludes his case with the sentence, "You have now our answer to the *Antitheses* compendiously indicated by us; I pass on to give a proof of the Gospel" (IV 2; ANF III, 347). But Tertullian could only have been thinking about the basic motifs of the work here, because in the following chapters he mentions numerous critical details and interpretations of Scripture that are found in the *Antitheses* but are not at all antitheses in the strict sense of the term and are only loosely connected with the main ideas.

13. Right before this quotation we read: "Marcion, finding the epistle of Paul to the Galatians (wherein he rebukes even apostles for 'not walking uprightly according to the truth of the gospel' [he thus applies the reprimand of Peter to all the apostles], as well as accuses certain false apostles of perverting the gospel of Christ) . . . " (ANF III, 348). One can hardly doubt, therefore, that in Galatians 1:2 Marcion was dealing with the whole question of the gospel.

14. There are two pieces of interrelated evidence for this: Tertullian, who in IV 1ff. proceeds to an examination of Marcion's Bible, turns *at the same time* to the *Antitheses* and immediately begins discussing (in sections 5 and 6) Marcion's attitude towards the apostolic age, the apostles, and the four Gospels in connection with Galatians 2. Maruta informs us, however, that the Marcionites replaced the Acts of the Apostles, which they rejected, with the "Summa," namely, the *Antitheses*.

That Marcion criticized the four-Gospel canon can be seen also in Irenaeus III 11.9 (ANF I, 429): "For Marcion, rejecting the entire Gospel, yea rather, cutting himself off from the Gospel, boasts that he has part in the [blessings] of the Gospel." Actually, the statements by Irenaeus taken directly from the Marcionite documents themselves also show that the *Antitheses* contained a critique of the first apostles and Gospel writers. See I 27.2 (ANF I, 352): "He likewise persuaded his disciples that he himself was more worthy of credit than are those apostles who have handed down the Gospel to us." III 2.2. (ANF I, 415): ". . . they object to tradition, saying that they themselves are wiser not merely than the presbyters, but even than the apostles, because they have discovered the unadulterated truth. For [they maintain] that the apostles intermingled the things of the law with the words of the Savior." III 12.12 (ANF I, 434): " . . . and [maintained] that the apostles preached the Gospel still somewhat under the influence of Jewish opinions, but that they themselves are purer [in doctrine], and more intelligent, than the apostles. Wherefore also Marcion and his followers have betaken themselves to mutilating the Scriptures, not acknowledging some books at all; and curtailing the Gospel according to Luke and the Epistles of Paul, they assert that these are alone authentic, which they have themselves thus shortened." III 13.1f. (ANF I, 436f.): ". . . who allege that Paul alone knew the truth and that to him the mystery was manifested by revelation . . . To allege, then, that these men [the apostles] did not know the truth . . ." The expression, "They boast that they have the Gospel," which Irenaeus uses twice with reference to the Marcionites (III 11, 14), presupposes a critique of other gospels, just as the other expression "peritiores apostolis" (IV 5 and elsewhere) presupposes a critique of the apostles. It is with respect to the drastic surgery that even the third Gospel required to make it fit the new doctrine that Tertullian's remark should be understood (IV 5; ANF III, 350): "Why did not Marcion touch [the Gospels of John and Matthew] — either to amend them if they were adulterated, or to acknowledge them if they were uncorrupt? . . . I will therefore advise his followers, that they either change these Gospels, however late to do so," etc.

15. Only in a few places can one question whether Tertullian is really reproducing Marcion's comments or putting words in his mouth. Tertullian is scrupulous in this regard. Cf. also his categorical remark in *De baptismo* 12 (ANF III, 675): "I have heard — the Lord is my witness — doubts of that kind: that none may imagine me so abandoned as to excogitate, unprovoked, in the license of my pen, ideas which would inspire others with scruple." If he does put words in Marcion's mouth, it is usually clear in itself, or else he inserts, as in II 17 (ANF III, 311), "You will perhaps say."

16. Above all, a critique of the story of the Fall.

17. The citations from the Gospel of John by the Marcionite Markus (in Adamantius) are not considered by Marcion himself.

18. It is noteworthy that Porphyry, too, began his extensive book on the Christians with a critique of the quarrel between Paul and the original apostles (Gal. 2). This can be found in Book I of the work (see my *Sammlung der Porphyrius-Fragmente*, No. 21, p. 53). Was Porphryry directly or indirectly familiar with the *Antitheses*?

19. From Origen's arguments with Marcion one gets the distinct impression that he had in front of him Marcion's explanations of a large number of biblical passages. Thus he can complain (*Comm. I 18 in Rom.*, Pt. VI, pp. 55ff., Lomm.) that the Marcionites have "not even lightly" ("ne extremo quidem digito") touched the difficulties found in Romans 1:24f. One could almost say that he had in front of him a part of the Marcionite Bible with commentary, but that is also the impression one gets from Tertullian's *Against Marcion* IV and V. One should consider these comments as similar in form to those in Bengel's *Gnomon*, not as running marginal notes on the New Testament but in the *Antitheses*.

20. It is not yet clear even in the work of the Presbyter cited by Irenaeus that both testaments were in *written* form.

21. A good overview of all the bad attributes of the World-Creator according to Marcion can be found in the pseudo-Clementine Homilies II 43.

22. The content of the *Antitheses*, therefore, corresponds exactly to the intentions that Marcion displays in his corrections of the gospel and the epistles of Paul. See above.

23. Tertullian used, in part literally, the same arguments against the Jews (*Adversus Judaeos*) as he does here against the Marcionites (*Against Marcion* III). Cf. III 8 (ANF III, 327): "Our heretic must now cease to borrow poison from the Jew."

24. For the fact that he did, however, make a certain distinction in the Old Testament, see below, Chapter VI, section 3.

25. Whether or not he valued some things in the Old Testament more highly, however, will be investigated later.

26. Supposedly, at the beginning of the *Antitheses* he commented on his hermeneutical principles and his rejection of the allegorical method.

27. Cf. Tertullian I 25 (ANF III, 291): " . . . what is happy and incorruptible can bring no trouble either on itself or anything else (for Marcion, while *pouring over* this opinion) . . ."

28. For the places where they are found, see Appendix V.

29. The antitheses of the Sermon on the Mount in Matthew 5 provide the nearest parallel to these. They too could have inspired Marcion, for although he did not accept the gospel of Matthew as valid, he was familiar with it.

VI. MARCION'S CHRISTIANITY AND HIS PREACHING

1. In so doing, it is not our intention to examine every particular; with reference to many of the details, it will suffice to have read them in the *Antitheses*.

2. Whether he harbored an *utter* antipathy to the latter will be examined later.

3. Some necessary exceptions will be found in what follows.

4. For the fact that the revelation of the redeemer-God as "the Alien" or the alien visitor contains a mystery that includes both remoteness and blessed closeness, see below.

5. See Tertullian, *De resurr.* 2 (ANF III, 546): ". . . under the pretence of considering a more urgent inquiry, namely man's own salvation—a question which transcends all others in its importance . . ."

6. "They call matter the power of the earth" (Esnik).

7. Cf. Tertullian, *Against Marcion* I 15 (ANF III, 282): "Then, inasmuch as He too has fabricated a world out of some underlying material which is unbegotten, and unmade, and contemporaneous with God . . . With this matter he further associates evil."

8. This assumption is further explained in Esnik (see Appendix VI), but it is highly unlikely that the mythological creation story, as he explains it, came from Marcion, since Marcion never went beyond the Bible in his treatment of "history." Furthermore, if Tertullian had read this mythological account in the *Antitheses* and had read there, among other things, that the World-Creator had stolen mankind from his partner, Matter, then he (Tertullian) would have severely taken his opponent to task.

9. The involvement of matter in creation pleased Marcion also because this doctrine taught that the World-Creator could not create out of nothing (unlike the other God). This indicates an interest that has nothing to do with the evil essence of matter.

10. Nothing is more certain than that Marcion, as a rule at least, did not speak of "principles" but of "gods," since he was a biblical thinker. Since the former term also appears (sparsely) in the tradition since Rhodon (in Eusebius, H. E. V 13), there is good reason to suppose that, since Apelles taught *one* ἀρχή, the two θεοί of his master were designated as two ἀρχαί by comparison. So far as we are able to determine, Marcion himself never referred to matter as θεός or even as ἀρχή, although he would have had to call it the latter.

11. It appears that Marcion did not identify the World-Creator with mammon, since the latter bears the predicate "unrighteous," but this is not altogether clear. Cf. Tertullian IV 33 on Luke 16:13, and Irenaeus III 8.1.

12. In the verse, "I put to death and I bring to life" (Deut. 32:39), which Marcion likes for its characterization of the World-Creator, the great inner contradiction of this God which determines all other contradictions manifests itself. Life, according to Marcion, cannot be genuine eternal life if its giver also kills. Hence love, grace, life, etc., are worthless in the World-Creator because they do not exclude anger and death.

13. Underlying this feeling there seems to have been a certain overwrought irritation on Marcion's part concerning life's vexatious troubles.

14. That is precisely why one may consider this God as the creator of the flesh and of its loathsome propagation only insofar as he in his weakness needed the assistance of matter and now must endure the fact that from this collaboration something dreadful has emerged. However, if one accepts here the influence of Syrian gnosis through Cerdo, it should be noted, on the other hand, that the terrible rage against the "flesh" leaves the impression of a resentment of a unique sort. Here again, therefore, a definitive judgment cannot be formed.

15. Thus, one can see the unique character of the World-Creator in mankind as well as in the world.

16. That according to Marcion God himself is the author of sin is a faulty conclusion drawn by Tertullian. Marcion expressly identifies the devil as the author, in addition to the evil constitution of mankind. See Appendix V.

17. The Jewish race is the worst. Nevertheless, Marcion left Luke 7:9 as it was ("Such faith I have not found in Israel"). "Why, however, might he not have used the example of faith in another god?" (Tertullian IV 18, ANF III, 374).

18. Marcion applies, as far as possible, the reproaches directed against the Jews in Romans 2:21f. to the God of the Jews himself, such as the reproach of theft (in the case of the Egyptians' gold and silver vessels). Again, the chosen people were authorized by their God to rob, deceive, and exterminate the heathen. In their doing so the moral commandments were not violated. Incidentally, compared with the World-Creator, Moses comes off as the better of the two (Tertullian II 25–28, ANF III, 318): "But (you say) God was even then mean enough in His very fierceness, when, in His wrath against the people for their consecration of the calf, He makes this request of His servant Moses: 'Let me alone, that my wrath may wax hot against them, and that I may consume them; and I will make of thee a great nation.' Accordingly *you maintain* that Moses is better than his God, as the deprecator, nay the averter, of His anger. 'For,' said he, 'thou shalt not do this; or else destroy me along with them.' "

19. In order to explain Marcion's remarkable attitude here, one may not work with the hypothesis that Marcion had not finished his critique of the text of Romans and might have had many corrections still to make. For it was this very epistle that, obviously, he had gone through with special care and had eliminated half the text.

20. Just as he distinguishes between "life" and "(eternal) life" and between Paradise and true blessedness.

21. From the numerous Pauline passages in which the law is mentioned and which Marcion retained (of course he deleted the statement in Galatians 4:4 that Jesus was subject to the law), mention should be made of the following, which further illustrate the fact that Marcion's position on the law was clear and unequivocal only in its main features and otherwise was quite complicated. First of all, he retained several references by Paul to the Old Testament: I Corinthians 9:8f. (here "according to the law" is set over against "according to men"); 14:19 (here Marcion's text is neither certain nor clear); 14:21 (here a promise of the law is applied to the new age, even though it was certainly interpreted differently by Marcion); 14:34 (here the prohibition against certain behavior by women in the assemblies is strengthened by the analogue in the Old Testament). Second, Romans 8:4 is retained, saying that the righteousness of the law has been fulfilled in the redeemed. Third, "law" is retained several times as the law of the good God. See Romans 8:2 ("the law of the Spirit of life"); 8:7 ("the mind of the flesh" versus "the law of God"); 13:9f. (Here are enumerated—and this is particularly important—only the commandments of the second table of the law, and then it is said that they are summarized in the commandment of love and that *therefore love is the fulfillment of the law*. There is therefore something unreprehensible in the law of the Creator-God, so that it can be recognized by the good God as his law. See also Gal. 5:4; this verse, which is likewise retained, says that the whole law is fulfilled in the commandment to love); and Galatians 6:2 ("the law of Christ," which in its content corresponds to the active love of one's neighbor that is also contained in the law of the World-Creator). On the other hand, after the words, "Honor your father and mother" in Ephesians 6:2, Marcion removed the Pauline addition, "which is the first commandment with promise," because this promise of a long life was offensive to him. Furthermore, it was certainly agreeable to him to avoid the explicit recollection of the law regarding an individual commandment.

From this (i.e., from the realization that Marcion discerns a dual goodness since he recognizes something of good even in the law) one first comprehends that he is saying of the Redeemer-God that he has redeemed mankind, not "by his goodness," but "by his *supreme and most excellent goodness*" (Tertullian I 17, ANF III, 283; cf. I 23, ANF III, 288: "a *primary and perfect goodness*").

22. Thus according to Tertullian. According to Epiphanius, the Marcionites read the canonical text here. Zahn (see Appendix IV) denies that Tertullian had a different reading from that of Epiphanius here.

23. This corresponds to the retention of the Pauline passages Galatians 5:4 and Romans 13:9, both of which say that love is the fulfillment of the law (see above, note 21). Marcion explains the aforementioned passage in such a way that he has Christ answer the question in the way it was posed by the questioner, who only wished to know the right way to inherit a long earthly life; but Christ inserted, for those who understood him, the thought, "Out of love for God we shall inherit eternal life."

24. Instructive in this connection is Marcion's antithesis concerning marriage, which he completely rules out for Christians. Christ forbade divorce; Moses, however, is chided by Marcion because he permitted it (see Tertullian IV 34 on Luke 16:18 and V 7 on I Corinthians 7:1ff.). According to Marcion, therefore, a marriage is supposed to be indissoluble once it is contracted; that is, he recognizes a conditional right of marriage.

25. Especially welcome is the explicit confirmation provided by Esnik's report (see Appendix VI) that true righteousness is found in the "alien" God. Jesus says to the "just" God: "I am rightly more just than you and have done great things for your creatures."

26. I Corinthians 1:30 (Christ being made our righteousness) appears to have been missing in Marcion's Bible, Adamantius notwithstanding. In Luke 14:14 Marcion probably left out "of the just" after "at the resurrection." In Romans 1:17 he deleted, "Just as it is written, 'The righteous shall live by faith,'" but only because the saying was introduced as the word of Scripture; in Galatians 3:11 he freely allowed the apostle to write, "You know that the righteous will live by faith." It is true that in Romans 10:3 he replaced "disregarding the righteousness which is from God" with the words "disregarding God," but he quietly retained, "they did not submit to the righteousness of God."

Anyone who objects that the Marcionite dialectic in these major ethical concepts ("just," "good," etc.) is unbelievable for that time has forgotten the statements of the Valentinian Ptolemaeus (Epistle to Flora, c. 5 in Epiphanius, Haer. 31.7), which contain precisely the same dialectic (independent of Marcion? Hardly): "If the perfect God is good in his very nature, as he then indeed is—for our Savior said about his Father, whom he revealed, that he alone is the good God—and if, furthermore, the wicked and evil one, afflicted with the nature of the adversary, is characterized by unrighteousness, then he who stands as the middle one between them and is neither good nor evil nor unjust, might, in a special sense, be called 'just,' as he is the leader in righteousness as he understands it. This God, then, will be lower than the perfect God and inferior to his righteousness." The highest God is therefore good and just, and the World-Creator has a righteousness as he understands it.

27. Therefore, Marcion could not leave Luke 10:24 standing: "The prophets wanted to see that which you see." Thus he wrote, "they have not seen what you see." He also had to remove the passages that said that the Father of Jesus Christ sent the prophets (Luke 11:49, etc.), that everything written by the prophets would be fulfilled (Luke 18:31), and that it was a hardening of the heart to refuse to believe the word of the prophets (in Luke 24:25 he substitutes "word of the Lord" for "word of the prophets").

28. It is certain that he allowed this verse to stand.

29. The expressions "the writing" and "the writings" are nowhere to be found in Marcion's New Testament. He removed "it is written" from several passages; see Romans 1:17; 12:19; II Corinthians 4:14; probably also 2:24 and I Corinthians 15:45, etc.

30. Zahn is doubtful, but according to Tertullian V 7 (see also III 5) it cannot be in doubt.

31. This and the preservation of the whole of Ephesians 5:22–32, to which Marcion for the most part must have been very unsympathetic, is most striking. On the probable motive for the retention, see Chapter VII.

32. One should also compare such passages as Luke 12:27 (Solomon) and 13:16 (the daughter of Abraham), etc.

33. For details see Appendix V. According to Marcion, a number of "messianic" prophecies were not messianic at all but were fulfilled already in David, Solomon, Hezekiah, etc. The main points of this messianic teaching were as follows: (1) The Messiah will be a pure man from the

house of David; (2) He is intended only for the Jewish people in order to lead them back from the dispersion; his appearing will benefit only such Gentiles as become proselytes; (3) When he appears, the rich and the nations will revolt against him, but he will defeat them and will rule the nations with a rod of iron, for he will be a "military and armed warrior"; (4) He has not yet appeared; this is shown by the details of Isaiah's prophecy about him that have not yet been fulfilled, as well as by the rich of the world who still exist at the present time. – The Christ of the good God explicitly warned about him (Tertullian IV 38 on Luke 21:8).

34. Apart from the great contradictions in the very nature of the World-Creator, which prompted him to give contradictory orders and laws, it is very definitely the "petty things" (*pusillitates*) in his nature (hence also in the nature of the world) that give Marcion special offense. He must have been a broadminded person in nature but along with that, as we have noted, extremely irritable about the disagreeable and petty things of life and the world. In addition, there was his strong abhorrence of bloodshed and war. He was, one would say today, a pacifist, and the Old Testament was an embarrassing book for him above all because of its bellicose spirit. Finally, the predilection of this God for the Jews was incomprehensible and repulsive to him, since this people was, according to its own sacred book, especially wicked.

35. Tertullian I 23 (ANF III, 288): "[Marcion's God] proceeded to the salvation of a human creature which was alien to him . . . That is rather a primary and perfect goodness, which is shed voluntarily and freely upon strangers *without any obligation of friendship*, on the principle that we are bidden to love even our enemies, such as are also on that very account strangers to us." Irenaeus III 11.2 (ANF I, 426): " . . . nor did [Christ] come to His own things, but to those of another."

36. " . . . [the God] who is beyond all principality, and beginning and power" must have been a solemn designation of Marcion's for this God, for Irenaeus refers to it (III 7.1, ANF I, 420) and, according to Tertullian, Marcion inserted in Galatians 4:26 the words: "This other [scil., divine administration] is above every beginning and power and principality." Irenaeus probably was familiar with this Marcionite text. It also follows from the full deity of this God that he was "tranquillus," imperturbable, etc. This is why Marcion's opponents ascribed to him the Stoics' conception of God. Marcion also emphasized the "patience" of this God, which explained for him, among other things, why this God had allowed the World-Creator to govern for so long (Tertullian IV 38; Celsus in Origen VI 52). On the other hand, it is advanced as a weakness in this God that he allowed the devil, etc., to exist.

37. The documentation for these statements can be found in Appendix V.

38. Although in the arguments of Porphyry against John 12:31 (Fragment 72, p. 90, of my edition) among other things the following sentences are found: "What is the reason for the prince being cast outside as a stranger to the world? And how did he rule if he was a stranger?" – this has nothing in common with Marcion's ideas.

39. Here one clearly sees in what sense the World-Creator is evil.

40. Marcion must have liked to stress the attribute of *wisdom* in the Redeemer-God. Irenaeus and Chrysostom attest to this, and in I Corinthians 1:18 Marcion inserted the word "wisdom." But wisdom for him was the wisdom of love, which attains the goal that the foolish and untamed zeal of the World-Creator misses.

41. One could suppose that Marcion was merely making a virtue out of necessity (since he was unable to point to any visible creation for his God) when he taught that *redemption* is the only worthy kind of revelation of the true God. But this explanation would do him an injustice. Marcion clearly recognized that physical creations cannot be evidence of goodness and love but that these can be expressed only in redeeming, loving activity. Paul of Samosata recognized the same thing but did not draw the same conclusion.

42. Tertullian I 19 (ANF III, 285): "Marcion's special and principal work is the separation of the law and the gospel."

43. On the names "Jesus" and "Christ" see Appendix III. Marcion's Modalism caused him and later his followers to leave out "God the Father" next to "Christ" in several places (see Galatians

1:1 and the spurious Epistle to the Laodiceans) or to put "Christ" in the place of "God the Father" (see the same spurious Epistle to the Laodiceans). Marcion's Modalism, incidentally, was not peculiar to him. It is the same as that which numerous Montanists and even the Roman bishop Zephyrinus professed.

44. It should be pointed out, however, that Marcionites were still writing the name "Chrestos" at the beginning of the fourth century (inscription of Lebaba) and certainly had not failed to notice how appropriate this name was for the personal manifestation of the good God.

45. Marcion also felt compelled to read a few other passages of the Gospel allegorically. Thus he noted that the "Great Supper" was "a heavenly banquet of spiritual satiety and pleasure" (Tertullian IV 31 on Luke 14:16ff., ANF III, 403), and "This is my body" he reinterpreted as "the figure of my body" (Tertullian IV 40, ANF III, 418).

46. One could again suppose that Marcion was making a virtue of necessity (since he could not use prophecies—which in the understanding of that time had the value of authoritative testimonies—to refer to his Christ), but again one would be doing him an injustice. According to the pregnant passage in Origen, *Comm. II 199f. in Joh.*, quoted in Appendix III, there can be no doubt that Marcion acknowledged only the evidences of the Spirit and of power, and thought nothing of authoritative testimonies.

47. The church, too, rejected this by its doctrine of parthenogenesis. Originally, the church had accepted the act of birth but later no longer allowed it to be construed as a natural act ("the perpetual virginity of Mary").

48. It appears also that Marcion or his disciples already considered that the divine Redeemer could have become man only by a "conversion." Whoever converts himself, however, ceases to be what he was. Since, therefore, that which is unending cannot cease, it also cannot be convertible

49. "Not truly, but seen under the appearance, as it were, of a greater glory" (Origen, T. V 283f.). Marcion found numerous proofs for Docetism in the Gospel. See his comment on Luke 4:30, etc.

50. Docetism was also an expression at that time for the belief that Christ was not a product of his time and that genius and divinity do not develop from nature.

51. See Tertullian III 9; *De carne Christi* 3; Ephraem, *Ev. Conc. Expos.* 255. One sees here also that for Marcion the Old Testament, despite its invalidity, can assist us doctrinally. Moreover, when he and his disciples, in response to the objections of the Catholics, appealed to the Holy Spirit in the body of a dove, even though they themselves did not acknowledge the entire story of the baptism, this was an *argumentatio ad hominem*.

52. According to the Gospel as Marcion read it, it was the disciples who, after the resurrection, took him for a phantom. Even the resurrected Jesus, however, did not make such a claim.

53. That is just the reason why the reproach of Marcion's opponents that everything here is lies and deception does not apply to him either. Instead, Christ ("His own consciousness . . . was enough for Him" [Tertullian, *De carne Christi* 3, ANF III, 523]) had to leave his opponents only with the mistaken impression that he had a fleshly substance. According to Hippolytus, *Refutation* X 19, Christ was "the inner man," but that is not clear.

54. "Christ announced that the Kingdom of God was new and unheard of" (Tertullian IV 24). This message is no more in need of "proof" than is the entire appearance of Christ, because it, like Christ's words and deeds, validates itself through its very content and power. See especially Origen, *Comm. II 199f. in Joh.*

55. On the great confession of Jesus (Luke 10:21f.): "[God] had concealed the greatness even of himself, which he was with all his might revealing by his Christ." " . . . [in the] destruction [of the things of the Creator], that he might refute them . . ." " 'All things have been delivered to me, . . .,' that is, *all nations*" (Tertullian IV 25).

56. Marcion saw in the parable a mode of expression peculiar to Jesus. That has to be compared with the fact that Marcion was a harsh opponent of the allegorical method of interpretation. We are not able, therefore, to get from Marcion a picture of Christ that is complete in every detail,

since in so many passages it must remain doubtful what he removed and what he left standing. It is very important to realize that he removed not only the baptism by John, the story of the temptations, the triumphal entry, and the cleansing of the temple, but also the parable of the prodigal son. For how can "the alien God" be the father to whose house the prodigal son returns? It clearly was necessary that the reassuring sayings about God's care for the sparrow and the hairs of our heads be dropped.

57. With respect to the tax collectors, see Marcion's comment on Luke 5:27ff.

58. See Marcion's comment on Luke 12:22ff.: " . . . it is in depreciation of the Creator that Christ forbids us to think about such trifles [food, clothing, etc.]." Therefore, it is most remarkable that he left standing Luke 12:30f. (" . . . and the Father knows that you need them. But seek the Kingdom of God and [all?] these things will be given to you"). How might Marcion have understood these last words? Certainly not in the obvious sense in which they ought to be understood. And it certainly would be incorrect to conclude from them that Marcion accepted a beneficient providence of the good God with respect to earthly things for his followers.

59. Marcion considered the doctrine of the World-Creator held by the Pharisees as hypocrisy also, since this doctrine did not recognize true goodness and gave that name to something else. See his comment on Luke 12:1 (Tertullian IV 28): "the leaven that is hypocrisy, i.e., the proclamation of the Creator."

60. Since Marcion, in attempting to adapt the Lukan text to his theology, proceeded as conservatively as possible and apparently failed to make deletions where they did not appear to be absolutely necessary, he was forced in many passages to offer highly strained, indeed sophistic, interpretations. He had to have Jesus give answers to something different from what the questioners had asked; he had to reinterpret or weaken the answers, mix extraneous elements into the explanation, accept offensive and ostensibly indulgent accommodations by Jesus, change the subject within the same discourse, assume a variety of subjects within one and the same statement, and the like. See examples in Luke 6:23,24ff.,35; 7:9; 9:21; 10:25; 11:42ff.; 12:46; 17:20; 20:27ff.; 21:25ff.; 22:70. The most objectionable thing to Marcion is that Jesus continually obscures the fact that he is the son of another God (see above; Marcion explains this also by the lack of understanding on the part of Jesus' hearers). Even at his trial Jesus did not profess to be the son of another God, "in order that he might be able to suffer" (Tertullian IV 41 on Luke 22:61f.). And according to Marcion (in Ephraem, *Evang. Conc. Expos.* p. 122f.), even at the Last Supper Jesus supposedly presented his body to be eaten "in order to conceal his greatness and to leave them with the impression that he was a body, because they were not yet able to understand him." Whether or not this is reliable is uncertain.

61. On Luke 8:25 Marcion remarks (Tertullian IV 20, ANF III, 378): "He [who commands the winds and the waters] is *the new master and proprietor of the elements, now that the Creator is deposed and excluded from their possession.*" But on earth Jesus wanted to give only samples of his superior power. He allows the dominion of the God of this world to continue so long as the world itself lasts (see below). Cf. the comment on Luke 8:27ff. (the demoniac): "[The demons were] in ignorance of what the power of the recent and unknown God was working in the world" (Tertullian IV 20, ANF III, 379). It is very understandable that Ephraem (*Evang. Conc. Expos.* 75) took offense at the stilling of the storm. He says that Marcion ought not to have left it in, since Christ had to use a "power and dominion" here that as the Son of the good God he did not have.

62. On Luke 11:22 (Tertullian IV 26): "The Creator subdued by the other God." But that too is only a "simulation"; the good God does not deal violently even with the World-Creator (see below).

63. Almost the whole of mankind was, after all, in the underworld. What has been left on earth until the imminent end of the world is only a very small remnant. Hence it is only in the underworld that the Redeemer, who goes down there, finds the majority of those to be redeemed. Cf. *Apox. Ezra* II 5 (*Violet*, p. 38): "I said, Lord, behold, those to whom you promised it, who are [here] at the end. But what shall those who went before us do?"

64. For an objection that can be raised here from the sources, see below.

65. The objection by his opponents that the creator of the world did not keep the soul (or the blood) of Christ because Christ arose, and that therefore the purchase had immediately become merely illusory was not, to the best of our knowledge, considered by Marcion. See Esnik for the doctrine as expounded by the Marcionites. I can only regard it as a later elaboration, for it neglects the biblical foundation that Marcion never abandoned—Tertullian certainly would have considered it if he had found it in Marcion's *Antitheses*—and it presupposes that the power of the Creator was completely broken already by the resurrection of Christ.

66. Marcion places the heaviest emphasis upon the forgiveness of sins. See his exegesis, as in Luke 5:20 (the forgiveness of the sins of the paralytic): "This novel benevolence of Christ."

67. This insufferably evident contradiction between the small number of the redeemed after Christ and the great number of those before Christ can be resolved if one looks at it from the early Christian viewpoint. According to this, Christ appeared at the end of the world-age, in which all that is evil was at its peak. This being the case, only a few can still be saved.

68. It is true that by his death Christ purchased the whole of mankind from the World-Creator, but he actually redeems only those who follow his gospel in faith.

69. "But will you have it that this faith of the woman consisted in the contempt which she had acquired for the law?" (Tertullian IV 20, ANF III, 380).

70. In the pre-catholic literature I am acquainted with the term "change" in Justin, *Apology* I 66. There it reads that our flesh and blood are nourished by the holy food in the Supper "in accordance with a change." What is meant is a mystical-sacramental alteration of our bodily nature. Marcion, on the other hand, is thinking about an inner transformation through *faith*. Paul speaks of the new creation. Marcion understood him. In *Apology* II 2 Justin calls the (hoped-for) conversion of a person living in sin a μεταβολή. That is the same use of the word that Marcion employs.

71. Through faith sinners are really transformed into something good.

72. Apelles caught the decisive significance of faith; see Rhodon (Eusebius, H. E. V 13, NPNF, Series 2, I, 228): " . . . those who trusted in the Crucified would be saved . . ." Cf. also "to those who believe," Hippolytus, *Refutation* VII 38 (conclusion).

73. According to a Marcionite statement in Esnik (Schmid, p. 144), people did and do *owe* Christ faith (and imitation), since *goodness* may not be rejected: "Marcion blathers that it is an obligation of the creature of the Just [God] to show adoration to the good Alien [God] by reason of goodness." I have no doubt that Marcion taught this.

74. Tertullian's critique is most scrupulous here (I 27, ANF III, 292–293): "Come, then, if you do not fear God as being good, why do you not boil over into every kind of lust, and so realize that which is, I believe, the main enjoyment of life to all who fear not God? Why do you not frequent the customary pleasures of the maddening circus, the bloodthirsty arena, and the lascivious theatre? Why in persecutions do you not, when the censer is presented, at once redeem your life by the denial of your faith?" Cf. Esnik (see Appendix VI): "Is it not therefore clear (since the good God imposes no suffering as punishment) that the Marcionites are not afraid of torture and do not shrink back from sin?"

75. When Apelles adds to the condition of faith, "only if they are found with good works," then that is, according to Marcion, either obvious or—if it is supposed to be something more than that—hardly in line with his intent.

76. Von Soden, W. Bauer, and Grejdanus have all denied, though in various ways, that Marcion had a deeper sense of guilt, if indeed any such sense at all, and have concluded from this that his piety and doctrine were fundamentally different from and far below Paul's. I do not deny that there is a certain difference. But to question Marcion's sense of guilt seems to me to be a kind of clerical heretic-hunting and to contradict that which we know about Marcion's concept of faith. I have, I hope, refuted their hypotheses in my *Neue Studien zu Marcion* (1923), and I believe that what is stated there does not need to be repeated. The Christians of this age and of the following ages almost all have emphasized the first half of the confession, "Rejoice, my heart; you shall be freed from the misery of this earth and from the burden of sin," more strongly than the second half.

But to question their sense of guilt on that basis is going much too far. If, however, one argues that Marcion's sense of guilt had to be deficient because the guilt is not related to the God who redeems us from it, one overlooks (1) that that deficiency is covered by the sense of inexhaustible thanks to him who first loved us and as *Alien* in his incomprehensible mercy made us to be his children, and (2) that, as has been shown, Marcion regarded the sinful condition, which manifested itself in moral waywardness and anarchy, as sin and guilt.

77. The good God is "the God of that age" (Tertullian IV 38) and does not claim to be the "God of this age."

78. Though after the transaction he should have kept the peace, now he is doubly jealous. Knowing the condition of faith that has been set down by his enemy, he seeks in every way to persecute, torment, and dissuade believers from their faith in order not to have to leave his children to the good God. If he was savage and cruel already before the appearance of Christ, his passions now surpass all measure and his "righteousness" is overcome by them.

79. This passage is important also because it is analogous to the Marcionite dialectic in the concepts of "righteousness," "law," ("goodness," etc.) and supports it in the face of objections in principle. Just as one can predicate "judging" and "damning" even of the good God, by the same token one can also predicate "good" of the just God and of the law.

80. Marcion does not delete the "woes" of Luke 6:24ff. but remarks, "The woe is not so much one of cursing as it is of warning." On the "woes" against the Pharisees in Luke 11:42ff. he remarks, "He uttered in order to tarnish the Creator as a cruel Being, against whom such as offended were destined to have a 'woe' " (Tertullian IV 28, ANF III, 395). In Luke 12:46 Marcion reads, "He will separate him [instead of 'He will cut him to pieces'] and will assign him a place with the unbelievers," and adds the highly forced remark, "[an act] of serenity and mildness simply to sever the man off and to assign him a portion with the unbelievers" (Tertullian IV 29, ANF III, 398). On Luke 17:1 (against the one who gives offense) he explains: "Someone else avenges the offense of his disciples." On Luke 12:49 ("I have come to kindle a fire") he remarks: "It is a figure." Luke 12:58f. he relates, naturally, to the World-Creator. Esnik says: "And if you ask whether the good [God] has torments at his disposal, the Marcionites say, 'They do not exist' . . . they say they have fled from the just [God] since he threatens terrible things in his laws, namely, 'The fire is kindled in my anger and will burn down to the lowest hell,' and 'All these [punishments] were preserved in my store,' and elsewhere, 'God judges with fire.' "

81. Since Marcion probably left the eschatological sections of the Thessalonian letters essentially unaltered, he must have taught a literal return of Christ. This was not the case with his disciple Apelles, who was in agreement with the Gnostics. See below (Chapter VIII, 3).

82. According to Tertullian (V 10), Marcion taught from I Corinthians 15:44 that at the resurrection the soul will become spirit and from I Corinthians 15:49 that the redeemed will have a celestial substance. Their bodies will not rise at all. However, a Marcionite did say to Jerome (*Lib. c. Johannem. Hierosol.* 36): "Woe to him who rises again in this flesh and these bones"; that is, the unredeemed will rise again entire, then to be engulfed by the hellfire of the World-Creator.

83. One sees here again a certain tie that binds the superior and inferior Gods (see above). Both maintain morality, a morality whose commandments, according to the judgment of the superior God, have also been transgressed by those who regard the just God as just; but no unity between these two Gods results from this.

84. Here, as in many other places, Marcion had the grammatical subject change: in verse 24 the destroyer is said to be the World-Creator, but in verse 25 the one who reigns is not he but Christ. This exegesis is wretched, but the thought guiding it is splendid.

85. At the end, therefore, it is revealed (as one had to suppose all along, given the inferiority of the World-Creator) that ultimately he performs the will of the good God, as an instrumentality of the latter, for even the good God does not intend that sinners will have eternal life. It is also revealed that despite the name "God" he is not a real God, because a real God does not die. What is he then? The World-Spirit, the World! It is perhaps with this in mind that the statement of Hip-

polytus (*c. Noet.* 11) is to be understood, namely, that the Marcionites, like the other heretics, were compelled against their will to acknowledge "that everything goes back to one" (and "that one is responsible for all things").

86. Tertullian I 21: "The churches of apostolic origin were corrupted from the beginning." It is true that the twelve made a good start at the beginning. (Tertullian III 22, ANF III, 340: "When the apostles girded their loins for this business [their mission], they renounced the elders and rulers and priests of the Jews. Well, says he, but was it not above all things that they might preach the other god? . . . What did the apostles thereupon suffer? You answer: Every sort of iniquitous persecutions, from men that belonged indeed to that Creator who was the adversary of Him whom they were preaching." Where did Marcion learn this, if not from the Acts of the Apostles?) But very soon their understanding was darkened.

87. The calling of Paul must have been understood by Marcion as a manifestation of Christ which was almost equal to his first appearance and activity. See the report of Esnik, which, to be sure, is not given in Marcion's own words, but does reproduce the attitude and the chief judgment of Marcion.

88. According to Esnik, the Marcionites asserted that they preached the unutterable words, for Marcion said that he had heard them. But that hardly stems from Marcion himself.

89. Marcion explains the "until today" in II Corinthians 3:15 as "until Paul, the apostle of the new Christ," who removed "the veil." Because of Marcion, Paul became altogether unacceptable to the catholic Christians, and Tertullian angrily called him "Marcion's apostle" and "the apostle of the heretics."

VII. THE HOLY CHURCH OF THE REDEEMED ONES AND THE ORDERING OF THEIR LIFE (CULTUS, ORGANIZATION, AND ETHICS)

1. According to Ephraem, the Marcionites called the church the bride of Christ.

2. Tertullian IV 5 (ANF III, 350): "[Marcion's gospel] too, of course, has its churches, but specially its own—as late as they are spurious; and should you want to know their original, you will more easily discover apostasy in it than apostolicity, with Marcion forsooth as their founder, or some of Marcion's swarm. Even wasps make combs; so also these Marcionites make churches."

3. On the baptism of the dead and the repetition of baptism see the next chapter.

4. Cf. my essay on bread and water in the Lord's Supper in *Texte und Untersuchungen*, Vol. VII, Pt. 2 (1891). Marcion's substitution of water for wine is explicitly attested by Epiphanius and Timotheus, see Appendix VI. The explanation of the biblical text, "This is my body," as "It is a figure of my body" (Tertullian IV 40), which is often alleged to be Tertullian's, actually belongs to Marcion. For Tertullian continues, "A figure, however, there could not have been, unless there were first a veritable body. An empty thing, or phantom, is incapable of a figure" (ANF III, 418). Marcion, therefore, understood the words of institution in a figurative sense. However, Tertullian's next words ("If, however, [as Marcion might say,] He pretended the bread was his body, because He lacked the truth of bodily substance, it follows that He must have given bread for us") are hardly directed against a statement by Marcion. It is most remarkable that in the Lord's Prayer Marcion changes "our bread" to "your bread." It is in this way that he wished to understand the petition concerning the bread in the Lord's Supper (just as many church fathers after him did, without altering the text), for the petition concerning bodily nourishment seemed to him to be "frivolous."

5. Cf. I 24 (ANF III, 290): "I rather think that by Marcion's rule the body is baptized." I 28 (ANF III, 293): "To what end does baptism serve, according to [Marcion]?"

6. Bousset, *Hauptprobleme der Gnosis*, p. 297, solely on the basis of these words, remarks, "The Marcionites were familiar with a baptism with oil." But then the Catholics were familiar with it, also.

7. One notices that "wine" is missing.

8. Prayers of praise and repentance are meant here. Confession of sin was practiced by the Marcionites, according to Aphraates III 6.

9. Marcion's version of the text of Galatians 4:26, "which holy church we professed," makes it certain that he, too, had a binding confession made at baptism and that the church was mentioned in it. This is important for the history of the Apostles' Creed. But it does not follow from this that here, too, he was claiming precedence over the great church in Rome (see Appendix VI on Marcion and the Apostles' Creed, and cf. the information on Apelles below). According to Esnik (see Appendix V), the Marcionites were "bound by baptism to an abstention from the eating of flesh and from marriage." Therefore, a vow was made.

10. For examples of "bishops," etc. in the Marcionite churches, see the next chapter.

11. Epiphanius, too, reports (*Haer.* 42.3,4) that among the Marcionites the mysteries were performed in the presence of the catechumens.

12. See also chapter 42: "they know no respect even for their own leaders."

13. If the marriage had already been contracted, Marcion respected it and the command of Christ regarding its indissolubility. He let stand the World-Creator's prohibition of adultery as well as the other main elements of morality (see above). Indeed, it remained important even for the Marcionite catechumens.

14. See the testimonies cited in Appendix V, especially Tertullian I 19 (ANF III, 293–94): "The flesh is not, according to Marcion, immersed in the water of the sacrament, unless it be in virginity, widowhood, or celibacy, or has purchased by divorce a title to baptism . . . Now such a scheme as this must no doubt involve the proscription of marriage . . . Hostile attacks are made against it as a polluted thing, to the disagreement of the Creator." IV 34 (ANF III, 405): "How is it that you on your side destroy marriage, not uniting man and woman, nor admitting to the sacrament of baptism and of the eucharist those who have been united in marriage anywhere else, unless they should agree together to repudiate the fruit of their marriage . . . ?"

15. Actually we do not know how many catechumens there were in the Marcionite congregations, compared to the number of professing believers. One may presume that the number was always very large. They were allowed to marry and to live in the married state. But "we will say nothing about his catechumens," says Tertullian V 7 (ANF III, 443), with Marcion's meaning in mind.

16. To call marriage "corruption"; Irenaeus I 28.1, "corruption and fornication"; Hippolytus, *Refutation* X 19) is the strongest expression of contempt possible for self-perpetuating humanity, which without redemption has no right of existence at all.

17. The documentation for this motivation is included in Appendix V.

18. Marcion brought the exhortation to complete chastity into his exegesis wherever he possibly could.

19. The Marcionites whom Esnik (see Appendix VI) knew permitted wine drinking, which surprised him. In the *Fihrist* (see Appendix VI) we read that the Marcionites avoided it. Since they celebrated the Lord's Supper without wine, it was probably as a rule avoided at other times as well. The *Fihrist* also talks about uninterrupted fasts among the Marcionites.

20. According to Esnik (see Appendix VI), the Marcionites appealed to the account of Jesus eating fish after the resurrection as justifying their permission to eat fish, too.

21. Carmen Pseudotert. *adv. Marc.* V 90: "The old man, whom you call an enemy."

22. Marcion speaks of his own followers as "wretched" and "despised" (IV 9.36). In their being such they should recognize that they are disciples of Christ; it is to be expected that they will incur misery and hatred at the hands of the world.

23. See Irenaeus IV 33.9; Tertullian I 24,27; Clement, *Stromateis* IV 4.17; the anti-Montanist in Eusebius, H. E. V 16:21; the *Acts of the Martyrs* by Pionius, etc. Cf. also the next chapter. It is probable that those heretics who, according to Clement of Alexandria (*Strom.* IV 4.17), rushed into death like the classical Hindu sophists so as to escape the detested Creator, were Marcionites. The anti-Montanist says that of all the heretics the Marcionites had the most martyrs.

24. Marcionite cynics in Hippolytus, *Refutation* VII 29.

VIII. THE HISTORY OF THE MARCIONITE CHURCH.
ITS THEOLOGICAL SCHOOLS AND THE SECT OF APELLES

1. The documentation not furnished here will be found in Appendix VI.

2. It would be a mistake if one read Tertullian III 12 to mean that there were also Marcionite Hebrew Christians.

3. The Marcionite bishop Asclepius in the region of Ceasarea in Palestine at the time of the Emperor Daza (Eusebius, *De mart. Pal.* 10.3); the Marcionite presbyter Metrodorus in Smyrna at the time of Decius (*Mart. Pionii* 21); the Marcionite presbyter Paulus in Lebaba in the Hauran (inscription). Successions of bishops among the Marcionites are mentioned by Adamantius (*Dial.* I 8): "Once Marcion died, there were among you many successions of bishops, or rather false bishops."

4. See below for the testimony of Tertullian.

5. Naturally, he also treated Marcion's church as a "school" in order to bring contempt upon it (see, e.g., Origen's *Comm. I 18 in Rom.*, T. VI, p. 55): "Marcion and all those who from his school produce, as it were, serpents' offspring . . ." Hippolytus, however, saw only a "school" even in the Roman congregation under the episcopacy of Callistus.

6. The sources give no answer to the question of the principal reason for the magnetism of Marcionitism. We are left, therefore, with conjectures. It was probably the paradox in the combination of the proclamation of the exclusively good God, Christ, the rejection of the Old Testament, an asceticism that promised to lead to a super-humanness, and the utter abhorrence for the "world," to which one felt vastly superior. On the influence of Marcion on the emerging catholic church, see the next chapter.

7. One should not be deceived by Jerome's polemic. He is copying the older polemic and is a Greek Christian as well as a Latin one.

8. It is strange that the memory of Marcionitism was kept alive in the West for the longest time by those who classified the "Sabellians" (whose doctrine continued to stir up people there) with the Marcionites as a scare tactic.

9. See Appendices VI and X. That Manichaeism occasionally displaced the much more profound and more spiritual Marcionitism can be explained by the decline of culture in general that was followed by a similar decline in religious culture. Another special magnetism could be found, moreover, in the organization of the Manichaean (in contrast to the Marcionite) church.

10. Celsus reports that the Marcionites even called themselves "rubbish" (after Phil. 3:8).

11. See Appendix VI. In addition to the Marcionite martyrs Metrodorus (presbyter) and Asclepius (bishop) there was, as late as the persecution under Valerian, also a woman martyr in Caesarea (Eusebius, H. E. VIII 12).

12. The question whether Marcionitism forms a part of the presuppositions of Mani's doctrine, i.e., whether Mani knew and used Marcion's writings, cannot be decided yet but probably should be answered in the affirmative. If it is to be answered negatively, it is certain nevertheless that already at the beginning of the fourth century (see the *Acta Archelai*) the Manichaeans were making use of Marcion's judgment about the opposition between Jesus and the Old Testament and were amply using the *Antitheses* (see Appendix VI). Mani wrote three treatises in the "Book of Secrets" against the Bardesanites (see Fluegel, *Mani*, p. 102). Marcion's name does not occur in the tradition about Mani.

13. The *Fihrist* (see Appendix VI) speaks of their Christianity as greater than that of the Manichaeans.

14. If the Marcionites adopted a secret code almost identical to that of the Manichaeans, it shows not only that they were drawing very close to Manichaeism but also that they were giving up their original openness, for one chooses a secret code only when one wishes to be read just by a select group.

15. The earliest reporter, Justin, faithfully reproduced Marcion's doctrine insofar as he did

not speak at all of principles in Marcion, but simply of two Gods, the World-Creator and the other, good God. Tertullian, too, however, speaks almost without exception of Gods and not principles. Nevertheless, Marcion did not avoid the expression ἀρχαί altogether (he used it for Matter). This is found in the testimony of his disciple Apelles (in *Anthimus of Nicomedia*; see Appendix VIII).

16. It should only be remembered here that these schools in several cases were, nevertheless, schismatic or even heretical and that, as a rule, the official church looked with suspicion upon the whole business of forming schools. Here began the great problem of church and theology, which in every stage of its development has always ended with the church becoming more theological, to be sure, but at the same time more and more vigorously rejected independent theology. Whether this happened in a similar way in the Marcionite churches we do not know. But it is not likely, for these churches were not established on a school-doctrine or on principles-doctrines. We also hear nothing of disputes in the Marcionite church, and according to the dialogues of Adamantius, the two Marcionites Megethius and Marcus coexisted peacefully even though one advocated the three-principle doctrine and the other the two-principle doctrine.

17. When Tertullian writes (*De praescr.* 42, ANF III, 264) that the Marcionites "amongst themselves swerve even from their own regulations forasmuch as every man, just as it suits his own temper, modified the traditions he has received . . . That was also fair for the Marcionites which had been done by Marcion—even to innovate on the faith, as was agreeable to their own pleasure," he is not relating this to the points above but to the principles-doctrine and related questions.

18. The high regard for the master who did not even claim a title for himself is shown in the unanimously attested continuation of and esteem for the unique self-designation "Marcionites" (cf. among other things the inscription of Lebaba). It is further shown in the description of Marcion as the "chief" of the bishops (Megethius in Adamantius I 8; was this common?), further still in the establishment of a Marcionite era (Tertullian I 19), and finally in the teaching that in heaven Paul sits at Christ's right hand and Marcion at his left (Origen, *Hom. XXV in Luk.*, T. V 181. This idea is reflected in the three-line inscription of Lebaba: in the first line one reads Marcion's name, in the middle line that of Jesus Christ, and in the third the name of Paul, though the latter as the name of a Marcionite presbyter). But at least at first Marcion was not awarded the name of "apostle" in his congregations; biblicism forbade that. It is Tertullian who writes (IV 9, ANF III, 355): "Christ . . . intending one day to appoint the shipmaster Marcion his apostle . . ." But Tertullian himself knows nothing of Marcion's own people regarding him as an apostle. Otherwise he could not have written in *De carne Christi* 2 (ANF III, 522): "Show me your authority. If you are a proph-et, foretell us a thing; if you are an apostle, open your message in public." Finally, it is only a polemical fencing stroke when Ephraem writes (*Hymn* 56): "Among the Marcionites it is not said, 'Thus says the Lord,' but 'Thus says Marcion.' " Nevertheless, the Marcionite church could not look at it any other way than that their founder belonged in the history of salvation in the broader sense of the term; for Christendom, after its second fall, which it committed by misunderstanding and backsliding from Paul (the first fall came between Christ and Paul), would have fallen back into the worship of the Creator God had not Marcion put it back on the right track. Marcion would con-tinue to play the role in his church, at least, that some dogmaticians of the seventeenth century ascribed to Luther when they devoted a special article to him, "De vocatione Lutheri." In addition, *one* later witness, Maruta, reports—certainly exaggerating—"Instead of Peter they set Marcion as head of the apostles."

19. Διαίρεσις is primarily a technical expression for the division of a discourse. But here the word is applied to things and facts, namely, all world phenomena, and that does not occur here only; see the philosophical-cosmological use of it in Athenagoras, *Suppl.* 10.3; 12.2; Tatian, *Orat.* 12.1. Perhaps Schwartz correctly substituted διαίρεσις for αἵρεσις in Tatian 5.2. (Origen, *De orat.* 3, writes, "Every body is divisible," and Athenagoras 4.1 writes, "In our case, they divided god from matter and point out that matter is one thing and god something else.") When Rhodon says that those Marcionite heads of schools were not able to find the διαίρεσις of the circumstances given in the world, that can only be an abbreviated expression for the fact that they did not find the *ground* of

the differences. Here it can only be a matter of the ultimate and deepest διαίρεσις, of the question of good and evil, and of the question "Whence evil?" (Tertullian I 2, ANF III, 272, also attests to that with respect to Marcion. But one may suppose that Tertullian heard it from Marcionite theologians and mingled it with genuine Marcionite teaching, for Marcion himself did not raise and solve problems but, unconcerned with problems, reproduced impressions: "While morbidly brooding over the question of the origin of the soul, his perception became blunted by the very irregularity of his researches; and when he found the Creator declaring, 'I am He that createth evil, . . .' ") They were not able to solve this problem by means of the church's doctrine of the *one* God, and they turned to the ready-at-hand conclusion that one must trace whatever is in conflict with God to a second principle. Rhodon also reproached these heads of schools with the charge that Justin had already made against Marcion himself: that they teach "simply and without proof" (Justin: "irrationally"), i.e., that they lack philosophical depth and sound argumentation (whether by reason or by authority).

20. It is also in Marcion's sense that he says that the Creator redeems *his* believers (naturally, this is to be thought of as an earthly redemption) and judges and punishes sinners (*Dial.* II 3f.).

21. Marcus was, therefore, really a representative of the dualism of "good versus evil" (without consideration of righteousness) that Hippolytus carelessly attributed to Marcion himself. Epiphanius' absurd report (see Appendix VI) that Marcion added the Devil to the two principles (the invisible good God and the visible Creator God) of his teacher Cerdo and, indeed, as the *middle* principle between the two, requires no refutation. For the fact that Epiphanius or someone else designated the Devil as the *middle* principle should not be considered a "refinement" since ultimately, according to Marcion, those who have fallen into the hand of the Devil are saved, whereas those loyal to the World-Creator are not.

22. "When the Demiurge formed man and breathed upon him, he was not able to bring him to maturity. But when the good God saw from above this vessel rolled up and palpitating he sent part of his own spirit and gave man life. Therefore, we say that the spirit that is of the good God saves" (*Dial.* II 8; cf. the same doctrine in Satornilus).

23. This expression can also be found in Rhodon in relation to the doctrine of Marcion's disciple Synerus (see Appendix VI).

24. The just God is called "the middle one" in Epiphanius also (6.8).

25. The doctrine of the three Gods (with the "middle one") and the false doctrine of the two Gods (the Creator of the world as the evil God) are very similar, as is obvious.

26. According to Hippolytus, Theodoret too ascribes the four-principle doctrine to Marcion (Appendix V). He makes a distinction there between πονηρός (evil) and κακός (evil), so that the doctrine is formulated as follows: "The good and unknown one, the just Demiurge (who is also πονηρός), the evil (κακή) matter, and the evil one (ὁ κακός)." Incidentally, Theodoret refers to a disciple of Marcion, Pithon, as the head of a school. Pithon is never mentioned elsewhere. Perhaps this is merely a mistake (for Prepon?).

27. With Esnik's Marcionites, as with Megethius, when it comes to creation and redemption, interest in the Jews is overshadowed by an interest in all of mankind.

28. For Shahrastani Christ is the son and envoy of the God of Light. He did not make him a middle principle, which allows for the mixture of good and evil: "The Light sent a Christ-Spirit into the mixed world, i.e., the Spirit and his Son."

29. The good God, however, must have collaborated in redemption.

30. Jesus, therefore, waives his right to kill the World-Creator and to take his children from him, and he pays a price. One should also notice here that the good God does not act according to the principle of "an eye for an eye, a tooth for a tooth."

31. This, to be sure, was not following the precedent of the master.

32. Tertullian, *De resurrectione* 2 (ANF III, 547): "We may ignore a certain Lucan, who does not spare even this part of our nature, which he follows Aristotle in reducing to dissolution, and substitutes some other thing in lieu of it. Some third nature it is which, according to him, is to rise

again, neither soul nor flesh; in other words, not man, but a bear perhaps—for instance Lucan himself."

33. This is not true of Epiphanius. When he and he alone claims that Marcion taught the transmigration of souls, it is both improbable in itself and refuted by Clement (see Appendix VI).

34. Cf. the odious and dubious suggestion by Hippolytus (*Refut.* IX 12 fin.) regarding the Roman congregation under the episcopacy of Callistus: "On the basis of this, first of all, they underwent a second baptism."

35. The custom, which was especially characteristic of the early inroads of the mystery religions into the congregations (though it should not be overlooked that the catholics must have freed themselves from it very soon), was also traditional among the Montanists (Filastr., *Haer.* 49) and the Cerinthians (Epiph., *Haer.* 28.6). The former reads, "They baptize the dead." The latter reads, "And a certain bit of tradition has come to us telling that some of them are said to have completed this life without being baptized, and others among them are said to have been baptized in the names of those, so that at the day of resurrection they might not suffer punishment and fall under the authority of the creator of the world."

36. See the complete evidence in Appendix VIII, my dissertation "De Apellis Gnosi Monarchica" (1874; it is outdated by the new version), and my essay "Rhodon und Apelles," (in *Geschichtliche Studien, Albert Hauck dargebracht,* 1916) which I am reproducing here in part.

37. Only Tertullian reports that sexual misconduct was involved here, while the Romans Rhodon and Hippolytus know nothing of it. Conversely, Hippolytus reports the sexual misconduct of Marcion, and Tertullian is silent about it (see above). Was it not just as spitefully concocted for Apelles as for Marcion?

38. "Afterwards a monstrous prostitute," claims Tertullian, which no one will believe. What we do know about her goes back to Rhodon and Tertullian. When Hippolytus wrote his *Syntagma,* he still knew nothing about her (hence Epiphanius also knew nothing). In the *Refutation,* however, Hippolytus is acquainted with her and her *Phaneroseis,* since in the meantime he had read Tertullian's treatise *Adversus Apelliacos* (since lost). Pseudo-Tertullian also was acquainted with this work and took from it his quotation about Philumene. In *De praescriptione* 6 Tertullian traces the heresy of Apelles directly back to Philumene.

39. Everything that Tertullian reports about Apelles' doctrine appears to have been taken from this work, as well as that which follows in the text above. According to Pseudo-Tertullian, who certainly copied Tertullian, the *Phaneroseis* seems to have enjoyed canonical authority among the sects. The expression, "private, but extraordinary readings" is rather obscure.

40. All this according to a fragment from Tertullian's *Adversus Apelliacos,* preserved by chance in an Augustine manuscript. That the heavenly apparitions appear in visions as "young men" (Tertullian, *De praescr.* 6 [a demonic angel is supposed to have caused them], et cetera; on this, see Jerome on Galatians 1:8) is also attested elsewhere. In the identification of the young man sometimes as Christ and sometimes as Paul, one recognizes the influence of Marcion still continuing. Christ appeared to St. Thecla in the form of Paul, which can be explained by her relationship with Paul. On the miracle, see the article by Buchholz, "Das okkulte Berlin" (*Berliner Zeitung am Mittag,* June 3, 1920). Here a participant in a spiritualist seance declares, "Recently a salt-barrel of mine got into a narrow-necked bottle." One probably may regard the bread as the consecrated bread on which the prophetess lived exclusively.

41. Rhodon speaks of several writings of blasphemous content that Apelles diligently composed as a refutation of the Old Testament. Origen and Tertullian (in the lost treatise against Apelles) were familiar with the *Syllogisms* and argued with them in great detail. Only Pseudo-Tertullian (after Tertullian) names the title. It is true that apart from the *Syntagma* of Hippolytus (who here and in the *Refutation* had in hand a confessional treatise by Apelles [or an earlier refutation? Rhodon?]), Epiphanius did not use the *Syllogisms* but probably, directly or indirectly, a treatise by Apelles (perhaps the same one Hippolytus used). Anthimus also was familiar with a treatise by Apelles.

42. See Anthimus, Appendix VIII. Cf. Apelles in Epiphanius, *Haer.* 44.1: "Marcion lied."

43. The four great specialized writings by Tertullian are directed against Marcion, Apelles, Valentinus, and Hermogenes. In the treatise *De carne Christi* it is almost exclusively the first three who are attacked. In *De praescr.* 37 they are distinguished from the other heresies as the "more prominent and more common."

44. Whether the congregation founded by Apelles was a formal church like that of Marcion, from which it had strictly separated, or a school-sect cannot be determined for certain. Its short life span points toward the latter. Epiphanius (*Haer.* 44.1) calls it a school.

45. Whether also in Egypt is not certain since Origen responds to Apelles only in his later works.

46. See Appendix VIII.

47. See Appendix VIII.

48. "Who prides himself in his (strict) conduct and his age," writes Rhodon bitingly.

49. It is possible that Hippolytus has precisely this discussion in mind, for in both places Apelles succinctly and clearly professes the one-principle doctrine.

50. Apelles, therefore, took the initiative.

51. That must have been done in an earlier passage not excerpted by Eusebius.

52. Rhodon probably suspected that Apelles had a secret doctrine which he did not wish to reveal (like the Valentinians and other Gnostics).

53. Romans 8:24 ("For in this hope we were saved"); I Corinthians 1:23; 2:2; 15:19 ("we have hope in Christ"); II Corinthians 1:10 ("in whom we have set our hope"). "To be found in" is also Pauline (Philippians 3:9), and Paul could even have written the clause, "Only if they are found in good works" (see II Corinthians 5:10 and even Galatians). For it is not to be supposed that Apelles meant it as the equivalent of "to hope in the Crucified One."

54. Cf. also the statement by Apelles in Hippolytus, *Refutation* VII 38: "[Christ at his ascension to the Father] left behind the seed of life for the world through the disciples for those who believe." The "seed" is reminiscent of I John 3:9. Marcion could not have expressed himself in this way.

55. This is Marcion's view as well, for he brings the good God and Christ together to the point of identifying them with each other.

56. The paraphrasing of "one principle" as "one uncreated" or "unbegotten God" called for by Apelles is worthy of attention. ($\dot{\alpha}\gamma\acute{\epsilon}\nu\eta\tau\sigma\varsigma$ is rare in the confessions of the early church—see Ulfilas' and Patricius' confessions—as is $\dot{\alpha}\gamma\acute{\epsilon}\nu\nu\eta\tau\sigma\varsigma$. Among the apologists the philosophical Athenagoras is the only one who uses the word $\dot{\alpha}\gamma\acute{\epsilon}\nu\eta\tau\sigma\varsigma$, and he does so very often. Justin, and he alone, also uses $\dot{\alpha}\gamma\acute{\epsilon}\nu\nu\eta\tau\sigma\varsigma$ often.)

57. One ought to note that for the sake of clarity Apelles uses the word "to hope" instead of "to believe" to describe saving faith. He gives the word "to believe" a broader meaning in which it expresses a conviction in general. On this matter cf. the line from Goethe: "Ask not through which gate you entered God's house, but remain in the quiet place where you first sat down."

58. That is very understandable, if his theology and Christology were like those of his younger contemporary, the Roman bishop Zephyrinus: "I know one God, Christ Jesus, and besides him there is none other."

59. Plato's doctrine of God also begins in this way, but then Apelles and Plato part company.

60. In these two convictions, too, Apelles goes along with Marcion, but not in the substantiation of the second.

61. That is, considering the state of the world and of humanity, how he can be at all, and how he can be a *single* being.

62. That is, I am convinced that he is and that he is one.

63. Even his always definite way of speaking indicates this, whether he is talking about the Old Testament, God, salvation, Christ, or Marcion.

64. See Norden, *Agnostos Theos*, pp. 19ff.

65. Furthermore, where he talks about the principles question and the "one principle," he does

not use the phrase "the one good God," for example, but "the one unbegotten God."

66. Rather, the Redeemer-God is in the Crucified One.

67. For himself Apelles identifies the Redeemer-God manifested in the Crucified One as the "one principle," but he does not demand this of others. Highly noteworthy here is the agreement and difference between Apelles and Augustine (*Confessions*, Prologue; see my essay in *Reden und Aufsaetze*, Vol. 5, pp. 69 ff.). Corresponding to the κινεῖσθαι are the "in thee" (*ad te*) and the "restless" (*inquietum*) in Augustine, but corresponding to the "hoping in the Crucified One" is the "preaching" (*praedicatio*), through which the *ad te* first receives its content, both recognizable and blessed for the subject. The difference here, however, is this: for Augustine the *praedicatio* has no foundation in and of itself. Apelles, on the other hand, bases everything on the *praedicatio*. He notes, however, that in his own case—he views this as subjective, not as something universal—a κινεῖσθαι cooperates with it.

68. Apelles himself never lost faith in his old confession, "one unbegotten good God," but he did differentiate the relationship to this God: everyone, he now taught, can experience redeeming love through the gospel, but it is not necessary for everyone to be convinced of the unity of the ground of the world, since this conviction is not necessary for salvation and, as experience shows, there are even good Christians who cannot be moved to that conviction. Did he not thereby at the end of his life extend the hand of reconciliation to his teacher Marcion, whom he once had so sharply attacked?

69. His opponent Rhodon amply characterized *himself* in the words, "But in the midst of my laughter I made known to him my contempt for the fact that he claimed to be teacher yet did not know how to prove that which he taught." We know that Rhodon himself was one of the run-of-the-mill philosophers of his day.

70. See the report by Pseudo-Tertullian: "The world was established as a copy of the higher world; with this world repentance was intermingled (by the angel creator)"; Tertullian, *De carne Christi* 8 (ANF III, 529): "They mention a certain angel of great renown as having created this world of ours, and as having, after the creation, repented of his work."

71. Jerome's claim that Apelles had his own Gospel (see Appendix VIII) cannot be believed. Pseudo-Tertullian testifies that Apelles used the Marcionite canon. The story of the lost sheep and Luke 8:20 are cited by him (Tertullian, *De carne Christi* 7, who assumes in the same chapter that Apelles rejects the Gospel of John), and the birth narrative is missing. To be sure, Apelles cites the saying (in Epiphanius, *Haer.* 44.2), "Become good moneychangers," as standing in the Gospel, but that is not decisive. After all, there is nothing to rule out the possibility that Apelles made changes in Marcion's Gospel, just as other disciples did. Hippolytus (*Refutation* VII 38) overstates the case when he says that Apelles took from the Gospels and the apostolic corpus whatever pleased him.

72. Epiphanius, *Haer.* 44.1 (also "the holy and good God from above") and Origen, *Comm. in Tit.* ("the unbegotten and good God").

73. Tertullian, *De anima* 23.36; *De carne Christi* 8. The souls were already male and female there in those upper regions (so says Philumene in her *Phaneroseis*). That the prophetess concerns herself with the sexual problem and locates the differentiation not in the body (which adapts itself accordingly) but in the spiritual nature deserves special attention. She must have attached some value, therefore, to her sex.

74. Epiphanius, loc. cit. and elsewhere.

75. Certainly, as Marcion taught, in inseparable unity as the "spiritus" that appears.

76. Hippolytus falsely asserts (*Refutation* X 20) that the World-Creator was not called God by Apelles.

77. The most important testimonies here are found in Tertullian, *De praescriptione* 34; *De carne Christi* 8; Origen, *Comm. in Tit.*; Pseudo-Tertullian; and Filastrius. Epiphanius speaks coarsely and falsely when he says (loc. cit.) that the World-Creator created the world "in accordance with his evil mind." In Hippolytus, *Refutation* VII 38, he is called "the just one."

78. See Tertullian, *De praescriptione* 7.33; *De carne Christi* 8; *De anima* 23; *De resurrectione* 5 ("that puny body, which they are not afraid to call evil"); Hippolytus, loc. cit. The complicated cosmology is naturally only the exposition of Apelles' view of the world. He saw in the cosmos a divine plan and the original operation of divine powers. Even in the soul he saw a greatness that belongs to the higher world. At the same time, however, he saw not only a very imperfect execution of the plan but also something devilish and evil, the effect of a satanic spirit that displays itself above all in the condition of men, who have in themselves, along with their heavenly part, the detestable flesh and who, insofar as they are Jews, have submitted themselves to the yoke of the deceitful "God." It was with great sensitivity that Apelles found the stamp of "repentance" impressed upon the whole world, to the extent that it had not been corrupted by the "superintendent of evil." What Valentinus conceived of as "pathos" Apelles understood more deeply as the painful consciousness of imperfection, with the wish to become better.

Hippolytus is in error when in *Refutation* X 20 he distinguishes still another evil angel from the fiery angel and designates Christ as a fifth entity. Apelles' World-Creator and the latter's relation to the fiery angel are not completely clear. Epiphanius says of him, "No good resulted," and when Apelles compares him with the lost sheep, it would suggest that a change for the worse had taken place in him. But that is not likely, since he begs the highest God to send Christ to redeem humanity. Who governed humanity before the appearance of Christ? Did the World-Creator lose all power in relation to the fiery angel? Did the Creator perhaps rule the heathen? Then they would be better than the Jews. That is indeed possible.

79. All witnesses confirm the rejection of the Old Testament ("Countless things profaned the law of Moses"), and several of them teach that to the rejection on religious grounds (Marcion) Apelles added a condemnation on rational grounds. The numerous fragments in Origen give a good picture of Apelles' boldness, acumen, and logical common sense (see Appendix VIII). It is interesting that he rejects, among other things, the story of the fall because it contravenes Pauline theology: "If God did not make man perfect, and now every person appropriates perfection of virtue for himself through his own diligence, does it not seem that man acquires more for himself than God gave him?"

From the general statements of his opponents concerning Apelles' critique of the Old Testament, one is not prepared for the fact that, nevertheless, something in the book is uttered by the World-Creator and indeed is even inspired by Christ. But the matter cannot be doubted, for Origen reports it casually (*Comm. in Tit.*: "He does not deny in any way that the law and the prophets are of God"), and Epiphanius (Hippolytus) does so explicitly and with the words of Apelles himself (*Haer.* 44.2: "Christ showed us what was said by him (and in which writing) and what was said by the Demiurge. For he spoke thus in the Gospel, 'Become experienced moneychangers.' Therefore I take out of each writing what is useful and treasure it").

Unfortunately, not a single Old Testament passage that Apelles traced back to the World-Creator or to Christ is mentioned by name. The distinction he finds in the Old Testament is Alexandrian Gnostic (see also the epistle of Ptolemaeus to Flora) and corresponds to that perspective's distinction in the make-up of the world. The world is something in between, with good and evil admixtures; the Old Testament, however, is something evil, with few intermediate and good admixtures.

The effort that Apelles exerts in the *Syllogisms* to discredit the Old Testament as a book of fables shows the strength of his reformatory intention to free Christendom from this book.

It remains doubtful whether Apelles regarded the story of the fall as just as much a fable as that of Noah's ark. If he did not—and considering the zeal with which he picks the story apart, that seems probable to me—then one has to assume from the alternatives he offers with his critique that he wished to highlight not so much the wickedness of the World-Creator as his weaknesses.

80. More exactly (Epiphanius 44.3): "For the salvation of those who come to a knowledge of him." Cf. Origen, *Comm. in Tit.*

81. See Apelles in Origen, *Contra Celsum* V 24: "He alone sojourned among the race of

men." "In the last times," Epiphanius 44.2.

82. In Epiphanius, loc. cit. (Hippolytus).

83. The accounts about the body of Christ all agree that it did not originate in the region of the higher God but belonged to this world. But the one account has Christ at his descent creating the body from the four elements that he finds in the terrestrial starry world, and at his ascension discarding it there again. According to the other account, Christ creates the body just on earth itself and also discards it there again before the ascension. The difference is insignificant.

It is clear that in this rule of faith is an imitation of the Old Roman Symbol (cf. especially the "was buried" and the "whence he also came" instead of "whence he comes," so that Apelles has a legitimate claim as a witness to this symbol (cf. Kattenbusch, *Das Apostolische Symbol*, II, 87, 639f.). One is reminded here also of the "holy church" in Marcion (see above).

Apelles, like other Gnostics, rejected the second coming of Christ. That follows from the "whence he also came" and from the teaching that Christ laid aside his flesh at the ascension. In this point also, therefore, he deviates from his master.

Since today again scholars are inclined to push the Old Roman Symbol back to about the year 200, it should be acknowledged on the other hand that the creed by Apelles in all probability presupposes it.

84. Cf. with the confession of faith in Epiphanius the passage in *De carne Christi* 7: "They confess that Christ *truly* had a body." After shedding his body, Christ is again only "spirit" (Pseudo-Tertullian).

85. But even the World-Creator must have been or yet must be saved by Christ. Otherwise he could not have compared him with the lost sheep.

86. *De praescriptione* 33. It follows from this that Apelles was just as rigorous in his asceticism as Marcion was. But was this still so at the end of his life when he declared that those who hope in the crucified one are saved if only they are discovered with good works? I believe that the question should be answered in the affirmative, for Apelles would hardly have lost his aversion to the flesh.

87. Almost inherent in Gnosticism for Apelles is the difference between the World-Creator and the God of the Law (God of the Jews). By placing the latter morally far below the World-Creator (and hence also below the world), he expresses his abhorrence of the Old Testament even more strongly than his former teacher had done.

88. With Valentinianism, whose doctrine of the aeons certainly remained completely foreign to him, Apelles shares the discriminating view of the world and the Old Testament that distinguishes divine, "intermediate," and evil components.

89. Like Apelles, Tatian was a strict ascetic and an opponent of marriage, and he conceived of the World-Creator in much the same way Apelles did. For his belief that in the words, "Let there be light," the World-Creator was petitioning the highest deity (Clement, *Eclogae* 38; Origen, *De oratione* 24) comes very close to Apelles' view that the Creator was assisted by Christ at the creation and that he also petitioned the highest God to send his Son to redeem humanity. Since both had their schools in Rome (Tatian's being the older, since Irenaeus already was acquainted with it), one may presume a certain connection here. However, nothing more specific can be said about it.

90. Despite his monotheism, Apelles is basically more "mythological" than Marcion. His two angels, the world-creating and the fiery angels, are in fact demi-gods (Marcion's World-Creator is not, according to his *theory*), and his doctrine of Christ's body, which he too regarded as unborn, is more brash that Marcion's Docetism, which survived the negative criticism.

91. His former teacher Marcion stood, as everyone knows, on the side of the Jews, since he regarded the Old Testament as a truthful book to be interpreted literally.

IX. MARCION'S HISTORICAL POSITION AND HIS HISTORICAL SIGNIFICANCE FOR THE EMERGENCE OF THE CATHOLIC CHURCH

1. As far as the relation of Marcion's Christianity to Gnosticism is concerned, I propose the following thesis: *Where Marcionitism was understood and appropriated superficially, i.e., according to its doctrines and not at the same time according to its motives, it could very easily appear and operate as "Gnosticism" and did so appear not only to its opponents but presumably also to many of its adherents.* For it had in common with many Gnostics: (1) the rejection of the Old Testament; (2) the conception of God as the Unknown; (3) the separation of the World-Creator from the highest God; (4) the conception of God as the absolute Good; (5) the conception of the World-Creator (= Lawgiver) as some kind of intermediate being; (6) the acceptance of the eternity of matter; (7) a docetic view of Christ; (8) the doctrine that the flesh is not resurrected; and (9) a dualistic asceticism.

But the very relationship between these doctrines shows that neither the essence of Gnosticism nor that of Marcionitism can be captured by them. For:

(1) In Gnosticism religion is determined by gnosis; in Marcion it is determined by faith in the crucified Christ. In the former an aristocracy of spiritual people is gathered; in the latter the humble brethren are the called ones.

(2) In the former the unnameable God reigns in the abyss and silence; in the latter God reigns as Christ. In the former the spirit of mankind is kindred to the highest God; in the latter this God is the absolute Alien and approaches us only through redemption.

(3) In the former extrabiblical myths predominate; in the latter they are absent.

(4) In the former the doctrine of the descent and ascent of the soul (spirit) is fundamental; in the latter it is not to be found. In the former the spirit returns to its abode; in the latter an Alien is supposed to become its abode.

(5) In the former an apostolic secret tradition is dominant; in the latter it is lacking.

(6) In the former the evil remain evil; in the latter they are capable of being redeemed.

(7) In the former one finds the magic of the mystery religions; in the latter not so.

In this way the most important principles of agreement and disagreement between Gnosticism and Marcionitism may be identified. Without a doubt the latter are the more significant. *At the same time they show most clearly the relationship with the doctrinal convictions of the great church.* From this perspective one could place Marcionitism in the middle between the great church and Gnosticism. But such an approach would be anything but enlightening, because in that age absolutely no one made or could have made such a judgment. From this perspective it is understandable, however, that Marcionitism, like the pre-catholic Christians, could form a church and, on the other hand, that the pre-catholic Christians had to throw it into the same pot with Gnosticism. It is also to be expected that just as, according to grossly exaggerated tradition, Marcion learned from Gnosticism, so also Gnostics learned from him. His *Antitheses* must have been especially welcome to them, and there are even some traces among them of the effect of this work. Furthermore, it is not improbable that the Valentinian Ptolemaeus learned from Marcion's double conception of the "just" (see above). On the other hand, it should be emphasized that if those nine points compiled above had been the most important ones in religion as a whole, all the Gnostic *schools* would have had to be swallowed up in Marcion's imposing *church*. The opposite, however, was the case; they remained in existence alongside the church, especially because Marcion's dualism was not genuinely metaphysical and because among the Gnostics the religious way of thinking and its presuppositions, as they are expressed in the seven points mentioned above, were different from those of Marcion *toto coelo*. A Valentinus would certainly have explained Marcion's religious teaching as a "peasant religion," i.e., as a kind of psychical religion. Thus the distinction we have to make in church history between the Gnostics and Marcion is a valid one, and its removal would seriously obscure the picture.

2. Marcion, according to Tertullian I 19 (ANF III, 285): "Marcion's special and principal work is the separation of the law and the gospel."

3. Marcion, accordir g to Tertullian I 20 (ANF III, 285): "For they allege that Marcion did not so much innovate on the rule (of faith) by his separation of the law and the gospel, as restore it after it had been previously adulterated."

4. Nevertheless, the view is highly worthy of further consideration and ought not to be rejected that, from *one* important perspective, Jesus' proclamation, Paul's doctrine, and Marcion's doctrine form a consistent line of development over against the Jewish religion.

5. On this see the Introduction. Paul confronted the early Christian syncretism of religious motifs and traditions by reducing the substance to clear-cut religious knowledge and precisely in this way put the *newness* of the gospel into focus.

6. There were actually three other alternatives, all of which were chosen. One could simply pass over those Pauline statements in silence and go on to the order of the day as if they did not exist at all (as was often done in Christendom before Irenaeus); or one could twist them, blunt them, and make subtle distinctions in them (which also happened); or one could explain this Paul as a terribly confused thinker and writer, full of contradictions of every sort, with whom any discussion was impossible. That was the judgment made by Porphyry.

The conclusion to which Marcion came (a fundamental Pauline dualism) was also shared by numerous Gnostics, and if one but assumed the perspective of a native Greek or Roman, it was almost unavoidable. For how could such a person recognize in the antitheses of "God and the God of this world," "spirit and flesh," and so on, anything other than the antithesis familiar to him from Plato and elsewhere? Marcion's greatness, however, lay both in the fact that he, too, recognized an antithesis here but *not* of the familiar religious-philosophical kind, *and in the fact that he was perceptive and honest enough to see, on the other hand, how many statements in the epistles are not in harmony with this antithesis*. The others, who made the apostle into a dualist, were helped by sophistic interpretations of the apostle's monotheistic statements and those acknowledging the Old Testament (in the same way that, vice versa, the church's theologians mishandled Paul's statements about sin, grace, and predestination).

Marcion alone drew the conclusion that is *absolutely unavoidable* if one has (erroneously) convinced himself that Paul separates the God of the gospel from the God of the law: he declared that non-Pauline elements have been inserted into the Pauline epistles, and those elements must be removed. This logical consistency in an age of confusion and eclecticism was a credit to Marcion, however wrong his starting point might have been.

This may be the place to examine briefly the main features of Marcion's relation to Paul. If one is convinced that Marcion in his high evaluation of the concepts of sin and grace, law and gospel, and obedience to the law and faith was really a disciple of Paul and sympathized with him, then one has to acknowledge, on the other hand, that *the Pauline way of thinking* (see Leisegang, *Der Apostel Paulus als Denker,* 1923) *remained absolutely closed off to him.* Whereas Paul's thought technique with respect to the first and last things was thoroughly dialectic (since for him God is "all in all"), this level remained incomprehensible and inaccessible to Marcion. His thought, rather, was completely dominated by the principle of contradiction and the utter inability to comprehend anything beyond it. That is clear everywhere, but it shows itself most clearly in the conception of "justice." Here he would have been required to reason out the problem dialectically (for according to Marcion, the good God also possesses justice, and the just law also possesses goodness). However, so far as we are able to determine, he remained stuck in this problem and never did reason it out. As one redeemed, therefore, he empathized with Paul and like him was inwardly controlled by faith in the crucified Christ. As a theologian, however, he stood almost at the opposite pole from Paul, forced the apostle down to his own level, and thus distorted him in the worst way. Still, does he not *finally* approach him when according to his eschatology, too, the Demiurge ultimately disappears and God appears as "all in all"? Viewed from this perspective, does he not differ from the apostle merely in his stronger pessimism about the world and its present course?

7. In its consequences it was actually incalculably great.

8. This is why Bunsen attributes the epistle to Marcion!

9. Other radical differences between Marcion and John are so obvious that it is unnecessary to mention them.

10. By moving in this direction, the Johannine conception of God in the first epistle goes beyond the Pauline conception (despite Romans 8:35; see Philippians 2:12) and is clearer. This is also precisely the direction, however, in which Marcion went, right up to the end.

11. Unfortunately, we do not know how large, in proportion to traditional Christians, was the number of Christians who in the postapostolic age and up until around the end of the second century rejected the Old Testament. Still, it is worth noting that Tertullian writes (V 20, ANF III, 472): "The majority of persons everywhere now-a-days are of our way of thinking, rather than on the heretical side." It is not entirely impossible that there was a decade in the second century in which the Christians who rejected the Old Testament outnumbered those who acknowledged it.

12. Marcion's whole undertaking is evidence that two or three generations after Paul there was no longer an authoritative knowledge about the historical course of affairs (apart from those writings that we, too, still possess), which curbed all subjectivity in the construction of the past. Otherwise, Marcion would not have been able to risk coming out with so revolutionary a view. Ritschl's thesis holds true here as well: "Nowhere is the historical memory shorter than under the domination of a tradition." In this case it was the arbitrary designation and esteem of the "apostolic" tradition. Placed under the protection of this label was the shaping of early Christian syncretism and all the religious motifs that one needed at the time. Marcion very correctly recognized of how little value this tradition was, but his remedy, though born of the fundamental ideas of Paul, was, historically speaking, worse yet.

The Acts of the Apostles, a basically reliable source for Paul's time, was certainly available, and Marcion was acquainted with it. But this book (which, incidentally, was nowhere yet considered to be sacred) Marcion judged to be a thoroughly spurious source and rejected it, since in his view it contradicted the epistles of Paul and furthermore was attributed to Luke, whose name the Judaizers had placed on the genuine Gospel when they adulterated it.

13. The agreement between Marcion and the Tübingen school is considerable. Both were correct that the motivating spirit of Paulinism, the greatness of the apostle's work, and one's understanding of the apostolic age must be perceived above all in the context of the struggle against the Judaizers — an historical insight of the first order that was lost in the long interval between Marcion and the Tübingen school and was not put forward as *historical* knowledge for the understanding of early Christianity even by Luther. Both were wrong, however, when they thought they could understand *all* of Paul's ideas and interests as well as all early Christian developments on the basis of that struggle. With Marcion this conviction had the result (as both the prologues to the Pauline epistles and his exegesis show) that in those passages of the epistles that he considered genuine he traced everything back to the opposition to the Judaizers in a highly forced manner. It was not essentially different with the Tübingen school, even if their method was not quite so grotesque. Since both were real critics and not sophists, they both saw the necessity, from the same point of view, of making major deletions in the Pauline epistles. In this the Tübingen school proceeded more radically than did Marcion, since they declared no fewer than six of the ten Pauline epistles to be spurious. Marcion, however, was the more audacious of the two in that he claimed to be able to recognize and remove the allegedly large number of large and small interpolations that the epistles had suffered at the hands of the Judaizers. Incidentally, the Tübingen school — i.e., the younger ones among them, after they had toned down the radicalism of the school (cf. the works of Hilgenfeld and Holtzmann) — also tried to remove a number of difficulties by the acceptance of tendentious interpolations. As critics, therefore, they became Marcionites.

14. It is quite possible that not only Marcion's native ability made him a church organizer on a grand scale but also his sojourn in Rome and his temporary membership in the Roman congregation. From the latter's concern for the universal church he may have recognized and learned

what should be done for Christendom as a whole and then from the start surpassed his "instructor" in drive and energy. If this is so, then there is in Marcion's "catholicism" a *Roman* catholic element.

15. *Before* there were two *connected* written testaments in Christendom, therefore, there existed two *opposing* testaments. The written New Testament was produced by Marcion as an adversary to the Old Testament. Only then did it appear in the catholic church, in opposition to Marcion, in the *higher stage* of peaceful unity with the Old Testament. See my work *Die Entstehung des Neuen Testaments*, Beiträge zur Einleitung in das Neue Testament 6 (1914), pp. 21ff.

16. This authority emerged only when the conception took hold that the entire genuine literary corpus of the apostle was *ipso facto* the holy foundation and rule of Christendom.

17. See *Die Entstehung des Neuen Testaments*, pp. 44ff.

18. See ibid., pp. 39ff.

19. The Roman community from which Marcion had come with his ecclesiastical foundation undoubtedly took the lead in the large countermovement that developed against him. It first learned what there was to learn from Marcion and taught it to the other congregations. It then produced in the building and securing of the new catholic church something stronger than Marcion had. The conceiving of the idea of episcopal succession and its connection with the guarantee of the "transmission of the truth" did not come from Marcion, even though we hear later on about "successions of bishops" in the Marcionite churches.

20. That even without the Marcionite movement the inner development of the church would have led to the creation of the New Testament, to its consisting of two parts (Gospel and Apostle), to Christian theology as a theology of the new *book*, and to the (relative) repression of cosmology is a thesis that is difficult to discuss. To me it does not appear certain at all. It seems more likely to me that without the Marcionite movement the church would have contented itself with the four Gospels (with a canonically uncertain status) alongside the Old Testament; that it would thus have hardly overcome the diffusion in its doctrine and come to a theology of the Book (even so, with the *two* testaments it now recognized and on other grounds it arrived at such a theology only very conditionally); and that cosmology would have claimed its place above soteriology. If, however, one objects that not just Marcion alone but Gnosticism also was involved here, he has failed to understand the numerical and material inferiority of Gnosticism *as a church-historical factor in comparison with the Marcionite church*. Indeed, Tertullian does call the Valentinians – only they can be meant here – "a most numerous association," but still only an "association" (*collegium*). He and Irenaeus certainly contended with them exhaustively, but by their very oddities the exotic secret speculations of the Valentinians invited exposure and rebuttal, and when they penetrated the Christian upper classes, they demanded special attention.

21. We should again be reminded here that such conservative critics as the editors of the *Novum Testamentum domini nostri Jesu Christi, Latine sec. edit. S. Hieronymi* (Wordsworth and White) wrote (Pt. II.1, 1913, p. 41): "Marcion's 'Apostolicon' was circulated also in Latin and was well known from *general* use . . . And at another time he gave abundant testimony that the Church ought not *also in the structure of the New Testament to be guided* by the heretics."

22. The two principal themes in Irenaeus, "The Creator God is also the Redeemer God," and "The Son of God became the Son of Man," on which the entire further development of the church's doctrine depends, are strictly anti-Marcionite. And yet Marcion is behind even them, since Irenaeus understood and developed them *soteriologically*, in distinction from the rational inadequacy of most of the apologists before him.

23. I have presented and substantiated these theses for years (though not, to be sure, with the necessary precision) in my *History of Dogma* and in my work on the origin of the New Testament. But in the textbooks and monographs on church history and the history of dogma that have appeared since then, these theses have not been given their due recognition. The history of the development of early Christianity up to the Catholic church must be constructed differently from the way it has been done to date. Marcion and his church must be given as prominent a place (and a similar and, in many respects, more far-reaching significance) in the second century as, *mutatis mutandi*, the

Reformation in the sixteenth century. Compared with Marcion, Gnosticism must be conceded a modest place in the history of the church (in the history of ideas it is otherwise), and the ancient catholic church must be seen as an (antithetic and synthetic) product of the influence of Marcion on postapostolic Christianity. There is a much greater difference in Christianity (the church) before and after Marcion than in the Western church before and after the Reformation!

X. MARCION'S CHRISTIANITY IN LIGHT OF CHURCH HISTORY AND THE PHILOSOPHY OF RELIGION

1. Or a book of fables and lies, which amounted to the same thing. The mediating view (itself highly deserving of attention from scholars), which distinguished various elements in the book (Ptolemaeus and pseudo-Clement, among others), also boiled down to a rejection of the Old Testament as a whole. This view, incidentally, could only have been the property of scholars and theological schools.

2. I pass over immediately to him, although the history of the ancient and medieval church still has something noteworthy to offer here as well. But it is not of such importance that it has to be mentioned. Especially relevant are Augustine and the Augustinian-Pauline and antinomian reactions in the church; in some respects they are all related to Marcionitism. An investigation of the subject "Marcion and Augustine" would be particularly interesting. Cf. also my essay, "Geschichte der Lehre von der Seligkeit allein durch den Glauben in der alten Kirche," *Zeitschrift für Theologie und Kirche* I (1891), 82–178, and the second section of the present chapter.

3. "No one is able to make final judgment according to any laws whatsoever except he who has and understands the gospel" (Wrampelmeyer, *Tagebuch über Luther des Cordatus* [1885], p. 55).

4. Frank has called attention to the relationship between Agricola and Marcion (*Theologie der Konkordienformel* II, 255).

5. The idea that the Catholic church was a compromise between contesting Petrine and Pauline factions can also be found in Morgan.

6. Hereby I object to the classifying of my arguments with those of Friedrich Delitzsch (*Die grosse Taeuschung*), which has happened several times. The latter are as outdated from a scholarly standpoint as they are objectionable from a religious standpoint.

7. Because of their significance the Marcionite words preserved for us by Origen (*Comm. in Joh.* II 199; see above) should be cited here in translation: "The Son of God needs no 'witnesses' (i.e., no prophets who have prophesied about him). For the convicting and heart-stirring power lies in the authoritative words of the Savior and in his miraculous deeds." And now very literally: "If Moses was believed because of his word and powerful deeds and did not need prophesying witnesses to precede him; and if likewise every prophet was accepted by the people as sent from God; how much more had not he who was much greater than Moses and the prophets the power to perform what he wished and to help mankind without any previous prophetic witness."

8. At that time no one could be a God who was not also a Savior. Only the few genuine Stoics thought differently about that.

9. "This small cell of the Creator"—how could a Hellene ever have spoken so disparagingly about heaven and earth? This world of physical and moral vermin!

10. The relationship with Tolstoy should be noted here.

11. Marcion explicitly set forth these equations. See above.

12. In any case, the Christianity of his day might well have judged the world more harshly than Marcion did by declaring that this aeon was completely *of the devil*. But the world was still good; only the age was evil, and as a reasonable being man could always elevate himself to the "good."

13. One is reminded again of Tolstoy.

14. Pascal, Pensees 340: "The first thing that God inspires in the soul, which he truly con-

descends to move, is a knowledge and a most extraordinary vision, by which the soul considers things and itself in a completely new way. This new light instills fear within him."

15. If today philosophy of religion is again defining the object of religion (the "Holy") as fundamentally the "Wholly Other," "the Alien," or something similar, and students of Pietism, Protestant orthodoxy, Catholicism, and the critical schools are arriving at this same basic definition; and if furthermore they teach that all "proofs" should be abandoned and wish to have us speak only of the phenomenon in itself, then they have every reason to remind themselves of their only predecessor in church history who knew this alien God, called him by name, and rejected all proofs and "testimonies" by which one could believe in him.

16. It ought to be remembered that "sensuality" and "cosmos" were very likely compatible and that it was perhaps through Gnostic influences that Marcion was prompted to separate them.

17. Alongside this work can be placed the doctrine of the two Mills (cf. John Stuart Mill's essay on nature, and see Jodl, *Geschichte der Ethik*, second edition, II [1912], 474f., 713f.), about which K. Thieme has rightly reminded me.

18. Max Scheler ("Von zwei deutschen Krankheiten" in the work *Der Leuchter* [1919], pp. 161ff.) reproaches Lutheranism with the danger of a misguided inwardness—whether rightly or not may be left undecided here. The reproach does seem, however, to be applicable to Marcion.

Index

182